LAST TSAR

S. S. OLDENBURG

LAST TSAR

Nicholas II, His Reign & His Russia

∾♋∾

Volume 3

THE DUMA MONARCHY, 1907-1914

Translated by Leonid I. Mihalap and Patrick J. Rollins
Edited by Patrick J. Rollins

∾♋∾

ACADEMIC INTERNATIONAL PRESS

1977

THE RUSSIAN SERIES / Volume 25-3

Sergei S. Oldenburg Last Tsar! Nicholas II, His Reign
and His Russia. Volume 3: The Duma Monarchy, 1907-1914.
Translation of *Tsarstvovanie Imperatora Nikolaia II.*
Volume II (Munich, 1949), Part III.

ISBN: 0-87569-073-4

Maps by Richard D. Kelly, Jr.
Composition by Jeanette Rawlinson and Jean MacNeil
Title page by King & Queen Press

Illustrations from Major General A. Elchaninov, *The Tsar and
his People* (London, 1917); *Finland: The Country, its People
and Institutions* (Helsinki, 1926); Thomas Michell, *Russian
Pictures* (London-New York, 1889); S.S. Oldenburg, *Tsarstvovanie
Imperatora Nikolaia II* (Vol. 2, Munich, 1949); Princess
Catherine Radziwill (Count Paul Vassili), *Rasputin and the
Russian Revolution* (New York, 1918); A.J. Sacks, *The Birth of
the Russian Democracy* (New York, 1918); *Stikhotvornaia satira
pervoi russkoi revoliutsii* (1905-1907), (Leningrad, 1969); Count
Paul Vassili, *Behind the Veil at the Russian Court* (London, 1914).

Printed in the United States of America

ACADEMIC INTERNATIONAL PRESS
POB 555 Gulf Breeze FL 32561

CONTENTS

❧

THE   EMP

LEGEND

————	Boundary of the Empire
+—+—+	Great Siberian Railway
▪—▪—▪	Chinese Eastern Railway
•—•—•	South Manchurian Railway
▒	Annexed 1858 - 1860
▥	Annexed 1864 - 1895
▨	Occupied 1871 - 1881

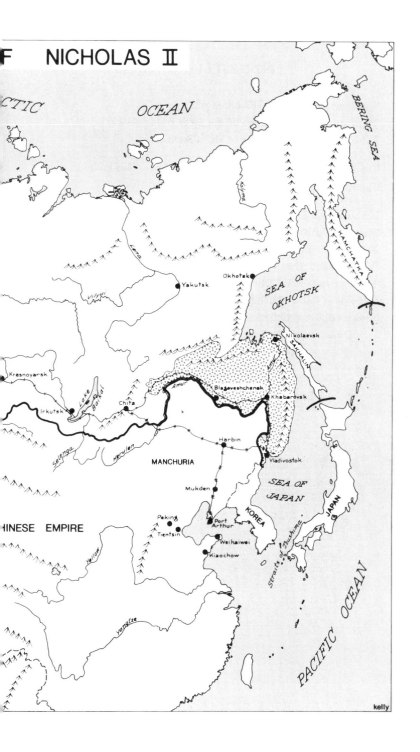

ARCTIC OCEAN

BERING SEA

KAMCHATKA

Yakutsk

Okhotsk

SEA OF OKHOTSK

Nikolaevsk

SAKHALIN

Krasnoyarsk

Lake Baikal

Irkutsk

Chita

Blagoveshchensk

Khabarovsk

Harbin

MANCHURIA

Vladivostok

SEA OF JAPAN

JAPAN

Mukden

Peking

Tientsin

Port Arthur

KOREA

Weihaiwei

Kiaochow

CHINESE EMPIRE

Yellow

Straits of Tsushima

PACIFIC OCEAN

Yangtze

Selenga

Kerulen

Amur

Lena

Kolyma

Vilyui

kelly

LIST OF ILLUSTRATIONS

CHAPTER THIRTEEN

THE ERA OF THE DUMA MONARCHY

Before 1905 it was a standard joke that Nicholas II was "quite amenable to a constitution as long as it did not preclude the autocracy." The idea seemed absurd, but the times proved more complex than most imagined and life refused to conform to a neat pattern. Following the reforms of 1905-7, a British reference work described the Russian government in this way: "In 1905 Russia became a hereditary constitutional monarchy, although legislative, executive, and judicial powers largely remain the prerogatives of the sovereign, who retains the title Autocrat." In other words, forms considered theoretically incompatible had been combined in practice. Continuity persisted without disruption. The representative system inaugurated by the emperor merely added a new page to an old book, the book of the Russian Empire. Nevertheless, during the years of transition Russia was changed more drastically and far more rapidly than during the reform era of Alexander II.

In the years that followed the upheaval, official policy adhered to the formula "reform, then pacification" and not [as often alleged] "pacification, then reform." The post-revolutionary period was necessarily one of revitalization. It was a period for adjusting to the reforms introduced earlier by Nicholas II—reforms instituted partly as a conscious plan for the improvement of national life and partly as "the lesser evil" that would eliminate the sources of discontent.

And the changes were enormous. During the heat of the struggle, Russian liberals and radicals were reluctant to acknowledge the transformation that already had taken place. Instead they compared the new order unfavorably to their own demands advanced at the height of the revolution. But in retrospect no one would deny that, compared to circumstances before 1905, Russia was adjusting to its new state of affairs.

The new order lasted about a decade. It has received less scholarly attention and is not as well understood as the preceding period. It is safe to say that this era disappeared from history even before it entered. Non-Russian historians have made scarcely any detailed and comprehensive studies of the period. Up to this point foreigners writing on Tsarist Russia usually have attributed the achievements of the pre-reform era to the period of the Duma Monarchy. They have been amazed to discover the great progress previously made toward the realization of civil liberties in Russia.

When the turbulent advance came to an end, society was aware of the halt but it failed to appreciate at once how extensively Russia had changed. "The great achievement of 1905 entailed such rapid change that our comprehension of events failed to keep pace," wrote the prominent Kadet Dmitry Protopopov.[1] Citing such changes as the abandonment of the radical movement by the well-to-do and the stratification and discord of the villages, Protopopov concluded that "these outwardly ugly and reprehensible developments undoubtedly are giving birth to a new world. A great change is occurring: the communal ant is being transformed into a free man; urban workers are forming unions and exhibiting a strong proclivity for education; porters, cabbies, and workers can even be seen reading newspapers in public. The emergence of a real patriotism can be felt across the land." Protopopov described all of this as the europeanization of Russia, and his observation contained a great deal of truth. During the period of the Duma Monarchy, Russia did resemble the countries of Western Europe in many respects.

THE NEW ORDER

As in the past, the emperor retained his full executive powers, but the popular representatives enjoyed an appreciable role in legislative and financial affairs. The legislative branch consisted of the State Duma and the State Council, both equal in their powers. The institution of a new law or the revocation of an old one required the consent of the two chambers and the approval of the emperor. The constitution was interpreted broadly with the result that many measures routinely adopted in the West by executive order had to pass through the Duma

The Tsar and His Heir

and State Council.[2] A similar principle regulated budgetary matters. Appropriations required by some specific legislation (the repayment of loans, for example, or the funding of the staffs of some departments) could be excluded from the budget only with the consent of the emperor and both chambers. All new appropriations, new taxes, state loans, or loans guaranteed by the government required the approval of the legislative bodies. If a new budget failed to win approval, the previous budget's provisions for expenditures and income remained in effect. The same procedure was followed for the annual quota of conscripts: both chambers had to approve any increase. Without their joint consent the annual levy remained set at the level of the preceding year.

The State Duma was elected for five years by means of a complex system. Voting rights corresponded closely to the general rights of citizenship, especially in the villages. The ballot was secret. Direct elections were held in the two capitals and the five largest cities, while in the provinces elections were conducted in two or three stages. Landowners were allocated the greatest number of electors. Large landowners voted directly for their electors. Small landowners gathered in special assemblies; the number of electors they chose was determined by the acreage that they collectively possessed.[3] Peasant organizations also selected electors. (All peasants elected a volost assembly which in turn chose the volost electors.) Two categories of electors were found in the cities—those elected by the working class and those chosen by the rest of the urban citizenry. Property owners and persons who paid substantial residence or business taxes formed one curia, while a second curia was reserved for renters and employees. There were also provisions for the selection of electors by cossacks and the nomadic peoples of the empire. Once all categories of electors had been chosen, they assembled in their provincial capitals and there they elected the members of the State Duma from among their own numbers. The law provided for the election of certain numbers of deputies from the various classes of citizens (peasants, landowners, and—in six provinces—urban workers).

The State Duma elected its own officers and adopted its own regulations to govern its internal procedures. Its rules of order required no other approval but were published and distributed by the Imperial Senate.

The emperor appointed one-half of the State Council, and the other half was elected in this manner: the clergy chose 12 representatives, the zemstvo assemblies 34, associations of nobles 18, the universities and academies 6, trade and industrial associations 12, landowner assemblies of the Polish Kingdom 6, and the non-zemstvo provinces 16 [10]—a total of 98 representatives. In principle the appointed members of the State Council could not be removed from office. Therefore, since their number considerably exceeded 98, annually on the first of January the government published a list of State Council members nominated by the tsar "to be present" at the sessions of the Council.

Both chambers had the right to submit inquiries to the various ministries concerning unlawful acts of the state. The Duma made extensive use of that prerogative. If a minister's response failed to satisfy the chamber, and if two-thirds of its members concurred, the president of the chamber could bring the matter to the attention of the emperor. All legislative sessions were open to the public except on rare occasions, usually when military questions were under consideration. The newspapers liberally reported the activities of the Duma and Council.

CIVIL RIGHTS

Subsequent legislation codified the civil liberties proclaimed by the October Manifesto. However, the need for certain restrictions became apparent immediately after the document was published. The status of the press changed markedly. The abolition of preliminary censorship followed on the heels of the manifesto. Prohibitions against the discussion of certain subjects disappeared. Departments with jurisdiction over the press confiscated certain issues of some periodicals, but publishers could be closed and their editions seized only with the approval of a court. The maximum punishment for publishing violations was a prison sentence not in excess of one year and four months. After the dissolution of the Second Duma, press controls were strengthened. Governors of provinces under states of emergency were authorized to fine newspapers (as much as 3,000 rubles) and jail editors (up to three months). Fines were an especially effective instrument for dealing with provincial newspapers. The arrest of editors, on the other hand, accomplished little, because the real head of the paper usually gave a subordinate the title of editor-in-chief.

Relaxed censorship allowed daily newspapers with sharply oppositional views to appear openly in Russia for the first time: *Rech* (the voice of the Kadets), the more radical *Nasha zhizn*, *Tovarishch* [Comrade], and later *Dni* [The Days] and *Pravda* [The Truth].[4] Also in evidence were monthly journals representing all shades of opinion, including Bolshevism. Books banned from Russia before 1905 (the works of Herzen, Tolstoy's attacks on the church, the books of foreign socialists and anarchists, and the like) were published freely. Of course the government continued to suppress blatantly revolutionary propaganda and expressly prohibited mutinous appeals, blasphemy, and insults to the sovereigns. Nevertheless, such leading figures of the 1905 revolution as Lenin and Trotsky and others who had fled abroad continued to print their views in the legal Russian press.

The "temporary regulations" of 4 March 1906 defined the freedoms of assembly and association. Organizations were permitted to form without prior approval, but they had to register their charters. If the government did not reject the charter within two weeks of its registration, the organization was legally recognized. Thereafter the organization could hold meetings without a special permit, even though attendance might be sizable. To stage public meetings organizations had to notify the government three days in advance. The assembly could take place if not prohibited one day before the scheduled date. The registration of organizations was entrusted to special boards consisting of government and elected officials.[5] Those bodies also had the power to disband any organization that deviated from the purposes described in its charter. As a result of this legislation, a great variety of associations and unions, especially trade unions, were formed in Russia.

The organizations that most often had their charters rejected were political parties. The Social Democratic and Socialist Revolutionary programs called for an armed uprising and a democratic republic. Obviously neither of those parties bothered to register with the government. Nevertheless, socialist fractions formed by Social Democrats and Trudoviks functioned openly in the State Duma; if there were no Socialist

Revolutionaries, that was because they boycotted the Duma after the Law of 3 June.[6] The charter of the Constitutional Democratic Party was not recognized because of the Kadets' prominent role in the Vyborg appeal. Consequently the Kadets existed in a semi-legal status. They published a journal, ran their own publishing houses, and maintained local committees which met openly—all without "official" recognition. Government officials were prohibited from joining the Kadets, but several professors, though members of the civil service, always held key positions in that party.

Under these new political conditions the emperor's role in affairs of state was much less direct than it once had been. The tsar was no longer "his own prime minister." Instead a council of ministers collectively considered issues and made decisions. Nicholas kept a vigilant watch to see that predatory precedents did not derogate his rights, which he perceived as inseparable from his duty as tsar. At the same time he scrupulously observed the legislative and executive order that he himself had proclaimed. The foreign expressions "constitution" and "parliament" irritated him. He much preferred to speak of "the renewed, altered order." Whatever the terminology, the tsar was extremely sensitive about the changes that had taken place. In many respects the new order ran counter to his own philosophy, but he conscientiously accepted it as the outcome of the long tortuous search for a solution to the tragic contradictions of Russian life. For twentieth-century Russia the Duma Monarchy, for all its theoretical and practical deficiencies, afforded that measure of freedom which Bismarck thought necessary in any state but which in excess would lead quickly to anarchy and the loss of all freedom.

The new system was harsher than its predecessor in only one respect: capital punishment. The death penalty became the government's answer to mass terror. Even though it enraged older writers like Tolstoy and Korolenko, punishment by death became as common in Russia as it was in France, England, and Germany. Stolypin concluded that no alternative would serve to suppress the bloody hooliganism into which the remnants of the revolutionary terrorists had degenerated.[7]

THE END OF THE REVOLUTION

June 3rd signaled the end of the revolution. Everyone, even its staunchest adherents, recognized that at once. The Law of

3 June offered a practical resolution of the antithesis of tsarist authority and popular representation, and the nation overwhelmingly accepted it without dissent. The ultra-conservatives were overjoyed. A telegram to the tsar from the Union of Russian People began by announcing that "tears of tender love and joy prevent us from expressing adequately the emotions that overcame us as we read your imperial manifesto, which with a single autocratic word put an end to the existence of the felonious State Duma." Other conservative and moderate groups sent similar protestations of loyalty.

The central committee of the Union of October 17 adopted a resolution which declared: "We are saddened to note that the revision of the electoral law proclaimed by the Manifesto of 3 June fails to adhere to the provisions of the Fundamental Laws, but we also feel that it is premature to pass judgment on this action and we consider the need for it—regrettable." The Octobrists placed the blame on the radical parties, which made it impossible to create normal conditions of life in the empire. Peter Struve, a former member of the Second Duma, provided this analysis in the *Birzhevie vedomosti* [Stock Exchange Gazette]: "The basic mistake lay in the fact that the Kadets could not bring themselves to break with the left." The liberal *Vestnik evropy* acknowledged that extreme necessity gave the government the right to deviate from legal norms and it concluded that supra-legal methods acquire a *raison d'être* once all other means have been tried without success. The Kadets, assembled in Finland in emergency session, adopted a resolution protesting the Law of 3 June, but a substantial majority defeated a motion to boycott elections held under the new law.

Facing the possibility of administratively imposed fines, the oppositionist press was restrained in its reaction to the new system. It was largely content to stress the contradiction between the Manifesto of 3 June and the Fundamental Laws, but the manifesto itself had acknowledged that discrepancy. The oppositionists proclaimed their indignation at this "violation" of the law, but their protests had a hollow ring. A year earlier they had responded to the dissolution of the First Duma (an imperial act strictly in accord with the law) by appealing to the nation to refuse to pay taxes or report for military service.

The defeat of the revolution was complete: it was beaten not only in a material and physical sense but also spiritually. The former coalition of oppositionist forces disintegrated. The alliance of zemstvos, cities, intelligentsia, and commercial-industrial elements with the revolutionary parties collapsed. For the first time in decades even the intelligentsia began to lose confidence in its hallowed convictions.

THE CONSERVATIVE RESURGENCE

The rightward shift among the zemstvos and municipalities began early in 1906, and each subsequent election produced greater representation for the right. The "third element" was vexed; many newspapers devoted space to "the reaction" and to discussion of the aroused "class-consciousness" of land- and property-owners. The movement was inexorable. The same elements which a short time before had been considered pillars of the Liberation movement were announcing their support of the government and sometimes proving even more conservative than the authorities. The same reaction could be discerned among the merchants and industrialists, including both Russian and foreign entrepreneurs. "The privileged classes . . . of course prefer Durnovo or Stolypin to Khrustalev," wrote *Russkaia mysl*. The governor of Ekaterinoslav, A.M. Klingenberg, wrote in a memorandum on the role of foreign capitalists in the revolutionary organizations that "after two years of insurrection, the majority of capitalists have sobered up to the point that they are no longer recognizable."[8]

On 11 June 1907, a week after the Second Duma had been dissolved, another zemstvo congress convened in Moscow, the first since November 1905. All but two of the 34 provincial zemstvos sent delegates. This congress, therefore, was a more faithful reflection of zemstvo opinion than the previous conventions in which many provinces had been represented by persons without proper qualifications. The change was pronounced.[9] The congress began its work by drafting and sending to the tsar a telegram protesting its loyalty and promising "to devote all our powers to assist Your Majesty in restoring justice, peace, and prosperity to our native land, which lies exhausted by sedition, violence, and destruction." The assembly also sent greetings to Stolypin and to the war minister, "a solid bulwark of the fatherland and order—loyal to the tsar's valiant army."

Alexander Guchkov, a delegate, spoke at a banquet and praised Stolypin: "In those dark days when many were overwhelmed by despondency, there appeared a man who—despite all obstacles, despite the loss of his family, despite all slanders—correctly assessed the situation and took the right road. If we have seen the last convulsions of the revolution—and there is no doubt that it is coming to an end—we owe it all to this man." Another delegate proposed a toast to Admiral Dubasov and the Semenovsky Regiment, "thanks to whom we now have the opportunity to assemble here in Moscow."

A zemstvo reform bill, intended for the Second Duma, came under sharp attack from the right. The congress objected to the projected expansion of voting rights, and only with serious reservations did it approve the draft of a bill for the creation of the small zemstvo unit. Although the left objected, the congress approved a resolution condemning terror. Liberals argued that the issue was beyond the competence of the assembly (M.A. Stakhovich was among those who raised this objection), but a vast majority carried the resolution. The zemstvo congress of 1907 reflected a striking change of mood among zemstvo circles. The leftist press attributed this new attitude to "class fears" stemming from the agrarian uprisings, but to some extent it demonstrated the zemstvoists' satisfaction with the government's reforms.

ELECTION OF THE THIRD STATE DUMA

The 1907 zemstvo congress has been called a "pre-Duma." It mirrored the views of that section of the population which had acquired decisive importance as a result of the new electoral law. As it was meeting, preparations were underway for the election of the Third Duma. New political alignments were taking shape. The Octobrists were destined to form the center in the new Duma, and some liberals already were expressing a desire to form a Kadet-Octobrist bloc for the protection of the constitutional foundations. Prince Eugene Trubetskoy,[10] the newspaper *Slovo*, and the Party of Peaceful Reconstruction urged their "neighbors on the left and right" to conclude a pre-election alliance.

Although their programs were similar in many respects, a political agreement between the Kadets and Octobrists was impossible. The line that separated the two parties was a political watershed that had been developing since the autumn of 1905. The Octobrists had backed the government in its struggle against the revolution and subsequently acknowledged the necessity, however "regrettable," of the Law of 3 June. The Kadets in contrast were and remained staunchly hostile to the government. More often than not they had voted with the revolutionary parties rather than the right, even in the Second Duma.

On the far right stood parties and groups (the Union of Russian People and others) whose basic position was to press for the tsar's unlimited power. Between the right and the Octobrists stood a few weakly organized groups of moderates and rightists. They accepted the new system but were not inclined to defend it against the crown, much less to extend it.

The election of the Third State Duma took place in September and October 1907. During the second phase of the election, the contest in the large cities was between the Kadets and the radicals. Paul Miliukov, who emerged at about that time as the undisputed Kadet leader, published a sharp attack on the extreme left in *Rech*: "Despite our previous cooperation, we [Kadets] now must admit that to our deep regret we and all of Russia do have enemies on the left . . . . Our enemies are those who have unleashed the base instincts of human nature and twisted the moderate aims of political struggle into a program of general destruction . . . . Indeed, we would be our own worst enemy if, for whatever reason, we acted out the old German folk tale and pressed on carrying the donkey on our back." The radicals did not take this lying down, and they reproached the Kadets for adopting this line only after the defeat of the revolution.

In the two capitals, Petersburg and Moscow, the Octobrists were victorious in the first curia and the Kadets in the second.[11] The voting pattern in the larger cities changed little from previous elections. The provincial electoral assemblies, however, produced the expected results. In the provinces Octobrists and rightists won over two-thirds of the seats in contrast to the Second Duma election in which they elected only about one-fifth of the delegates. The membership of the new

The Taurida Palace—Home of the State Duma

Duma consisted overwhelmingly of representatives elected under the banner of cooperation with rather than struggle against the government.[12]

Approximately 300 of the 442 Duma members were Octobrists or deputies representing parties and groups farther to the right. (The numbers in both groups were roughly equal.) Parties opposed to the government won only in Siberia, in the Caucasus, in the Polish and Lithuanian provinces, and in the Ural provinces of Perm, Ufa, and Orenburg. Nine deputies from large urban centers and six elected from the workers' curia[13] rounded out the oppositionist forces.

A BAD START

The first session of the Third Duma opened without formal ceremonies on 1 November 1907.[14] Preliminary caucasus had revealed that there would be no single majority united around a common program. With difficulty the Octobrists and rightists reached agreement on the election of a presidium. By an almost unanimous vote the Octobrist Nicholas Khomiakov,[15] son of the prominent Slavophile and godson of Gogol, was elected chairman of the Third Duma. By agreement with the right an Octobrist also occupied the post of second vice-chairman, while rightists took the offices of first vice-chairman, secretary, and senior assistant to the secretary. The left was allotted the posts of junior assistants to the secretary, and for that reason the Kadets refused to participate in the presidium.[16] Stolypin asked the emperor to receive the new Duma, but Nicholas replied that it was "still too early. It has not yet proven itself satisfactory, not proven itself in the sense of the hopes, which I have for it, for cooperation with the government. Premature actions and precedents ought to be avoided on my part."[17] The following days revealed that the deputies of the Duma center indeed were not at all favorably disposed toward the emperor's desires.

During the election campaign, Octobrist speakers frequently had reproached the first two Dumas for failing to thank the tsar for introducing representative government. Therefore, one of the first moves of the Octobrists and some rightists was to propose a salutation from the Duma to the tsar. The proposal, inspired by the motives of utter loyalty, suddenly embroiled the Duma in a bitter political struggle. Rightists in the committee charged with drafting the statement insisted that the text include the term "autocracy;" the Kadets demanded a reference to "the constitution." The committee could not agree. On 13 November the matter came before the general session of the Duma, and a stormy debate erupted. At the heart of the matter was the essential nature of the Russian governmental structure, whether it was an autocratic or constitutional system.

Guchkov spoke from a decidedly constitutional stance, but he opposed the use of constitutional language in the message to the emperor. The rightists attached fundamental importance to the inclusion of the word "autocracy." Nicholas Markov argued that "the title of autocrat exists, and if you reject it you become a violator of the Fundamental Laws. If you eliminate the word 'autocrat,' we will not endorse your message." The session dragged on far into the night. F.N. Plevake, a famous lawyer, delivered an impassioned speech. Addressing the right, he recalled that the emperor himself had granted the Duma its legislative rights: "He himself would tell you that you are children. He would say, 'I gave you the toga of a man, but you ask again for a child's smock!' " The gap between the center and right grew more discernible. Finally the Kadets and Progressists informed the Octobrists that they would vote for the greeting if it contained no reference to "autocracy." As a result by the vote of 212-146 the Duma rejected the rightists' salutation, "To His Majesty the Sovereign Emperor, Autocrat of All the Russias." Thereupon the right wing refused to join in the message and instead sent the tsar a separate greeting (bearing 114 signatures).

The Duma's message had been adopted by a completely unexpected coalition of center and left, and the vote received a great deal of attention. *Rech*, the voice of the Kadets, declared that "on the night of 13-14 November the Duma wrote an end to the neither-nor status of this great land, and in the twenty-fifth month of the Russian constitution it declared that the constitution of Rus does truly exist." *Tovarishch* proclaimed that "autocracy in Rus is dead beyond recall." *Rus* spoke of "the descent of the spirit of the people upon the Octobrists," while in *Moskovskie ezhenedelnik* [Moscow Weekly] Prince G.N. Trubetskoy announced: "The Manifesto of 17 October was registered once and for all in Russia on that memorable day of November 13th." *Novoe vremia's* Menshikov wrote that "the first victory of the left was unexpected and thunderous" and added: "Instead of an unsuccessful siege of the government, they will launch a Japanese-style flanking movement—a maneuver that seems peaceful, loyal, and devoted but ends: please allow us to bind you hand and foot."

The emperor was outraged that the Duma, for whose loyalty Stolypin only recently had vouched, should put to a vote—and reject!—his title which was confirmed by the Fundamental Laws. Nicholas never forgot this episode, and it determined his attitude toward the new Duma and toward the Octobrists in particular.

Nevertheless, the majority that emerged on 13 November had absolutely no correlation with the general political structure. The Octobrists had sided with the Kadets in the heat of battle, but fundamentally they remained opposed to the Kadets. Cooperation with the government and suppression of the revolution remained the foundation of their program. That was the banner that had carried them to victory in the election, and their course was parallel to that of the right, not the left. The vote of 13 November was fundamental and stipulative, but it could not alter the basic political alignments.

STOLYPIN SETS THE OCTOBRISTS STRAIGHT

Under different circumstances the new Duma might easily have been sidetracked into the oppositionist camp and thus into a deadlock. Stolypin, however, managed to restore the situation. He believed sincerely in the necessity of a representative system. He believed that the Duma contained a majority that wanted to cooperate with the government, and he knew that he could not get a better Duma without causing serious upheavals. Therefore, Stolypin made it clear to the Octobrists that he could go so far and no farther: if the Octobrists wished to avoid a break with the government, they first of all had to forego an alliance with avowed enemies of the regime—to renounce any coalition like the one that materialized suddenly on the 13th. Just three days later, on 16 November, Stolypin came before the Duma to speak in behalf of the government. Members of the center and right gathered and accompanied the prime minister into the chamber, greeted him with a noisy ovation, and interrupted him several times with their applause. "The historic Autocratic Power and free will of the monarch," stated Stolypin, "are the most valuable heritage of the Russian state system . . . and are destined, in times of upheaval and peril for the state, to save Russia and guide her along the path of order and historical truth. The autocracy of the tsars of Muscovy bears little resemblance to the autocracy of Peter, just as Peter's autocracy has little in common with the autocracies of Catherine II and the Tsar-Emancipator. The Russian state has grown and matured from its own roots, and as the roots developed and changed so too did the supreme power of the tsar. It is impossible to graft some foreign flower to our Russian roots, our Russian trunk. Let our own precious Russian flower bloom, let it flourish and unfold through cooperation between the supreme power and the representative institution which that power has created."

The Duma majority—from the center to the right—loudly acclaimed the speech of the chairman of the council of ministers. The Duma's attitude toward Stolypin became even more evident on the following day when the Kadet speaker Rodichev, responding to the prime minister's remarks, attacked Stolypin personally. The deputies sprang from their seats and demanded that Rodichev desist and sit down. Although Rodichev subsequently apologized to Stolypin, the Duma expelled him from fifteen sessions.

Once the sessions of 16 and 17 November demonstrated that the Duma majority was uniting behind Stolypin, the emperor's negative opinion of the assembly gradually began to soften. He responded drily to the greeting from the Duma: "I am prepared to believe the sentiments expressed in it. I expect productive labors." He responded gratefully to the telegram sent by the rightist deputies and told them: "I believe that the Duma created by Me will turn to its tasks and that it will justify My hopes by adhering strictly to the Fundamental Laws that I have established." On 19 November the emperor received Duma chairman Khomiakov for the first time and, as the newspapers noted, the reception was most gracious.

PARTIES AND ALIGNMENTS IN THE THIRD DUMA

The Duma took up the declaration of the council of ministers and at the conclusion of the debate it rejected all proposed plans of transition. The Octobrist program narrowly failed by a vote of 182-179 when deputies of the left and right combined to defeat the center. The assembly then debated the message to the emperor, and after that the Duma settled down. It became obvious that the Duma would be controlled by a majority of Octobrists and rightists.

The Octobrists were the most numerous party in the Duma and occupied a commanding position in the center. The Octobrist left wing contained deputies whose views were close to those of the Party of Peaceful Reconstruction; the right included deputies who had voted against the party leadership on 13 November. Alexander Guchkov was clearly the recognized leader of the Octobrists and in general the most prominent figure in the Third Duma. He spoke less often in general sessions than in party caucases. A.V. Trykova, writing in *Russkaia mysl*, observed that "the leader of the Third Duma is chary of speech-making. There is no doubt that his hand guides the bulky ship through the reefs, even though he rarely shows himself on the captain's bridge." Guchkov was firmly committed to constitutionalism and to the enhancement of the rights of the State Duma. But he was also a gradualist who hoped to achieve those ends without revolution. He believed that the Duma had to "grow into" the state system. To accomplish that the Duma had to learn to cooperate with the government, to conduct itself in a business-like manner, and to avoid the biased partisanship that presumably was incumbent upon parties of the opposition. The Octobrist ranks included many other distinguished spokesmen and even more business-like workers who could boast of long experience in zemstvo and municipal affairs—men like N.V. Savich, Professor M.M. Alekseenko, E.P. Kovalevsky, Baron A.F. Meyendorf, Count A.A. Uvarov, V.K. von Anrep, and many others.

The right wing of the Duma formed a more "democratic" composite in that it included many peasants and priests. On the extreme right was a fraction of about fifty deputies who identified with the Union of Russian People. They were critical of Stolypin's government and were quite prepared to play the role of an "opposition of the right." The rightists lacked any single recognized leader, and they often bickered among themselves. The leading ultra-conservative spokesmen were G.G. Zamyslovsky, N.Ye. Markov, V.M. Purishkevich, and V.V. Shulgin.

The moderate rightists, together with a small group of nationalists on their right, numbered about a hundred deputies. Their leader, even less conspicuous than Guchkov, was P.N. Balashov, and their most prominent speakers were Count V.A. Bobrinsky, Bishop Evlogy, and P.N. Krupensky. The right-moderates aligned with the Octobrists to form the main "Stolypin majority" in the Third Duma. However, whenever the nationalists sided with the extreme right, the combined forces of the left and right were sufficient to override the center. Such was the case when the Octobrists and right-moderates were out-voted on the question of the council of ministers' declaration.

Heterogeneous elements made up the opposition. The Progressists (Party of Peaceful Reconstruction) were not far removed from the Octobrist left wing, and in some instances they joined the Duma majority. N.N. Lvov was their leading spokesman. The Kadets formed the largest opposition party, but they no longer exercised the leadership that they had enjoyed in the first two Dumas. Miliukov, elected for the first time to the Third Duma, was the Kadets' leader, but their best spokesmen were F.I. Rodichev, A.I. Shingarev, and V.A. Maklakov. (Maklakov was the leading representative of the party's right wing.) The Muslim deputies usually voted with the Kadets. The Poles, on the other hand, remained aloof in order to emphasize the fact that they represented the Polish and not the Russian people. On the extreme left were two groups of about 34 deputies characterized by their extraordinary drabness: the main spokesman of the Trudoviks was the Lithuanian A.A. Bulat; two Georgians, N.S. Chkeidze and E.P. Gegechkory [both Mensheviks], led the Social Democrats.

Relations between the majority and the oppositionists were strained. Early in 1908 the majority instigated a demonstration against Miliukov, who during the Christmas recess had traveled to the United States to lecture on "the Russian liberation movement." Such an "appeal to foreigners" enraged the conservative press. When Miliukov returned and took the speaker's rostrum, a majority of deputies walked out of the assembly. The majority also demonstrated its contempt for the opposition when it chose the Duma's committee of imperial defense. Contrary to a general agreement on proportional representation, the Octobrists and rightists excluded from this committee all Social Democrats, Trudoviks, Poles, and even Kadets. The majority contended that those parties could not be trusted with sensitive military information. The committee of imperial defense, headed by Guchkov himself, subsequently became a very important body. In general the Octobrists and rightists did not miss any opportunity to express their loyalty to the crown, and early in January 1908 some 300 deputies were introduced to the emperor at Tsarskoe Selo.

TSAR AND DUMA, THE UNEASY PARTNERS

Nicholas entrusted the Duma entirely to Stolypin and rejected every effort to involve himself in legislative affairs. In January 1908 the Moscow nobility sent an appeal approved by a majority of rightists to which the emperor replied: "I am certain that as in former times the nobility of Moscow will render Me the service that I expect of it, and that it will dedicate all its strength to realize My instructions on the renewal and reinforcement of our great Russian state." Guchkov noted that the tsar's response made "an excellent impression. It is the highest tribute, the best possible proof of the stability of the constitutional system."

Generally the majority jealously guarded the Duma's rights, although in customary style the radical press alleged quite the contrary. At one point the government proposed to reduce the staff of a department created by imperial decree during the interval between the Second and Third Duma. The moderate-right leader Count Vladimir Bobrinsky proposed a reduction of one ruble in the department's budget in order to emphasize the Duma's prerogative to make such a decision. That reduction came to be known as "the constitutional ruble."

Debates over the budget afforded the Duma great influence over the entire governmental apparatus. Individual bureau chiefs literally quivered before the Duma's finance committee, which had the power to slash staffs and allocations. General debates on estimates for the various ministries opened all ministerial activities to public scrutiny and gave members of the opposition a golden opportunity to criticize the government. They used those debates to broadcast their propaganda, especially since the leftist press printed their speeches in full whereas all other papers severely edited them.

From the very outset the Duma paid particular attention to the requirements of public education. Its first budget provided an 8,000,000 ruble appropriation for public schools. The committee on imperial defense, working behind closed doors, developed a lively exchange with the military departments and generously responded to the requests of the army.

Stolypin and the Duma majority found the basis for amicable cooperation, even to the extent of a prearranged language for their dialogue. Government actions that displeased the center were attributed to "irresponsible influences," and by threatening to resign Stolypin found that he could get almost any concession he wanted from the majority. (Such exchanges always occurred in private, of course, for Stolypin obviously could never put before the Duma a "question of confidence" in the government.) During consideration of the restructuring of the railroads, Miliukov demanded the establishment of a "parliamentary investigating commission." Finance minister Kokovtsov quipped, "Thank God, we have no parliament," a remark that the chairman of the Duma, Khomiakov, characterized as "unfortunate." Thereupon the ministers took the position that they would not address the Duma, and Stolypin announced that he would resign unless the Duma found an acceptable way out of the situation. The incident was closed when Khomiakov "apologized" before the Duma.

At another point Guchkov, debating the annual estimates for the war ministry, sharply criticized the prevalence of persons "irresponsible by their very position, at the head of responsible and important branches of military life," meaning the grand dukes. He was particularly critical of the council of imperial defense whose chairman was Grand Duke Nicholas Nikolaevich. On that issue, however, both Stolypin and Minister of War Rediger were somewhat sympathetic to Guchkov's argument.[18]

The Duma majority was completely receptive to the emperor's desire to construct the Amur Railroad. It initiated its own revision of the relationship between Finland and the empire and even summoned Stolypin to an interpellation on that question.[19]

The first session of the Duma produced only one serious clash with the government. Nicholas deemed it essential to begin rebuilding the fleet, and a proposal to construct four battleships of the new dreadnought type was introduced into the Duma. The Duma, however, refused to appropriate the funds without a prior reorganization of the naval administration. The emperor was extremely annoyed. He complained to Stolypin that he "felt like rebuking" the State Duma for "its blind and entirely unjustifiable refusal of credits for the reconstruction of the fleet—and that just before the arrival of the King of England." Nicholas nevertheless permitted the government to follow prescribed legislative procedures to gain approval for the funds. Stolypin addressed the State Council on the subject: "All the arguments and evidence adduced by the legislative establishment to deny the funds are designed to compel the government to resort to purely executive alternatives inherent in the supreme power. They say: 'Do as we say, and you will get the money.' " The Duma's objective, Stolypin argued, was a parliamentary system: "It would establish invidious precedents to pave the way for an unconscious transition to [parliamentarianism]." The Duma refused to yield and thereby delayed the naval reconstruction program,[20] but that was the only major confrontation to occur during the first session of the Third Duma.

In an appraisal of the Third Duma, Prince Meshchersky wrote: "As long as Stolypin is head of the government, [the Duma] will be impudent, it will be stupid, and, though I think it will manage at length to be wise, one hardly could consider it dangerous."

CLOSING THE BOOK ON OLD BUSINESS

During the winter of 1907-1908, the government disposed of a series of matters left over from the revolution and war. The Social Democratic deputies of the Second Duma received sentences of four-to-five years at hard labor for attempting to create a revolutionary organization in the army. Members of the Peasants' Union were imprisoned for fifteen months in the

Peter and Paul Fortress for inciting agrarian riots. Members of the First Duma who signed the Vyborg manifesto were sentenced to only three months' imprisonment in the fortress; they were also deprived of their voting rights, which for them was a far more telling punishment. *Tovarishch* commented that "they were accused of setting the country on fire but were punished only for reckless driving in the city."

The trial of General Stessel and other high-ranking commanders at Port Arthur lasted more than two months. For surrendering Port Arthur, Stessel was sentenced to death, but his sentence was commuted to ten years in the fortress. The rest of the accused were acquitted.[21] A little later, Admiral Nebogatov, who had surrendered the remainder of his detachment after Tsushima, also faced a court-martial and was acquitted. The "ataman of the Urals," Lbov, who was sort of a twentieth-century Stenka Razin, was caught and executed on 1 May 1908. He and his band had been swaggering all over the Urals for some time, and his elusiveness had become legendary.

THE LAST STAND OF STUDENT RADICALISM

Russian life was settling into new ways. Equilibrium was returning gradually—an equilibrium more stable than what had existed before the Japanese war. Not only did the zemstvo, urban, and commercial-industrial elements abandon their former prejudiced opposition but a completely new attitude began to prevail among the students, who earlier had stood foremost in the struggle against the government. The winter of 1907-1908 passed, like its predecessor, without serious disturbances.

Every political party had a student following, and they met as literary circles under various names. They functioned without interference in the educational institutions, which were administered independently by councils of professors. That new regime afforded opportunities to unite and organize not only to left extremists, who had always formed clandestine organizations anyway, but also to moderates and rightists. Thus there were student organizations aligned with the Kadets, Octobrists, and Union of Russian People. The Kadet students adhered closely to the views of the professors and formed the moderate element in the student body. They contested the dominance of the left extremists and spurned demonstrations and strikes as critical tactics of political struggle. For two years life in the universities proceeded almost uneventfully. The radicals occasionally staged one-day strikes to protest one thing or another, but the only evidence of these disruptions was a slight decrease in the number of students attending lectures.

The revolutionary parties made one final effort to mobilize the student masses in the fall of 1908. The policy of the new minister of education, Alexander N. Schwartz, abetted their cause. On assuming his post, Schwartz announced that in the absence of new legislation old procedures were to be followed. Therefore, he reinstituted the use of transfer examinations in the middle schools and ordered that women no longer were to be permitted to audit courses in the universities. Women admitted to higher courses had been doing this since 1906 with the tacit consent of the authorities.[22] At the same time the ministry raised the question of dismissing several leftist instructors.

The Kadet papers denounced Schwartz's actions, as did the Octobrist *Golos Moskvy* [Voice of Moscow].[23] On 20 September 1908 the students of St. Petersburg University met and decided to strike. In order to avoid a confrontation, the council of professors decided to close the university, but the minister refused to permit it. Proclaiming its cause as "the struggle for university autonomy," the strike spread rapidly from St. Petersburg to other universities. At a demonstration in the capital one radical declared: "If the student body does not act now, we can say this for our universities: Rest in Peace."

The course of the strike revealed how much times had changed. The student moderates organized and campaigned against the strike by demanding a general referendum by secret ballot on the strike question. The leftists relied on their usual tactic of mass meetings. In a strange development at Moscow University a student rally by a voiced vote approved the obstruction of classes as a strike tactic, but in a written ballot that same body called for an end to the strike altogether! The authorities adopted a wait-and-see attitude. There were no mass arrests or exiles, and likewise no public demonstrations. After two weeks or so, one institution after another passed resolutions for the resumption of classes. For the first time in the history of the student movement moderate elements used their own resources to break the monopoly of the extremists, and radical control of the student movement came to an end. As a focal point of revolution, the universities proved indeed to be "deceased." In the years to come peace and quiet reigned in Russia's institutions of higher education.

THE REVALUATION OF VALUES

By the eve of the revolution of 1905 the Russian intelligentsia had acquired a complete set of values that denied the historic principles and foundations of the Russian state. Against traditional formulas like "For Faith, Tsar, and Fatherland" or "Orthodoxy, Autocracy, and Nationality" the intelligentsia counterpoised the negation of religion, the negation of monarchy, and the negation of the national idea. Love for the people, for "the masses," replaced their devotion to their native land. They approved of Lermontov, who had written: "I love my country, but with a strange love . . . for my soul is not satisfied by blood-drenched glory nor by peace steeped in fulsome arrogance;" but they scorned Pushkin for his "To the Slanderers of Russia" or his "Stanzas" to Emperor Nicholas I, which in their view were "disgraceful pages" that marred the work of the great poet.[24]

The defeat of the revolution not only disappointed the intelligentsia but also led them to reassess their values. The new order, even the demise of the radical movement in the universities, gave a strong impetus to this development. Before the revolution, anyone who criticized the left was subject to attack, but once the circumstances changed and such criticism no longer provoked retribution, many persons formerly silent began to speak out. The religious values of the intelligentsia were the first to be reappraised; then the examination extended to their conceptions of nationality, the state and Russia as a great power. The conference on religion and philosophy[25] and the establishment of the journal *Novyi put* testified to the intelligentsia's revived interest in religion even before 1905. But what earlier had concerned only a few now came to engage a wider intelligentsia following. Monthly journals, including even the Marxist *Sovremennyi mir* [The Contemporary

"The Tree of Russian Liberty" by a Socialist Cartoonist

World], began to carry articles on religious-philosophical themes. Symbolist literature, once universally derided,[26] finally gained acceptance, and there appeared a new literary trend, the vulgarized "modern style." Leonid Andreev, for example, turned from realist fiction to symbolist drama with plays like *Anathema, Tsar-Hunger*, and *The Black Masks.*

Certain negative tendencies accompanied this healthy reexamination of the "canons" of the intelligentsia. An epidemic of "saninism" swept the country. That term came from Michael Artsybashev's novel *Sanin*, a work preoccupied with eroticism and "free love."[27] Though denounced by both conservative and radical critics, *Sanin* was immensely popular among the intelligentsia and semi-intelligentsia. The novel's popularity came as a shock even to leftists, and it was published only because preliminary censorship had been abolished. Thus before the censors were able to proscribe *Sanin*, thousands of copies were in circulation all across Russia. Politics, once such a dominant factor in the life of the intelligentsia, had led to frustration, and they filled the vacuum in their lives by turning to whatever presented itself.

ORIGINS OF THE ANGLO-RUSSIAN RAPPROCHEMENT

Foreign affairs seemed subordinate to domestic affairs during the revolutionary period, but in fact a fundamental reorientation of Russian foreign policy was taking place. Before 1905 the cardinal features of Russian policy had been the alliance with France, good relations with Germany, cooperation with Austria in the Balkans, competition with England along the entire Asian "front," and open hostility toward Japan. But the Treaty of Portsmouth ended the bitter relations with Tokyo, and the British Liberals, who came to power in 1906, were disposed to modify England's traditional policy of hostility toward Russia. Besides a genuinely pacifist disposition, the new British attitude reflected the influence of France and their own concern over the growing rivalry with Germany. The development of a new type of battleship [the dreadnought] considerably depressed the value of older combat ships and seriously threatened England's traditional naval hegemony. The new dreadnoughts gave Germany, which just recently had begun to build a navy, a viable opportunity to challenge England for supremacy on the high seas.[28]

England sent a new ambassador to St. Petersburg in May 1906; he was Sir Arthur Nicolson[29] and his instructions were to achieve a rapprochement between England and Russia. He found the new Russian foreign minister, Alexander Izvolsky, quite receptive to this end. Initially the British government counted heavily on the Kadets for support in this matter, but Nicolson soon concluded that it was not the Duma but Stolypin who held the key to success. Nicolson was greatly agitated, therefore, when British Prime Minister Sir Henry Campbell-Bannerman spoke at an interparliamentary banquet after the dissolution of the First Duma and exclaimed, "The Duma is dead, long live the Duma!"[30] No less upset than his ambassador was the King of England, Edward VII. At the request of the Russian government the visit of a British squadron, scheduled for the summer of 1906, was cancelled. The incident, nevertheless, did not prevent the two governments from beginning a search to resolve their differences on Asian questions.

The published diplomatic correspondence indicates that England initiated the move for an understanding.[31] The Russian government went along because in principle it seemed inadvisable not to seek some amicable agreement as part of its larger policy of healing the wounds of war and revolution. The idea of an Anglo-Russian rapprochement seemed consistent with a general trend toward liberalism and was popular with Russian society. Unaware that the British had taken the initiative, Russians assumed that the imperial government was committed to a "constitutional course" because of its desire for an understanding with England. The press, therefore, forgot the long-standing conflict between Russia and England and ignored even the most recent incidents in order to promote Anglo-Russian cooperation. Meanwhile, it never occurred to the emperor to alter Russia's domestic policy for the sake of wooing England. If the existence of the Duma facilitated a rapprochement, that was only because it helped the British overcome their deep-seated antipathy toward "tsarism."

The negotiations dealt with Tibet, Afghanistan, and Persia (Iran). Tibet was nominally part of the Chinese Empire. Before the war with Japan, Russia had attempted to use its subjects, the Buriat-Lamaites, to influence the government of the

Dalai Lama and to counter British influence. England took advantage of the Russo-Japanese War to send a military expedition to Tibet. The Younghusband expedition occupied the forbidden city of Lhasa, and the Dalai Lama fled to Mongolia. England then forced the Tibetan government to agree to a treaty which gave London control over its foreign relations. Afghanistan was an old bone of contention between Russia and England. The Afghan boundary dispute produced the only incident that nearly led to war during the entire reign of Alexander III. All Russian plans for an invasion of India were predicated on the occupation of Afghanistan. In Persia the British resisted the spread of Russian influence, supported liberal and revolutionary elements against the shah, and opposed the construction of Russian railroads for fear that Russia would gain access to the Indian Ocean by way of the Persian Gulf and the port of Bender Abbas.

In 1906 England offered major concessions, although it remained inflexible on Afghanistan. The British were willing to renounce their domination of Tibet, and they offered the Russians a sphere of influence in northern Persia, which was the country's most populous and fertile area. The negotiations proceeded for a year [June 1906-August 1907]. At first they were shrouded in secrecy and were not even mentioned in the press until the spring of 1907. The reports produced great satisfaction in France and great concern in Germany. Russians, preoccupied with the Second Duma, took little note of them at first. France and Japan concluded an agreement in the spring of 1907,[32] and the official Russian press stressed St. Petersburg's warm approval. Then in the summer of 1907 Russia and Japan signed agreements which liquidated the last issues remaining from the war.[33]

On 21 July [3-6 August] 1907 the tsar and the kaiser met in the Baltic in the waters off Swinemünde. It was their first meeting in two years, since Björkö. Though attended by great ceremony, the conference was politically insignificant. Nicholas outlined the basis of Russia's agreement with England, and William tried to appear unconcerned. The collapse of the Björkö agreement injected a certain strain into the relations of the two emperors. Nicholas believed that the kaiser had misconstrued the treaty by insisting on its literal interpretation, while William felt that the tsar had yielded to the pressure of his ministers and abrogated obligations that he personally had assumed. Thus the toasts given at Swinemünde were remarkably noncommittal. Nicholas mentioned the "continuation of kindred relations and traditional friendships;" William said something about "the unchangeable friendship between our dynasties and our people." Even so, the meeting at Swinemünde gave foreigners the impression that Russia's freedom of action had been limited in so far as its agreements with Japan and England were concerned.

THE ANGLO-RUSSIAN AGREEMENTS OF 1907

England and Russia signed their far-reaching agreements on 18/31 August 1907. England yielded Tibet, and both powers recognized China's sovereignty over that country. Russia renounced its designs on Afghanistan, and both governments pledged to respect Afghanistan's independence and inviolability. Persia was divided into three zones. The Russian sphere of influence was the northern zone with the cities of Tabriz and Teheran, the southern coast of the Caspian Sea, and the central region up to Ispahan and Khanikin. The British sphere was defined as the southeastern region bordering on Afghanistan and India. In between was a "neutral zone" which included almost the entire shore of the Persian Gulf. Both countries mutually pledged to protect Persia's independence and territorial integrity.[34]

The Russian press on the whole approved of the accords. *Novoe vremia* referred to the agreements with Japan and England as the "liquidation" or settling of old accounts: "The agreement of 18 August signifies a new era in Asian alignments; it signals the abandonment of that Indian conquest that once fired the Russian imagination." In defending the agreement before the council of ministers, foreign minister Izvolsky used a similar argument: "We must put our Asian interests in proper perspective, otherwise we ourselves will become an Asiatic country, and that would be the greatest of misfortunes for Russia."

Johannes von Miquel, the German charge d'affaires in St. Petersburg, sent these observations to Chancellor Bülow: "It seems to me that the novelties introduced into Asia by these agreements are not as great as expected. The importance of the Russian-English agreement will be felt less in Asia than in Europe, where its consequences will be apparent for some time to come." Miquel emphasized that the agreement was "more likely English handiwork than the result of Russian policy," and he noted the anti-German tone that accompanied reports of the agreement in the Russian and British press. British conservatives, however, sharply objected to the accords. Lord Curzon, the former viceroy of India and organizer of the Tibetan campaign, was particularly outraged. Nevertheless, the British Parliament ratified the agreements.

THE DOUBLE-HEADED EAGLE

If one were to credit the remarks of the German charge d'affaires, then the tsar had no desire to join England in a pact directed against Germany. But neither did Nicholas have any reason to oppose an English accord, particularly when it offered Russia considerable advantages simply for abandoning ambitions that hardly could be realized anyway in the foreseeable future. All the same, the emperor was not writing off Asia. His strong interest in the construction of the Amur railroad demonstrated his continued concern for the Far East. When Stolypin appeared before the Duma to defend this project, he argued that "the Russian people always have been conscious that they are settled and firmly established astride two parts of the world, that they beat back the Mongolian invasion, and that the Orient is dear and close to their hearts. Our emblem, the legacy of the Byzantines, is the double-headed eagle. True, one-headed eagles are strong and mighty, but you will not change our eagle into a one-headed eagle by severing the head that faces east—you will only make it bleed to death." Stolypin's statement was a better expression of the emperor's view than Izvolsky's contention that Russia's interests in Asia had to be put "in proper perspective."

Not only what was said but also what was left unsaid in the Anglo-Russian agreement gave Russia undeniable advantages in Asia. Moreover, the agreements with Japan on northern Manchuria, Mongolia, and Chinese Turkestan had little resemblance to the view, especially common in Russian society, that Russia was a humiliated and weakened power. Indeed, what was remarkable was the swiftness with which Russia recovered its prestige as a world power. Russia remained the major power in Asia. The war had exhausted Japan more than Russia, and thanks to the emperor's wisdom and firmness Tokyo had failed to obtain the indemnity it so earnestly desired. Japan knew that Russian power was to be taken seriously: Japan had tested that power in battle, and the Japanese rulers knew very well that the good fortune that enabled them to conclude the war on favorable terms was unlikely to smile on them again.

Nicholas did not want the British agreements to lead to a break with Germany, but powerful influences led in that direction. Russian society was consumed with the thought that an alliance with England and France inevitably meant "constitution," whereas friendship with Germany promised only "reaction." Foreign minister Izvolsky did not immediately adhere to that view, but he found supporters in the Duma not only among the majority but also among the opposition in the person of Paul Miliukov. Meanwhile the intelligentsia began to take an interest in foreign affairs. Peter Struve, not at all embarrassed to exploit Stolypin's epigram about "a Great Russia" and "a great upheaval" wrote:[35] "There is only one way to create a Great Russia, and that is to channel all our resources into the one region that is truly accessible to the realistic influence of Russian culture. That region is the entire basin of the Black Sea, the region, that is, where all the European and Asiatic nations converge on the Black Sea."

None of these ideas were new, of course. They represented a return to the Near Eastern policy of Nicholas I and Alexander II. The Russian government had followed a different course in later decades as it became more aware of the pitfalls and narrow opportunities along that ostensibly natural route. Then, suddenly, one whole generation later, the Russian intelligentsia set out on the road already traveled by the Russian state. To most Russians that course seemed easier and was more understandable than the ambitious Asian policy of the emperor.

And so by the summer of 1908, without any formal change in Russian foreign policy, the world was introduced to a new international combination: Russia, France, and England. On 28 May/10 June 1908 King Edward VII of England arrived at

Reval. A fierce parliamentary debate preceded his visit. Representatives of the British left protested the government's rapprochement with tsarism and discoursed at length on "Russian atrocities." Sir Edward Grey[36] countered decisively. He reminded the house of the epidemic of revolutionary terror and pointed out that the signers of the Vyborg manifesto had been jailed for committing an illegal act "not for their liberal convictions." The debate revealed that the major British parties, the Liberals and Conservatives, were equally in favor of the rapprochement with Russia.

Less than a month after the visit of Edward VII, the President of France, Armand Fallières, paid a state visit. In the French parliament only the socialists protested, but even they were not particularly vehement. "The President," cried the "communard" Vaillons, "may hear gunfire in Russia: her best citizens are being shot." Stephen Pichon, the foreign minister, resolutely condemned slurs like that. Such was the international setting in July 1908, when the revolt of the Young Turks erupted and ended all possibility of maintaining the status quo in the Balkans.

∽ဝ၇∾

CHAPTER FOURTEEN

THE THEORY AND MECHANICS OF AGRARIAN REFORM

In an address to the State Council on 11 March 1908 Stolypin succinctly set forth the government's number one priority: "Many believe that without the complete restoration of calm to the villages, everything must remain as it was. The government has a different idea . . . . The government intends to suppress—by force if necessary—any attempt to create disorder. But the government is also convinced that it must commit all of its moral resources to the regeneration of the country. Reconstruction must, of course, begin at the bottom. It should be possible to begin with the weathered stones of the foundation and rebuild in such a way as to strengthen the entire edifice without causing it to tumble down."

The imperial government recognized the need to improve the conditions of rural life and had wrestled with the problem for years. Finally, after great thought, debate, and preparation, it had decided on a course and moved forward with determination and energy. Any resolute action on so controversial an issue as land reform was bound to provoke bitter controversy. And indeed, both conservatives and radicals attacked the Law of 9 November 1906.[1] Within the Duma only the centrists and moderate rightists wholeheartedly supported the principle of extending private property to the villages. On the right, especially among peasants and priests, the obshchina had many defenders. Nicholas Markov announced that he would vote for the law only because he considered it improper to oppose the will of his tsar. The law already was being implemented, otherwise it would have cleared the Duma only with great difficulty.

"Only peasant emancipation and the railway construction program compare in significance to the agrarian reform which abolished the commune," wrote Peter Struve in *Russkaia mysl*. "It is clear," he added, "that without the Law of 3 June the State Duma never would have accepted Stolypin's agrarian reform. It is also clear that, even with the 3rd of June system, the Duma never would have agreed to the reform except for its prior enactment without the Duma under Article 87."[2] Agrarian reform, therefore, was achieved in the traditional manner, by command of the sovereign. But even though the Rubicon had been crossed, the Duma majority had the opportunity to work with the government in the further development of the legislation.

Implementation of the reform actually had been underway since 1 January 1907. The basic principle underlying that great task was the right of peasants to depart freely from their communes and to acquire personal title to their lands—individual, not family ownership, was to be the key. As prime minister and minister of interior, Stolypin took the lead in carrying out the reform. He demanded an equal commitment from the local authorities. The administration was not supposed to stand by idly waiting to see whether the peasantry wanted to take advantage of the new legislation. In January 1909 he assembled the members of the land settlement commissions[3] and told them: "You are pledged to explain the new law thoroughly to the people and to make it easy for them to take advantage of it. A key has been placed in your hands. You must rely on your own intelligence and use that key to unlock the door to a better future for our people. Get to know the power that is in your hands and understand this, that I cannot tolerate failure—in my view an uninspired worker is no worker at all."

Local commissioners drawn from the bureaucracy and zemstvos responded eagerly to the government's energetic initiative. The responsibility for actually carrying out the reform was delegated to district land settlement commissions, most of whose members were elected officials.[4] In the first two years 374 district commissions set to work; within five years there were 463. The number of surveyors employed by the commissions expanded in five years from 200 to more than 5,000.[5]

An essential feature of the reform was the reorganization of landholdings, and in that respect the government's basic goal was to eliminate strip farming. Special legislation on land reorganization later emanated from the Duma and State

Council. The manifold responsibilities of the land commissions included the transfer of already consolidated holdings to private ownership (without resurveying), the division of consolidated lands into individual allotments, the creation of small farmsteads (the *otrub*), and the resurvey of communal lands to eliminate strips though without immediately converting the land to private property.

With a view toward creating viable independent peasant proprietors, the government encouraged communes to make a final redistribution of their lands. Then the authorities assisted in the transfer of title to the land and in the consolidation of peasant holdings into compact farms. Peasant allotments in villages which had not reapportioned their lands since emancipation were considered to have reverted automatically to individual ownership. Individuals separating from their communes received allotments equal to their share of the communal land as established by local custom. Independent proprietors retained their rights to pasture, forest, and other common lands.

The land resettlement process followed four stages: (1) entire communities or individual peasants submitted applications for a redivision of the land; (2) the land was surveyed and mapped to indicate the new demarcation of holdings; (3) boundary markers were actually set in place; and (4) the peasants, singly or collectively, approved the new boundaries; when disputes arose, the land commission made the final decision.

THE CAMPAIGN AGAINST THE COMMUNE, 1907-1911

The following statistics reveal the complexity and pace of the land reform. During the first five years of the reform, the authorities received 2,653,000 applications for individual allotments. Preliminary surveys were made for 1,327,000 householders (with 12,406,000 desiatins); 1,700,000 surveys were completed; and 891,000 householders accepted final settlements totaling 8,067,000 desiatins.[6] Although the figures seem enormous and even though eight million desiatins represented more than the combined area of Holland and Belgium, the figures represented only a modest beginning. The area converted to private ownership constituted only about five percent of the communal land in Russia, exclusive of land already

The Emperor Examining a New Type of Plow

privately owned by peasants. That figure, however, did not include 1,715,000 desiatins converted to private ownership but not yet reapportioned, nor did it reflect the work completed in eliminating scattered strips but short of conversion to private ownership (some 6,000,000 desiatins in six years). In other words, during the first phase of their operations, the land commissions altered the status of about 17,000,000 [?] desiatins.

The pace of the reform varied widely throughout Russia. It enjoyed rapid success in New Russia (the provinces of Taurida, Ekaterinoslav, and Kherson), in the neighboring Ukrainian provinces of Kharkov and Poltava, and in the northwestern provinces of St. Petersburg, Pskov, and Smolensk. Resettlement moved forward with equal speed in the western region, where the problem was not the dissolution of communes but the consolidation of holdings into farmsteads, and in the lower Volga region (in the provinces of Saratov and especially Samara). In short, the reform was an immediate success either in territory settled comparatively recently or in areas that bordered on districts where private ownership was prevalent, as in the northwestern provinces around the Baltic.

In the north and northeast (Arkhangel, Vologda, Olonets, and Perm) still another extreme appeared, for there the reform remained a dead letter. Olonets did not record a single resettlement in five years, in Arkhangel only 200 desiatins in a total of 335,000 were reorganized, and the pattern was the same in the others. In those provinces with their vast amounts of open land and great distances the need for mutual support was stronger than the desire for freedom in the disposition of the land.

Between those extremes were the original Great Russian provinces where 2-5 percent of the peasant holdings were reorganized as private property. In each of those provinces several thousand peasants (about 5,000 in Kazan, 9,000 in Tver, and so on) decided to disregard the conservative majorities and demanded their allotments from the communes.

CONSERVATIVE MISGIVINGS

The government's land reform program went beyond the Law of 9 November. It already had established a land reserve

(1906), which made certain appanage and state lands available to the peasantry, and the Peasant Bank aggressively continued to purchase land from the nobility. In the fourteen months following the first of January 1906, the bank purchased 7,617 nobles' estates, a total of 8,700,000 desiatins— more land than the bank had acquired in the preceding quarter of a century. After 1907 the bank's purchases diminished somewhat. The bank's policy of selling or leasing land to peasants on very favorable terms contributed to the liquidation of large estates, an economic development that seriously concerned some observors.

V.I. Gurko in an important speech to the congress of the United Nobility early in 1909 declared that the breakup of large-scale enterprises was reducing the country's economic productivity. He pointed out that small-scale agriculture was not as prevalent in Western Europe as it was in Russia. The policy of the Peasant Bank, he said, produces a situation in which "everyday in Russia the total area of rented land decreases by 3,000 desiatins; everyday 3,000 desiatins of arable land is doomed to be fragmented into small plots .... We are witnessing the most energetic fulfillment of the Socialist Revolutionary program whose aim, as you well know, is the expulsion of all property owners from the countryside." Gurko also stressed the contradiction between the government's policy of buying up nobles' estates for resale to peasants and the Law of 3 June: it appeared that the government was working for the economic destruction of the very social element to which it offered a decisive political role in the State Duma.

The historian V.I. Gere warned against the cultural consequences of destroying the landowning nobility. In 1906 he wrote: "If the hearths of the gentry are allowed to go out, then the hearths of culture also will be extinguished, and the dark gloomy night of barbarism will reign all across our vast Russia."

The government, not entirely oblivious to those concerns, directed its attention to land organization and agricultural development, leaving it to the natural law of supply and demand to find the proper correlation of great and small ownership. The Peasant Bank stopped its massive accumulation of land, but the landholdings of the nobility continued to dwindle steadily. To a rather considerable extent the nobles were losing their taste for the land. Many landowners left their estates for good after the disturbances of 1905-1906. Thus, however willy-nilly, the development of Russian agriculture had to be entrusted to the more efficient peasant landowners whose economic importance increased with each passing year.

"THE WAGER ON THE STRONG"

While officials throughout Russia struggled to translate the complexities of land reform into reality, the Duma and State Council thoroughly and sometimes angrily debated the new legislation. The Law of 9 November, approved and amended by the Duma's land committee, came before the general membership of the Duma on 23 October 1908. About half of the assembly, 213 deputies, signed up to speak on the bill. Almost all of the peasant deputies felt obliged to address the subject. The committee spokesman, the Octobrist S.I. Shidlovsky,[7] declared that the agrarian legislation represented a genuine return to the liberal course of the great reforms of Alexander II, a course abandoned by the government during the period of "reaction."

The objections raised by the opposition were basically political in nature. A.I. Shingarev reminded the Duma that the Law of 9 November emerged during the heated activities of the courts-martial. Rodichev argued that it was "impossible for a country that does not enjoy the rule of law to support an intensive economy." Miliukov tried to discredit the law by contending that its true authors were V.I. Gurko and the council of the United Nobility. The Progressist N.N. Lvov emotionally answered that charge:

This ukaz reflects far more than the specific interests of the nobility—it embodies our nation's interests . . . . It is essential above all that our peasant begins to sense that he is an owner and master. Only through private property can you give him this attitude. If it is in the interests of the nobility to insist on introducing private property into peasant life, if the interests of the nobility consist of leading the peasantry out of their present condition by instilling among them the solid foundations of private property in order to teach them to respect the rights of others as well as their own—then we must support those 'interests' and in doing so we will accomplish a great task. I will not hesitate to go over to the side of those who seek to achieve that!

Among radical leftists, the Trudoviks clung to their agrarian socialist ideology and consistently defended the obshchina.

The Social Democrats also opposed the reform, but Count V.A. Bobrinsky reminded them that their stand ran counter to their own program, and he quoted Lenin from the journal *Zaria* [The Dawn]:[8] "The lands should be taken away; but as for turning them over to the peasants, that would stand in contradiction to the aggravation of the class struggle. No, we oppose the sale of land as private property."

The right also criticized the reform. Deputy Shechkov from Kursk argued that the abolition of the commune was inconsistent with the Russian class structure and violated the right of collective ownership. V.A. Obraztsov, a member of the Union of the Russian People, received a thunderous ovation when he warned the Duma that the peasantry, having received the freedom to dispose of its land as it pleased, would sell its property and spend the proceeds on alcohol. "If, instead of providing allotments to the land-hungry and landless, the Duma wants to breed a proletariat—to breed millions of landless peasants, then we will go back home and report that the State Duma and the government are solving the land problem in reverse." Count V.A. Bobrinsky, the leader of the right moderates, answered that charge by citing Professor Petrazhitsky:[9] "If we think the peasants are like those who would roast and eat the cow given to them to provide milk for their children, then they require general supervision. However, if we recognize that the time has come to make proper economic use of the land, it follows that the peasants must be given the right to own the land." Speaking for the government, Deputy Minister of Interior Lykoshin charged: "To assert that peasants, given the right to dispose of their land as they please, would turn, almost to a man, into drunkards and sell their plots for half a kopeck to buy a class of vodka—that is a slander against the Russian people."

Stolypin himself spoke on agrarian reform only once, on 5 December 1908, during an item-by-item reading of the bill. His purpose was to defend the principle of individual ownership against attempts to substitute ownership by peasant households. As a result of his speech, Stolypin's agrarian policy came to be known as "the wager on the strong."

Exceptional problems require exceptional measures . . . [he said]. But when writing legislation for the entire country, we must bear in mind above all the sober and strong peasants, not the drunkards and weaklings . . . . We must be confident, gentlemen. There was a moment not too long ago when confidence in Russia's future was shaken . . . . At that moment the only confidence not shaken was the faith of the Russian tsar in the strength of Russia's toilers and peasants . . . .

Is it not clear that the bondage of the commune and the yoke of family ownership create bitter slavery for a nation of ninety million persons? Have we already forgotten that we have traveled that road before and that our gigantic experiment as guardians over the bulk of our people already has proven to be a colossal failure? Gentlemen, we cannot return to that road, nor can we allow only the upper classes the illusory luxury of freedom. We must deal with life itself . . . .

Gentlemen, it is impossible to provide armor for everyone going into battle and there is no spell to be cast that will protect every warrior from injury. Likewise, gentlemen, it is impossible to design a law only for the feeble and powerless. No! In the world struggle, in the competition among nations, the place of honor can be won only by those who are willing to expend the full measure of their material and moral resources.

THE STOLYPIN MAJORITY

The question of agrarian reform produced the following alignment of the Duma: Octobrists, moderate-rightists, nationalists, a section of the right, the Polish Kolo, and some of the Progressists rallied in support of the Law of 9 November.[10] The extreme left, the Kadets, and most of the extreme right formed the opposition. The majority was an impressive one, and the Duma even managed to introduce some amendments that increased the pressure on communes to cooperate in the transition to private property. Most of the Duma's revisions, however, were scuttled by the State Council.[11]

After considerable delay in the legislature, the new agrarian law finally won approval and was published on 14 July 1910. By then it actually had been in operation for three and a half years. The law was not put into practice without some resistance. Peasants who favored retention of the obshchina sometimes vented their hostility against those who were withdrawing to form private farmsteads. Violence occurred frequently during the first years, and the oppositionist press even predicted "civil war in the villages." But no civil war developed. The government was strong enough to maintain order, and the instances of violence became increasingly rare.

Alexander Krivoshein, appointed director of the main administration of land organization and agriculture [i.e. minister of agriculture] in the fall of 1908, set out to increase the rate of agricultural development through improved programs of state assistance. He initiated a program of loans for land reclamation, expanded agricultural education, and established model farms and experimental stations on state-owned lands. The attention of Russia focused increasingly on agriculture. During the first decade of the emperor's reign, agriculture had been a stepchild of Witte's economic policy. That negative legacy began to change.

After land reform, the main concern of the government during the period of the Third Duma centered on military reorganization, based on experiences in the Japanese war, and on naval reconstruction and the development of public education. Those, indeed, were the most urgent problems of the day. The Duma supported the government on the agrarian question, and it played a major role in the reorganization of the army. In naval affairs, however, it quickly became a stumbling block. On the other hand, it became an accelerator in the realm of public education. In the spring of 1908 the Duma committee on public education drafted a twenty-year plan (1909-1928) for the gradual introduction of elementary education throughout the empire. Count Bobrinsky, who had christened the Second Duma the "Duma of national ignorance," once remarked that the Third Duma had to strive to become the "Duma of national education." The Duma did much to merit that title.

THE COLLAPSE OF THE BALKAN ENTENTE

The Austro-Russian agreement of 1897, confirmed in 1903 at Mürzsteg in a meeting of the two emperors, was predicated on two principles: the solidarity of the two monarchic states and their mutual renunciation of any attempt to alter the status quo in the Balkans. As ambassador to St. Petersburg, Baron Alois Aerenthal[12] was considered a russophile and a convinced supporter of monarchical solidarity. As Austria's foreign minister, he was destined to become the destroyer of the Austro-Russian accord.

Austria's response to the Russian revolutionary movement was to introduce universal and equal suffrage. Liberals and socialists contended that this move would strengthen the unity of the Austrian empire. Instead, the first election under the

new law demonstrated that national differences had penetrated even to the masses. The empire's socialists themselves
split into particularist factions reflecting their diverse national
origins. The reform set the masses in motion, but it did nothing to build imperial unity. The question of the Austrian succession remained open and, in anticipation of the event, many
observors dated the disintegration of the Danubian monarchy
from the death of Emperor Franz Joseph, who was 78 in
1908.

The conviction that time was working against the empire
prompted Austro-Hungarian statesmen to adopt a risky policy
—a kind of preventive attack against the empire's potential
successors. Against Russia this policy expressed itself as an
increasing encouragement of alleged Ukrainian separatism. In
the Balkans Austria wanted to demonstrate its strength, and
it must be said that Germany did not lift a finger in any serious
effort to restrain its ally from that course of action.

On 14/27 January 1908 Baron Aerenthal informed the
Austro-Hungarian delegations that he had instructed the ambassador in Constantinople to raise the question of Austrian
concessions regarding the construction of a railway through
the Sanjak of Novi Bazar, a Turkish province that separated
Serbia and Montenegro. Under the terms of the Treaty of
Berlin [1878], Austria had the right to maintain small garrisons in the sanjak. From an economic standpoint the railway,
paralleling a line through Serbia, would create a new direct
link between Austria and the Aegean port of Saloniki and thus
reinforce the Central Powers' access to Turkey. The railway
project clearly deviated from the established Austro-Russian
policy. In his memoirs Baron M.A. Taube correctly describes
this as the first move in a series that ultimately led the world
to war.

The Russian government and press reacted sharply to the
Austrian effort to upset the status quo. The German ambassador, Count Frederich Pourtales,[13] apparently with little
understanding of Russian domestic affairs, dismissed Russia's
concern as an outgrowth of "reactionary tendencies" which
presumably went hand in hand with "Pan-Slavic ambitions."
Receiving the Austrian ambassador on 15/28 February, the
tsar told him that he valued Emperor Franz Joseph's friendship. Even though the policy of cooperation with Austria never

was popular in Russia, said Nicholas, he intended to pursue it, although Baron Aerenthal's statement "made it difficult." In a note referring to Germany Izvolsky declared that "the international agreements that we have undertaken with the sole aim of protecting ourselves from complications in Asia do not contain any threat to Germany." Nevertheless, an anti-Austrian and anti-German tone swelled through the Russian press, and the radicals' commentary was scarcely discernible from that of *Novoe vremia.*

The Russian government revived a plan for a railroad from Serbia to the Adriatic Sea—across the projected Austrian route —and the kaiser promised the tsar Germany's support. The Balkan situation was changing in that England was beginning to shift its backing from Austria to Russia. At their meeting at Reval Nicholas II and Edward VII discussed the possibility of broad autonomy for Macedonia.[14]

Then suddenly in early July 1908 a revolt broke out in Turkey. It was led by nationalist officers who were members of a secret society known as the Committee of Union and Progress. They were known more commonly as the Young Turks. Sultan Abdul Hamid II, whose absolute power had remained unchallenged for thirty years,[15] found himself without support. Only one army corps stationed in Constantinople remained loyal to him, but the provincial garrisons, beginning with the Balkan units, went over to the revolution. Unwilling to commit his only loyal troops to battle, the sultan decided to give in and restore the constitution of 1876, which he had abrogated in 1877. The Young Turks became masters of the country, including the capital, even though an old liberal functionary, Kiamil Pasha, became premier [grand vizier].[16]

The Turkish revolution took place in isolation from the non-Turkish nationalities which formed a majority of the population of the Ottoman Empire. The Young Turks were Turkish nationalists committed to the indivisibility of the empire. After visiting Constantinople, Guchkov compared the Young Turks to the Octobrists, and radical journalists in Russia had a field day ridiculing him. The election of a Turkish parliament was scheduled. As a result, all demands on Turkey and all plans for Macedonian reform were tabled.

NEGOTIATIONS AT BUCHLAU

With the outcome of the Turkish revolt in doubt, all powers with an interest in the Turkish succession began to prepare their claims. Izvolsky went abroad for a meeting with Aerenthal at Castle Buchlau on 3/16 September. Various versions of the details of this meeting have emerged. The German secretary of state for foreign affairs, Baron William von Schoen, sent Bülow an account of a conversation with Izvolsky on 13/26 September. According to Schoen, Aerenthal made the following proposal at Buchlau: Austria would limit itself to the annexation of Bosnia and Herzegovina, give up its drive toward Saloniki, pull its troops out of the Sanjak of Novi Bazar, and support Russia's demand for unfettered transit of its warships through the Straits. Simultaneously Bulgaria would declare its independence—a mere formality in as much as Turkish sovereignty had been a fiction for some time.

Izvolsky apparently approved this plan in principle. It is important to recall that in the Reichstadt agreements of 1876 and again in the alliance of the three emperors in 1881 Russia had recognized Austria's right to annex Bosnia and Herzegovina "whenever it becomes necessary."[18] On that point, therefore, the Russian foreign minister's hands were tied; it was simply a matter of obtaining some compensation. Izvolsky believed that Austria's renunciation of the sanjak, the right of free passage through the Straits, and Bulgarian independence (besides an attractive commercial agreement for Serbia) afforded Russia sufficient compensation. He also appears to have believed that this revision of the Treaty of Berlin would be part of a single package, presumably to be recognized by a new international conference.

Unfortunately on 24 September/7 October 1908 Baron Aerenthal announced Austria's annexation of Bosnia and Herzegovina.[19] This step became necessary, he explained, in order to bestow representative institutions upon those provinces so that their inhabitants would not be disadvantaged in comparison to their neighbors under Turkish rule. At the same time Prince Ferdinand of Bulgaria proclaimed his country's complete independence and assumed for himself the title of tsar. These actions clearly repudiated obligations assumed under the Treaty of Berlin, even though they actually only confirmed long-standing realities.

THE BOSNIAN ANNEXATION CRISIS

In international relations "no one makes sweet music." Russians, and especially Serbs, recoiled in anguish at the news. Belgrade viewed Vienna's action as the first step toward Austrian hegemony in the Balkans. As the Serbs saw it, Bulgaria had "received its independence from the hand of Austria," and the annexation of Bosnia and Herzegovina represented a wilful occupation of Slavic territory. Slav sympathizers sprang to life in Russia and launched an intense campaign against the Austrian coup. The Young Czech leader, Dr. Karel Krámař, and other Slavic leaders visited Petersburg during the spring of 1909, and that summer an All-Slavic congress convened in Prague with several members of the State Duma in attendance. The Russian government tried to combat this agitation, for example by prohibiting discussions after lecturers had spoken. Meanwhile, moderate deputies competed with leftists in denouncing the government's efforts to restrain the movement. At one meeting even V.A. Bobrinsky announced that if the government accepted the annexation it would have to "dissolve the Duma and arrest us all." The campaign embraced the political spectrum from the moderate right to the Kadets. Only the extreme left and right remained aloof: both agreed that a break with Austria and Germany would lead Russia to war and eventually to revolution.

Austria's violation of the Berlin accords displeased London and Paris and they backed Russia's demand for an international conference. England, however, would not endorse Izvolsky's dream of adequate compensation—the opening of the Straits.

Izvolsky, insisting that the conduct of foreign policy was the prerogative of the emperor, refused to explain his meeting with Aerenthal to the council of ministers. Obviously the foreign minister was embarrassed by the turn of events and stunned by the public reaction. His only defense was that his bargain with Aerenthal was conditional, but those who regarded the annexation itself an outrage also regarded any mention of compensation as a shameful irrelevancy. Moreover, as *Vestnik evropy* explained, "the only way to wrest that territory from the hands of the Austrians is by force of arms." But Russia knew that it was unprepared for war. Izvolsky offered to tender his resignation but the emperor would not allow it.

In the end there was no formal resolution of the annexation crisis. After more than five months, the Bosnian question ceased to inflame the Russian public. In the Duma agrarian reform and then the Azef affair pushed foreign affairs into the background. Austria and Bulgaria, meanwhile, came to an understanding with Turkey; financial compensation helped reconcile Constantinople to the loss of another portion of its empire. Russia assisted Bulgaria in that matter by yielding to Belgrade several years' payment of the indemnity imposed on Turkey after the war of 1878.[20] Then without waiting for a conference of the powers Russia formally recognized Bulgarian independence. The Bosnian question remained unresolved, however, and agitation remained strong among the Serbs, who were counting on Russian support.

BERLIN'S FRIENDLY MEDIATION AND ITS SIGNIFICANCE

The Austrians then decided to press their advantage by forcibly establishing their supremacy over the Balkans. Vienna threatened Serbia with war unless Belgrade accepted the annexation. The Serbs firmly insisted that only an "international tribunal" could resolve the issue.[21] The situation grew perilous. At that point Berlin offered to mediate and proposed a compromise: The German government would use its influence to persuade the Danubian monarchy to abandon the use of force against Serbia and also would bring Austria to seek formal approval of the Bosnian annexation from the powers, if for its part Russia would promise in advance to recognize the annexation. On 8/21 March 1909 Bülow instructed his ambassador, Pourtales: "Your Excellency will declare to Mr. Izvolsky in most precise terms that we expect an unequivocal answer—yes or no. We will be compelled to regard any evasive, conditional, or vague response as a rejection of our offer. In that event we shall withdraw and allow events to run their course. The responsibility for any further consequences then would fall exclusively on Mr. Izvolsky."[22]

While somewhat short of an ultimatum, the German demarche contained an obvious threat. To "allow events to run their course" implied an Austrian attack on Serbia. If Russia chose to interfere, then in accord with the terms of the Triple Alliance Germany would be obligated to come to the aid of its ally. Still, the German proposal offered a way out of the impasse, and on 9 March Nicholas wired the kaiser that your proposal "indicated a desire to find a peaceful solution," and "I have instructed Izvolsky to meet you half-way." But the tsar also warned that "a final rupture between Russia and Austria would adversely affect our relations with Germany. I need not repeat that I would find such a development unbearable."[23]

On 11/24 March Izvolsky gave the German ambassador an affirmative answer. Pourtales, overjoyed, telegraphed Berlin: "One cannot rule out the possibility that the trend is reversed" and that "Russian policy now will find a new orientation in the sense of a rapprochement with Germany." It is hard to imagine how anyone could have been more badly mistaken!

The Russian public had little inkling of the course of these negotiations. Therefore, on 14 March, when the newspapers carried the communique to the signatories of the Treaty of Berlin and reported that Russia already had agreed to the annexation, a tempest erupted in the press and the Duma. The public wanted to know the purpose of Russia's insistence on an international conference when the government now had recognized the annexation even before England and France, who had relatively little interest in the matter. One popular rumor held that Germany had threatened Russia with war if Petersburg would not agree immediately to the annexation. Some papers wrote of the "diplomatic Tsushima" and decried Russia's humiliating defeat. While much of the resentment was genuine, the reaction also reflected a strong element of politics. Oppositionists seized the opportunity to emphasize and exaggerate yet another failure of the "tsarist government." Partisans of an Anglo-French orientation exploited the opportunity to widen the breach between Russia and Germany.

The entire course of Austrian policy, from the sanjak railway to the threats against Serbia, revealed unmistakably Vienna's incapacity or unwillingness to respect the age-old traditions of Russian foreign policy. Germany, meanwhile, by siding openly with Austria in the Bosnian crisis, departed from the precepts of Bismarck, who cautioned in his memoirs that under no circumstances should Germany choose between Russia and Austria. Thus, although the Bosnian crisis found its solution, it inflicted a deep wound on the balance of power.

The Emperor and His Entourage at Poltava, 1909

THE AZEF AFFAIR

A sensational revelation from the revolutionary movement provoked great consternation in Russian society early in 1909. Both revolutionary parties, the SRs and SDs—their influence ebbing even emong students—were in a state of depression and despair. They continued to slaughter policemen and to carry out "expropriations," but the latter more and more resembled simple acts of robbery. Although the authorities uncovered several revolutionary plots in 1907 and 1908, those years passed unmarred by major terrorist acts. Then in January 1909 the foreign press reported that one Evno Azef, a member of the central committee of the SRs, had fled from a party court and had been denounced as a "provocateur." For some ten days Russian censors prohibited the Russian press from publishing this report and they confiscated all papers that carried it. Suddenly on 19 January A.A. Lopukhin,[24] a former director of the police department, was arrested in St. Petersburg, and for the next few weeks the Azef affair was the major topic of conversation. The Duma received two resolutions for inquiries into the matter, one from the Kadets and another from the socialists.

Although the general public had never heard of Azef, he was very well known to revolutionaries who regarded him as a revolutionary technician without peer. He was the leader of the SR Battle Organization and a member of the party's central committee. (He had represented the SRs at the Conference of the Opposition and Revolutionary Organizations of the Russian Empire in the fall of 1904.) Now suddenly it turned out that he was an Okhrana agent, and the SR's informant was none other than the former director of the police! That in itself was so bizarre that the rumor-mills immediately bloated his importance to fantastic dimensions. From some newspapers one gathered that Azef was simultaneously responsible for the revolution and the struggle against it. Though much about him remains obscure, a more accurate reconstruction of his true role is now possible.

Azef came from a poor Jewish family that lived in Rostov-on-the-Don. At the age of 22 he went abroad and enrolled in the Karlsruhe (Germany) Technical Institute. In that same year, 1893, he contacted P.N. Durnovo, then director of the police department, who employed him as an informer in a contingent of agents who spied on Russians studying abroad. In 1899 Azef returned to Russia, obtained employment as an engineer, worked with the Socialist Revolutionary underground spreading propaganda, and continued to file reports with the Okhrana. His energy and "long meritorious service" helped him rise in the ranks of the party.

After 1903, Azef's reports to the police became less candid and his revolutionary work more determined. The explanation, according to some informants, was the Kishinev pogrom; others attributed the change to the influence of the SR terrorist Gregory Gershuni. The arrests and deaths of other leaders placed Azef at the top of the Battle Organization, second only to Boris Savinkov.[25] Azef hardly found his promotion cause for celebration, for he lived under the constant threat of exposure and death. He was afraid to get drunk because he might reveal his secret; since he talked in his sleep, he followed the practice of locking himself alone in his room. Meanwhile he drew liberally on the funds of both sides, though in fact he received more money from the revolutionary treasury than from the police. He indulged his fancy for fine restaurants and cafe singers and explained to his comrades that high living was the best way for a terrorist to distract the police. He spent great sums of money on [his mistress], a cabaret singer.

As long as the revolution seemed to be succeeding, Azef favored it more than the police. When the tide turned, Azef resumed his activities as agent-informer even more zealously than before. By 1907 he had completely disorganized the revolutionary terror. His comrades, however, grew suspicious of their systematic failures. Finally V.L. Burtsev,[26] a publicist primarily concerned with the history of the revolutionary movement, openly accused Azef of double dealing. Because of Azef's exemplary revolutionary past, the party leaders at first were skeptical of Burtsev's allegation. But Burtsev contacted Azef's former chief, Lopukhin (since dismissed without a pension), and Lopukhin confirmed, first to Burtsev, and then to SR representatives who visited him in London, that Azef was a longtime Okhrana agent. The SRs convened a party court. Initially Azef defended himself with vigor, but after two sessions he fled and disappeared without a trace.[27]

ON MANNERS AND MORALS

Azef's exposure was a deadly blow to the Socialist Revolutionary Party. Several terrorists committed suicide. The leftist parties, however, tried to convert the setback into a bludgeon against the government. They immediately took the offensive and charged the government with "provocation." In the Duma the Social Democrats and Trudoviks directly accused the police of using their agents to organize terrorism "for the purpose of expanding the reaction and justifying emergency measures." Their allegations disregarded the fact that terrorist activity had dwindled practically to nothing once the government mounted an attack and began the so-called "reaction."

According to the government, Lopukhin's arrest was necessary because he betrayed the identity of a secret agent to the revolutionaries and thus deprived Azef "of any possibility of warning the police of the criminal plans of organizations." The French socialist leader Jaurès, writing in *L'Humanite* before Lopukhin's arrest, alleged: "The government apparently considers itself guilty in the Azef affair, since it does not dare to apprehend Lopukhin. In any country when an official betrays a secret confided to him in the line of duty, he is arrested immediately and punished appropriately." Eventually Lopukhin was sentenced to five years at hard labor, but by that time the Russian public had all but concluded that he was an innocent victim.[28]

In this instance the Duma did not yield to the agitation of the left. "Thanks to the Azef affair, the Socialist Revolutionary Party has suffered a serious defeat," declared the Octobrist von Anrep, "and now it seeks to vent its wrath." V.A. Bobrinsky reiterated that view: "Now, drowning and choking in slime, they seek to throw mud on the government as well." On 11 February 1909 Stolypin came before the Duma to deliver the government's explanation of the Azef affair. He argued that the term "provocation" had no applicability: "According to revolutionary terminology, anyone who furnishes information to the government is a provocateur . . . . That definition is no accident—it is most advantageous to the revolution. But the government must declare with complete frankness that it defines a provocateur only as one who freely initiates a criminal act and entices lesser associates to join him . . . . Is it not an absurdity then to speak of provocation in connection with such [terrorists] as Gershuni, Savinkov, Kaliaev, Schweizer, and the like?"[29]

Stolypin filled in the details of Azef's activities as an agent and Socialist Revolutionary. He stressed that it was precisely from the moment that Azef reached the top of the organization that "every effort of the central apparatus came to naught, the revolutionaries were thrown into confusion and in due course exposed . . . . Just as light was useful to the government, so darkness was essential to the revolution. Imagine, gentlemen, the complete horror of a young man or woman, seduced into criminality yet idealistic and willing to sacrifice themselves—imagine their revulsion on discovering all the filth that encrusts the leadership of the revolution: would the revolution not find it far more profitable to spread monstrous calumnies about the crimes of the government . . . would it not be better for the revolutionaries to blame the government for the chaos within their ranks? (Laughter and applause)."

Stolypin concluded his defense of the government's policy with a reminder that the struggle against the revolution was a means not an end. But, he said, when people resorted to bombs in place of rhetoric, merciless punishment became the only possible response. "We, the government, are only seeding forests so that you will have something to build with. Our enemies point to those forests as though they were ugly buildings that we erected, and they take up axes and furiously assault the trunks. Inevitably the trees will fall, and they even may bury us in their ruins. But do not let that happen before it becomes possible to find beneath the ruins . . . the foundation of a renewed Russia—free in the best sense of the word: free from poverty, from ignorance, from injustice—and loyal to the last man to the emperor and to Russia!"

Nothing of substance emerged during the subsequent debates. Finally a majority of centrists and rightists voted to accept Stolypin's explanation and to reject the inquiries demanded by the Kadets and socialists. "The mountain gave birth to a mouse," wrote *Novoe vremia*'s Pertsov. The public's interest in the Azef affair faded fast, although the legend of Azef, "the omnipotent provocateur," proved more tenacious.[30]

In evaluating the Azef affair one could conclude that Azef's exposure was incomparably more beneficial to the government

than his continued services might have been. The moral defeat
that it inflicted on the terrorist organizations destroyed them
more certainly than arrest or repression. The SR Battle Organization was never resurrected. The leftist press was somewhat successful in foisting on a credulous public the impression that the Azef affair also "scandalized" the government.
That might have been the case had Azef held a major position
in the police or administration. But in fact the government
was well aware of the kind of person it was dealing with; it
never entrusted him with secret information, and he was used
only as a spy in the opposing camp. His arrest would not have
prevented one single assassination;[31] to have refused his services would only have made it easier for the terrorists. The
government, locked in a death struggle with the revolution,
had no reason to spurn the opportunity for its intelligence
service to penetrate deeply into the enemy's central apparatus.

VEKHI

The most vivid example of the ideological reappraisal of the
intelligentsia's traditional outlook appeared in the spring of
1909 in a collection of essays published under the title *Vekhi*
[Signposts].[32] A total indictment of the intelligentsia, *Vekhi*
was all the more impressive because its contributors had no
common assumption as their point of departure. The introduction announced that "the aim of these articles is not to
judge the intelligentsia in the light of some cognitive truth,
nor do they proceed from a haughty contempt for the past
but rather from the pain of the past . . . and a vital concern
for the future of our native land. The Revolution of 1905 and
the events that followed provided something of a national test
of those values which Russian public opinion has cherished as
its most sacred possession for more than half a century." The
authors proclaimed the "theoretical and practical superiority
of life over the outward forms of social organization," and
they asserted that "the path followed by society until now
has led it to a hopeless impasse."

Vekhi's contributors approached the subject from various
perspectives. Nicholas Berdiaev[33] cited several examples to
demonstrate that the intelligentsia had no interest in objective
truth but used philosophy merely to support their political

views: "They took up Kant only because critical Marxism promised to base its socialist ideal on Kant. Then they turned to the practically indigestible Avenarius, because they suddenly imagined that Avenarius in his most abstract and purest form was the philosophy of the Social-Democratic Bolsheviks . . . ." Sergei Bulgakov described the revolution as an "historical judgment upon the intelligentsia." "No intelligentsia is more atheistic than the Russian intelligentsia," he wrote. "To our intelligentsia a bit of education or enlightenment is synonymous with religious indifference." Russians vainly imagined that irreligiosity was the means by which they participated in a truly European civilization but, he observed, the West contained not only "poisoned fruit" but also healthy roots. Against the pointless theomachistic heroism of the intelligentsia Bulgakov asserted the humility of Russian saints and ascetics.[34]

Michael Gershenzon[35] condemned the intelligentsia's isolation from the people: "A crowd of sick men quarantined in their own country—that is the Russian intelligentsia . . . . [The people] do not see us as thieves, like their brother the village *kulak*, nor even as plain foreigners, like the Turk or Frenchman. They see our human and recognizably Russian features but do not sense a human soul in us, and therefore they hate us passionately . . . . Such as we are, we not only cannot dream of merging with the people, but we must fear them more than all of the government's executions, and we must bless this regime which alone, with its bayonets and prisons, still protects us from the people's wrath."

Bogdan Kistiakovsky[36] argued that the intelligentsia suffered from a total disrespect for the conservative viewpoint. He found telling examples in the history of the Social Democrats and quoted Lenin at the 1903 party congress on the necessity of cruelly suppressing dissent even within one's own ranks. ("Frightened remarks about the state of siege and exceptional measures do not scare me one bit," said Lenin. "As for our own unstable and wavering elements, we not only can create a state of siege but we must do it.")

Peter Struve discussed the intelligentsia's "irreligious apostasy from the state" and deplored their narrow interpretation of politics as the framework of life itself, the "alpha and omega of their existence . . . . Thus they transform a limited instrument into an all-embracing goal." Simon Frank[37] denounced the intelligentsia's "wilful nihilistic materialism" which proclaimed the "satisfaction of the needs of the majority" as the ultimate good. The intelligentsia is bound to "a religion dedicated to earthly requirements," and the typical intelligent is "a militant monk of the nihilistic religion of secular welfare."[37] Finally, Alexander Izgoev exposed the seamy side of the life and psychology of the students, who were considered the "avant garde" of the intelligentsia.[38]

"Our warnings are not new," advised [Gershenzon in] the foreword to *Vekhi*. "The same thing has been repeated tirelessly from Chaadaev to Soloviev and Tolstoy, by all of our deepest thinkers. No one listened to them; the intelligentsia ignored them. Perhaps now, awakened by the great upheaval, they will listen to softer voices."

Vekhi did indeed create a great uproar, all the more because the contributors were prominent representatives of the intelligentsia. The left-wing press bitterly attacked them. In *Vestnik evropy* Prince D.I. Shakovsky characterized them as "blind leaders of the blind," and *Sovremennyi mir* labelled them "creators of a new racket." Some writers and publicists headed by Miliukov even issued a collection in response to *Vekhi*.[39] Merezhkovsky denounced the *Vekhi* group with uncharacteristic passion at a meeting of the Religious-Philosophical Society. The intelligentsia, he said, were like a peasant's overworked and exhausted horse, and *Vehki*'s contributors were peasants flogging the horse to death.

Only the conservative press found any merit in *Vekhi*. Archbishop Anthony of Volynia addressed a long letter to Struve: "We do not know what should delight us more, the scientific character and wisdom of your arguments, the tone of conciliation and love in your appeal to those of different views, your belief in the power of the human conscience even for those who deny it both in theory and practice, or finally the Suvorov-like[40] courage with which like Saul who came to see the light, you turned to your former brothers lost in false euphoria."

Vekhi had considerable influence among students who, in a sense, represented the "ultimate" in public opinion in that they were the first to dismiss ideas that began to appear out of date. *Vekhi* was fashionable for a time. Then, even though the novelty began to fade, the ideas that it suggested or, more precisely, the doubt that it cast over the past traditions of the intelligentsia left a deep mark on the outlook of Russia's educated classes. Finally, it should be noted that the authors of *Vekhi* scrupulously refrained from drawing any political conclusions.[41] They even referred to the "disgusting triumph of reaction," and some remained active members of the Kadet Party.

THE DUMA AND THE ARMY

The Duma's committee on imperial defense established an excellent relationship with the war department. It attentively examined every military project and frequently increased the army's appropriations. The committee was most solicitous toward any proposal to improve the material status of the officer corps. At the same time it often busied itself with organizational matters that were beyond its jurisdiction. Guchkov's celebrated speech against "irresponsible persons" [the grand dukes] in the war department was a case in point. As a result rightists began to charge that the centrists' special concern for the army was politically motivated. In his memoirs Count Witte somewhat indirectly made the same accusation. He wrote that Guchkov allegedly told some Russians living in France that "the revolution failed in 1905 because the army remained loyal to the emperor . . . . If another revolution should occur, it is essential that the army be on our side; therefore I occupy myself exclusively with military questions and military affairs in the hope that, should the need arise, the army will be more loyal to us than to the tsar's court."

That the Third Duma's concern for the army was prompted primarily by a genuine desire to enhance its fighting efficiency is all but beyond question. Guchkov's attitude toward the revolution of 1905 was clear enough. Still, the possibility remains that the Duma's centrists welcomed the opportunity to prove to the army that not all of the people's representatives were its enemies like the radical intelligentsia. Moreover, following the example of parliaments everywhere, the Russian Duma hoped to expand its powers and exploited any ill-defined area to do so. That was the issue behind the major political crisis that emerged in the spring of 1909.

In the summer of 1908 Admiral Evan Dikov, the naval minister, submitted the proposal for a new table of organization for the naval general staff. A non-controversial matter, it cleared the Duma without debate. Only when the bill reached the State Council did someone [P.K. Schwanebach] point out that the approval of staffs exceeded the competence of the legislative branch, which constitutionally was limited to the approval of military appropriations. The State Council, therefore, rejected the bill. The navy reintroduced the bill into the Duma, this time seeking only an appropriation. However, the committee on imperial defense, looking to its own interests, contended that it had no desire to "weaken" the naval bill and restored it to its original form. Early in January 1909, the Duma approved the bill and sent it to the State Council.

On 23 February Stolypin fell ill with the flu and later developed pneumonia. That same evening Guchkov entered the debate on the military estimates with this significant statement:

We have been wrestling with this question for a year and a half now. The government has yet to see us refuse any appropriation . . . . Not only have we refrained from cutting the war department's estimates, we have even encouraged it to seek new funds . . . . Certain material improvements have been achieved. However, in those areas of military affairs that are beyond our power the situation is not so promising . . . . Take for example the area of the military command. Can you assure me that the military districts are in the hands of officers who in peacetime are capable of training our army for combat and then of leading our troops to victory? . . . We cannot continue indefinitely to formulate our foreign policy on the basis of military weakness . . . . We know, the government knows, our enemies know—but the agonizing question remains: does the Supreme Leader of our army know the state of our defense establishment?

War minister Rediger responded to Guchkov. He admitted the need "to upgrade, to refresh" the army's commanders, but he added that "in selecting officers for the top posts one must use the material and candidates that are available."

Rediger's response caused Nicholas Markov to rise in protest: "I have been delegated by the rightist faction to declare that we interpret the minister of war's explanations to be in agreement with Mr. Guchkov's evaluation, but since the so-called war minister was sent here in the name of the Sovereign Emperor, it is our opinion that he had no right to respond in that manner . . . . We consider it an insult to the Imperial Russian Army to declare that it lacks suitable material to make good commanders." General Rediger repeated, however, that "at this moment the commanders of our army are not ideal," and Guchkov welcomed his "courageous admission." On the following day the Kadet's *Rech* gleefully recalled that "former deputy Zubarov once said that under the present circumstances our army will always be defeated. A.I. Guchkov with characteristic skill has expressed the idea differently—much more clearly and more graphically."

The emperor was extremely displeased that his war minister not only failed to protest the Duma's intrusion into a matter beyond its competence but also appeared to agree with Guchkov's criticism. On 11 March Rediger was fired. Chief of the General Staff General V.A. Sukhomlinov succeeded him. To be sure, even in parliamentary countries it was not customary for the legislature to criticize high-ranking military commanders.

THE NAVAL STAFFS CRISIS

Those were the circumstances in which the State Council took up the naval staffs bill for the second time. The government contended that the Council should accept the Duma's version in order not to delay and complicate the matter. The cabinet's solution was an amendment to the effect that approval of the bill in its present form was not to be regarded as a precedent. The Council's finance committee approved that solution, but a minority of rightists disagreed, and a violent debate erupted when the bill came up for general consideration. Stressing the tsar's exclusive jurisdiction over military appointments, P.N. Durnovo, the leader of the rightist group, declared that "such intrusions, regardless of their insignificance, establish dangerous precedents for the leadership of the country's defenses and, quietly and slowly but inexorably, they erode the foundation on which the military power of Russia has been erected."

Count Witte emerged as an unexpected ally of the right. In an impassioned speech he argued: "What appears at first to be a trifling matter conceals an especially significant question concerning the prerogatives of the Imperial Power. We should not forget that the Imperial Army has marched over practically all of Europe and has created this immense Russian Empire . . . . Is it not premature, gentlemen, to exchange the Imperial Russian Army for an army organized by chance and dilettantes?"[42]

Finance minister Kokovtsov, substituting for the ailing Stolypin, reminded the State Council that it already had accepted a variance in that area when it approved a bill to staff the operations section of the port of Vladivostok. Therefore he urged the Council to approve the current proposal "because of its practical urgency." Witte caustically objected: they want to pass off the project as a minor matter, "and then what—no more after that?" So unmistakable a violation of the emperor's prerogatives was, said Witte, "an operation under chloroform."

The State Council approved the bill by the narrow margin of 85-73, but the debate went on. M.O. Menshikov used the pages of *Novoe vremia* to defend the rightist position (against A.A. Stolypin, the prime minister's brother). The fact that the ministers voted with the left against the emperor's prerogatives was, charged Menshikov, "a state scandal." The emperor himself did not act immediately on the bill. Once again, as in the issue of the autocracy and the zemstvos a decade earlier, a struggle was taking place before the throne. Once again, Witte appeared in the role of defender of monarchical rights. Stolypin, slowly recuperating from his illness, left the capital to spend four weeks at Livadia. Nicholas deferred his decision because he did not want to express his will in the absence of the prime minister who enjoyed his confidence.

At that point a counter-revolt against the Young Turks broke out in Constantinople, but within twelve days they brought in fresh troops from Macedonia and occupied the capital. The Young Turks retained their power and deposed Sultan Abdul Hamid II. On the day the newspapers carried that report Menshikov published an article titled "Our Young Turks" (parodying Guchkov's widely reported remark). Menshikov berated the Octobrists and charged that the "left-Octobrists" were trying deliberately to reduce the tsar's power through the naval staffs question. "To mistake them for rightists is the same as confusing snakes with eels. They look alike, but they are entirely different creatures."

The leftist press began to discuss the forthcoming resignation of the cabinet. Stolypin returned to Petersburg on 20

April, and on the 25th the emperor sent a letter announcing his decision. Having "weighed every consideration," he had decided not to confirm the bill. "There can be no question of confidence or no confidence. Such is my will. Remember that we live in Russia and not abroad or in Finland. Therefore I do not permit even the thought of someone's resignation. Of course, there will be talk in Petersburg and Moscow, but the hysterical shouts will die down soon enough . . . . I repeat that I categorically reject in advance a request by you or anyone else to be relieved of his office."[43]

Nicholas did everything possible to soften his disapproval of the government. An imperial rescript, published on 27 April 1909 and addressed to Stolypin, instructed the prime minister to spell out rules for determining which military and naval questions were to be approved directly by the emperor and which were to be introduced into the State Duma and State Council: "The entire conduct of the Council of Ministers under your leadership, which merits My full approval, has been directed toward strengthening the foundations of the state system that I have established; that serves as My guarantee that you will successfully execute My present charge to you . . . ." Nicholas had found it necessary to draw the line decisively against any intrusion of the Duma into the realm of the military administration. His decision created deep disappointment in the Duma center and partly explained the public's unfriendly attitude toward Sukhomlinov, the new war minister charged with implementing the emperor's orders.

THE DISINTEGRATION OF THE CENTRIST BLOC

The conflict over the naval staffs bill also marked a turning point for Stolypin's cabinet. *Vestnik evropy* observed that "having remained in power, the cabinet has moved considerably to the right." The naval staffs crisis produced the first serious conflict in which the emperor disagreed in principle with his council of ministers. It also marked the first occasion in which the emperor demonstrated that he had no intention of allowing his right to approve or reject legislation to lapse into a mere formality. The crisis somewhat diminished the prestige of the council of ministers. Rightists immediately sensed the significance of the tsar's action. In *Moskovskie vedomosti* Lev Tikhomirov called the Rescript of 27

April the "second instance" (after the Law of 3 June) in which the Fundamental Laws had been corrected "by direct action of the sovereign's will." Tikhomirov's statement was inaccurate in that the Rescript of 27 April did not violate any law.

The State Duma's reaction was to pass a bill granting Old Believers[44] the right to form communities and citizens generally the right to convert from one faith to another. A majority composed of the center and left passed that measure, and the same coalition approved the "Dubrovinsky inquiry" into unlawful actions of the Union of Russian People that allegedly were taking place with the approval of the administration. (The Octobrists' main speaker on the inquiry was A.D. Protopopov.[45]) Guchkov himself took the floor to speak on the issue of the Old Believers[46] and used the opportunity to expand the framework of the debate. What had been done, he asked, to realize the promises of the Manifesto of October 17? "You know it is not enough. You know that a thick cloud developed and descended over that question. Well, what is there now to prevent us from acting in the area of religious freedom? What kind of arguments can be invented now as restraints on the question?"

The government's majority had fallen apart. Peter Balashov, the leader of the moderate rights, summed up the results of that session and spoke during an interview of "a newly forming majority." Guchkov, hoping to minimize the effect, replied that such a majority existed only on religious and national minority issues. On other matters the former majority still survived. But the Octobrists, too, were breaking up. Part of the right wing openly rejected Guchkov's policy. Guchkov resigned as chairman of the fraction, and in winning re-election he also managed to expel his major opponents from the fraction. As a result some twenty former Octobrists assumed the position of right-moderate "outlaws" [*dikii*].

FOREIGN INTERLUDES IN 1909

In the early part of June 1909 the State Duma's chairman, Khomiakov, led representatives of both chambers on a visit to England. The delegation included members of all fractions from the nationalists to the Kadets. The Russian deputies received a most cordial welcome and were honored with receptions and banquets everywhere they went. The parliamentary visit marked a new stage in the development of the Anglo-Russian rapprochement. The British Labor Party injected a note of dissonance when it issued a manifesto that studiously distinguised between the Duma and the emperor. The Russian delegation protested and characterized the statement as an affront. Even Miliukov, the most liberal member of the delegation, declared at a banquet given by the lord mayor of London: "As long as Russia has a legislative body that controls the budget, the Russian opposition will remain the opposition *of*, not *to* His Majesty." Miliukov's statement prompted a flurry of comment in Russia. *Sovremennyi mir* declared that "Miliukov's fall will become a great asset to the enemies of the people's freedom." Responding in Parliament to a Laborite attack on Russia, Sir Edward Grey alluded to the statements of the Russian deputies as proof of the existence of a Russian constitution.

On 6 June 1909 Emperor Nicholas visited with Emperor William in the Finnish skerries. Although their meeting was friendly, the following day *Novoe vremia* observed that "there can be no talk of any change in our country's predetermined foreign policy." After celebrating the bicentennial of the victory at Poltava, the emperor left Russia for a tour abroad. He visited England and France, attending naval reviews in both countries. At Cowes, where he had been a guest fifteen years earlier following his betrothal, Nicholas recalled those days and told the English people that "I shall always remember the happy days that I spent with your beloved and revered Queen Victoria." To King Edward's remarks about the English visit of the Duma delegation Nicholas replied: "May the cordial reception which Your Majesty and Your people accorded the members of the State Duma and Me and My squadron during the winter be a token of Our two countries' warm relations founded on common interest and mutual respect."

"GIVE RUSSIA TWENTY YEARS OF PEACE"

Russia enjoyed a remarkably bountiful harvest in 1909, and grain exports reached an unprecedented total of 748,000,000 rubles. Signs of recovery appeared in all sectors of the economy. Meanwhile the country's interest in politics was declining

Barents Sea

SIBERIA

White Sea

Archangel

URALS

Gulf of Bothnia

FINLAND

1 Petrozavodsk

Vologda

Viatka

Perm

Helsinki

Reval

St Petersburg

Novgorod

Kostroma

Kazan

Ufa

Baltic Sea

Riga

3 Pskov

Tver

Yaroslavl

Nizhni-Novgorod

Simbirsk

Orenburg

4 Mitava

Kovno

Vitebsk

Vladimir

Penza

Samara

Vilno

Smolensk

Kaluga

Moscow

Riazan

Saratov

STEPPE REGION

Minsk

Mogilev

Tula

Tambov

Grodno

Orel

Warsaw

POLAND

Chernigov

Kursk

Voronezh

5

Zhitomir

Kiev

Poltava

Kharkov

8

Astrakhan

Kamenets - Podolsk

Ekaterinoslav

Novocherkask

CENTRAL ASIA

6

Kherson

7

Sea of Azov

9

Stavropol

Caspian Sea

Kishinev

Simferopol

Ekaterinodar

11

Temir-Khan-Shura

Novorossisk

Vladikavkaz

12

10

Kutais

Baku

Tiflis

Elisavetopol

Kars

Erivan

Black Sea

Legend

Provinces are named for capital cities
except those that are numbered.

1 Olonets
2 Estland
3 Lifland
4 Kurland
5 Volyn
6 Bessarabia
7 Tauride
8 Don Cossacks
9 Kuban
10 Black Sea
11 Terek
12 Daghestan

☐ Central Black-soil Region

THE PROVINCES OF
EUROPEAN RUSSIA
in the
2nd half of the
19th century

scale

0   100   200   400

miles

kelly

noticeably. The oppositionist press interpreted that as "the reaction," the failure of public spirit. "One reads the papers, but as soon as he has finished he has forgotten what he read . . . . In the election of a deputy to the State Duma less than a third of 80,000 eligible voters participated.[47] As many as 10,000 notices of pre-election meetings were sent, and occasionally a hundred, sometimes two hundred, but at the most five hundred people attended." Thus lamented *Vestnik evropy*, which also observed that at the same time "it is impossible to find a seat in a restaurant that offers music, and advance reservations are necessary to attend an operetta . . . . Private interest rules the day."

Stolypin appraised the situation quite differently. In an interview with the editor of the Saratov paper *Volga*[48] he declared: "Judging from the newspapers, one would gather that our country is enveloped by pessimism and general depression. But I have observed, and I think you could confirm, that it is already possible to detect a cheerful atmosphere welling up in this province, and that indicates that the whole country gradually is being drawn into brisk activity.

The cheerful optimism noticeable in our province coincides with the introduction of the land reform. My assumption is that our first step is to create a citizen, a peasant proprietor, and when that is accomplished he will feel a citizen's responsibility for Russia. First a citizen, then a citizen's sense of responsibility for his country. Unfortunately, too many would go about this in reverse."

Stolypin took note of the selfless and tireless effort required to reorganize the landholding system. He spoke of reforms that lay ahead—local government and the zemstvos— and he commented on the university that was scheduled to open in Saratov: "A newspaper in a university town has a great purpose: to make our youth patriotic! to develop in them a spirit of healthy enlightened patriotism! I recently visited Scandanavia. I was pleased to see the spirit and pride of local young people marching in orderly ranks with their national flags." Stolypin then concluded: "Our basic goal is to strengthen the lower classes. They possess the entire power of the nation. There are more than a hundred million of them! Believe me, once the roots of our country are healthy and strong, the Russian government will speak with an entirely different voice before Europe and the entire world. Harmonious, cooperative efforts based on mutual trust—that is the motto for all Russians! Give Russia twenty years of peace at home and abroad, and you will not recognize her!"

CHAPTER FIFTEEN

A FRENCHMAN'S APPRAISAL OF THE TSAR

Reflections of former French President Émile Loubet appeared in the New Year's edition of the Viennese *Neue Freie Presse*. Referring to Nicholas II, he wrote: "The Russian Emperor is alleged to be susceptible to diverse influences. That is quite incorrect. The Russian Emperor carries out his own ideas. His proposals are maturely considered and thoroughly worked out, and he applies uninterrupted concentration to their realization. Occasionally it appears that he might have forgotten something, but he remembers everything. For instance, during our meeting at Compiegne we spoke privately about Russia's need for land reform. The Emperor assured me that he had been thinking about it for some time. When the reform finally was carried out, the ambassador informed me of it and at the same time graciously recalled our conversation."[1] President Loubet concluded: "Beneath the Tsar's shy, somewhat delicate features is a powerful soul and a resolutely courageous heart. He knows where he is going and what he wants to do." That constancy, that capacity to return to what apparently had been put aside was a characteristic exhibited in both the domestic and foreign policies of Emperor Nicholas II. Though hurdles sometimes stood in his way, he never lost sight of his destination.

THE POTSDAM AGREEMENT

Like Stolypin the emperor recognized that Russia needed long years of peace at home and abroad. Therefore he was greatly concerned over the deterioration of Russian-German relations. With few exceptions animosity toward Germany flared through every segment of Russian society after the Bosnian crisis early in 1909. Moderate liberal circles acclaimed Peter Struve's "Great Russia" program, a Slavophile legacy which aspired to Russian hegemony in the Near East. Proponents of

Struve's program failed to realize that its inevitable consequence was conflict with Germany, Austria-Hungary, and Turkey. The emperor, however, was not so blind. While making every effort to build new relations—that was the purpose of his journey to Italy and the Racconigi agreement of 1909[2] — he did not ignore the question of improved relations with Germany.

Russia's foreign minister, A.P. Izvolsky, had concluded the Anglo-Russian agreement of 1907 and thereby acquired the reputation of an antagonist of Germany. That explained why the Duma opposition, which was so hostile toward the other ministers, accorded Izvolsky such respect. Izvolsky, moreover, considered himself more liberal than other members of the cabinet. In the summer of 1910 his opposition to the government's policy toward Finland prompted him again to ask to be relieved of his duties.[3] At that point Izvolsky's departure suited the emperor.

In the middle of August 1910 the emperor and the imperial family traveled to Germany. They spent two and a half months in peaceful rustic surroundings at Castle Friedberg in Hesse, the empress's native land. That was the imperial family's longest foreign sojourn during the entire reign of the emperor. While there A.I. Nelidov, the imperial ambassador to France, passed away. On 21 September the emperor appointed Izvolsky to Paris. S.D. Sazonov, the deputy foreign minister and a relative of Stolypin by marriage, succeeded Izvolsky as foreign minister.[4]

Nicholas was reluctant to leave Germany without an opportunity for a frank discussion with Emperor William. The Prussian minister to the court of Hesse wrote to his master that the tsar "on several occasions has stressed his desire to resume the tone of your formerly friendly relations." The kaiser was rather skeptical, and he wrote on the margin of his envoy's report: "Neither the tone nor the desire are of any use now—after the Triple Entente and six new Russian army corps." Coincidentally the *Post*, a German newspaper of little importance, printed an article belligerent toward Russia. The Russian press responded in kind, and the "atmosphere" seemed unpropitious. Nevertheless, at the summons of the tsar Sazonov journeyed to Germany and met with the new chancellor, Theobald von Bethmann Hollweg. A short time later, on 22-23 October 1910, the two monarchs met at Potsdam and discussed their policies at length.

Proceeding from the solidarity of their monarchical interests, Nicholas and William mutually pledged not to support any policy directed against the interests of the other. Germany promised not to encourage Austria's aggressive Balkan policy, and Russia pledged to remain aloof from any British undertaking against Germany. The agreement supported the Near Eastern status quo and discriminatory commercial interests in Persia, whose frontier eventually would be reached by the Bagdad Railway then under construction.[5]

After the meeting of the monarchs, the two ministers exchanged views. The tsar found the results of that discussion as reported by Sazonov "quite satisfactory."[6] The kaiser was overjoyed that Nicholas "spoke so frankly with him about politics." The meeting at Potsdam failed, however, to restore completely the former cordiality in Russo-German relations, and the results were dimmed by the following incident.

Sazonov suggested that the results of the negotiation be written up,[7] and Bethmann agreed to draft a declaration. The main points were that Austria had promised to refrain from an "expansionist policy" in the East, and that Germany "was not obligated and had no intention to support such a policy should Austria-Hungary pursue it." For its part, Russia declared that it "was not obligated and had no intention to support a hostile British policy toward Germany, should England pursue one." It went on to discuss the maintenance of the status quo in the Balkans, the localization of conflicts, and other matters.

Sazonov, however, objected to the declaration on the grounds that the obligations were unequal: Germany was making specific commitments only with regard to the Balkans, whereas Russia was invited to bind itself to more general commitments. On 21 November German State-Secretary Kiderlen telegraphed Ambassador Pourtales: "For us the commitment in connection with England is the alpha and omega of the entire agreement." The emperor found a way out. He charged Sazonov to make the following declaration: His Majesty has given the German Emperor his solemn word not to support a British policy directed against Germany; the German Emperor has promised not to encourage Austrian expansionism in the

Balkans. The verbal assurances of the two monarchs are more valuable in the eyes of the Sovereign than an exchange of notes. His Majesty relies on the assurance of the German Emperor and assumes that he will respect his assurances.

Confronted with that statement, the German government had to content itself with a verbal understanding, but Berlin still did not like the secret nature of the agreement. Kiderlen bitterly summarized the Russian reply by quoting from Heine's song: "But don't greet me under the linden" [i.e. in public]. Nevertheless, when the German chancellor announced to the Reichstag that Germany and Russia had promised at Potsdam "not to enter into aggressive combinations against one another," the Russian government expressed its complete satisfaction with the wording.

The Russian press gave the Potsdam agreement a cool reception, and Miliukov proclaimed his objections before the Duma: "It means that our agreements with our allies have ceased to be offensive and that we are left with only a defensive role." At that the rightist deputy Berezovsky exclaimed, "He wants war!"[8] In fact no general Anglo-Russian agreement existed, and the Franco-Russian alliance was, and since the time of Alexander III had been, a strictly defensive pact. French foreign minister Pichon, responding to questions in the Chamber of Deputies, gave assurances that the Potsdam agreement was in no way inconsistent with the Franco-Russian Alliance.[9] However, London clearly was put out; the new British ambassador, Sir George Buchanan,[10] who arrived in St. Petersburg in October 1910, worked strenuously to neutralize the effects of Potsdam.

During an interview with a *Novoe vremia* correspondent, Sazonov called on the Russian press to restrain itself toward Germany. "In all candor I must say that at times you are too harsh. A milder tone would be more conducive to the interests of both nations. If I were a magician, I would roll the scroll of fortune so as to shorten time by five years. By then mutual distrust and irritations will have dissipated by themselves. Time has a way of applying balsam to burning sores."[11]

DEFENSE POLICY AND THE DUMA

Profiting from the lessons of the Japanese war, the reorganization of the Russian defense system continued apace. In the summer of 1910 an imperial decree revised the mobilization plan and deactivated four fortresses in Poland. As a result the army's centers of concentration shifted eastward away from the frontier. This move was designed to overcome two problems. First, because of its relatively undeveloped rail network, the Polish salient could be squeezed as if in a vise by coordinated Austrian and German attacks along the flanks. Second, rapid advances in the development of artillery had reduced the effectiveness of fortresses and turned them into potential traps for their garrisons. Therefore, the plan called for the Russian army to concentrate beyond the reach of the enemy and then pass over to the offensive.

The German military attache reported that the revised plan reflected "purely strategic considerations." The French high command received advance notice; the technical adjustment fell within the terms of the Franco-Russian military convention. The French press was greatly agitated, however, because reports of the new plan appeared almost at the same time as the Potsdam meeting. French journalists warned that Russia would refuse to attack Germany when the opportunity arose, that Russia was prepared to surrender the Kingdom of Poland, and that other dire consequences were in the offing. In February 1911 the *Journal* published a sensational article titled "The End of an Alliance". After competent authorities explained that those fears were unfounded, the alarm subsided.[12]

The naval staffs crisis helped to clarify the relationship between the Duma and the war department. Detailed regulations promulgated on 26 August 1909 specified those matters to be considered in the higher reaches of the government and those to be submitted for consideration by the State Duma and State Council. The Social Democrats demanded an inquiry into the regulations, but after lengthy debate, with Stolypin himself taking part, the Duma defeated the SD's resolution.

In his speech of 31 March 1910 Stolypin warned that "the history of revolutions, the history of the fall of nations teaches us that armies fall into chaos when they cease to be united— united by their obedience to a single peremptory sacred will. Allow the seed of doubt to undermine that principle, infect our army with the slightest notion that it depends on some collective will, and its power will cease to rest upon the one immutable principle that unites it—the Supreme Imperial

Power." Stolypin went on to assert that "up to now the State Duma generally has respected the rights of the army's Supreme Leader, and the government never has encroached upon the rights of the State Duma."

Actually the Third Duma never did take a formal stand on critical matters of defense policy. The legislature battled over the navy for two years, from 1908 to 1910, as the Duma consistently struck credits for dreadnoughts from the naval appropriation while the State Council repeatedly restored them. Finally, during an intersessional recess, the emperor ordered work to begin on two ships. Upon its return the Duma had the opportunity to deny the funds and thus halt construction, but it chose not to contest the modernization of the fleet. In 1911 four dreadnoughts were launched.[13]

THE RUSSO-JAPANESE RAPPROCHEMENT

General P.F. Unterberger, the governor-general of the Amur [1905-1910], was bombarding St. Petersburg with increasingly alarming reports of rumors of an approaching Japanese invasion and complaints about the inadequacies of Russia's Far Eastern defenses. His cables caused the emperor great concern. Meanwhile intelligence reaching the foreign ministry gave quite the opposite picture of Japan's intentions, and in this instance the diplomatic sources proved correct. Tokyo was seeking cooperation rather than a renewal of hostilities with Russia, because another war, whatever the outcome of the initial battles, offered only to reverse all the gains won in the conflict of 1904-1905.

The United States had reached a position diametrically opposed to Japan's policy in China, and England's primary interest was to attract Russia to its side against Germany. Russia and Japan, however, had a common interest in excluding any new competitor from Manchuria. Therefore both countries saw little merit in the plan of the American secretary of state, Philander C. Knox, who called for the sale of all Manchurian railroads to an international company and strict adherence to the principle of the "open door" in Manchuria. Russian cooperation with Japan came under attack from the Duma opposition, and Miliukov contended that "by backing Japan we are not betting on the winning horse."

In the Russo-Japanese Convention of 1910, signed on 21 June/4 July, the two governments promised to assist one another in all matters respecting their Manchurian railroads. They also agreed to maintain the status quo in China [Manchuria] and pledged to communicate with one another on all measures necessary to that end. The substance of the agreement was a deal in which the two powers would work against the influence of third parties in China. It was based upon the following tacit demarcation of spheres of influence: Korea and southern Manchuria to Japan; northern Manchuria and Outer Mongolia (and possibly Chinese Turkestan) to Russia.[14]

Late in the summer of 1910 Stolypin and agriculture minister Krivoshein traveled through western Siberia on an inspection of Asiatic Russia.[15] Several months earlier, in the fall of 1909, finance minister Kokovtsov had visited Manchuria and Vladivostok. At Harbin he met with Prince Ito, one of Japan's leading statesmen. Their meeting ended tragically when a Korean revolutionary killed Ito on the platform of a railway station in Kokovtsov's presence. The assassination had no effect on Russo-Japanese relations. The reports of all three ministers indicated that each recognized the great importance of Russia's Asiatic possessions and that each properly appreciated the emperor's policy of expanding Russian influence in Asia, a policy that he had pursued since the first day of his reign.

THE BLOODLESS CONQUEST OF OUTER MONGOLIA ·

China had fallen into a state of total decay. The "Iron Empress," Tzu-hsi, died at the end of 1908 after forty years of autocratic rule, and her son, the "captive emperor" Kuanghsü, died at the same time. The crown passed to his two-year-old nephew, Prince Pu-I; his little-respected father [Prince Chun] became regent. During Kokovtsov's Far Eastern tour, a young Chinese general lamented to him that "China has no head." A revolutionary party was intensifying its propaganda, especially in the south, while at court individual dignitaries struggled for power. At the same time, in an effort to tighten its control over the outlying provinces, the Chinese government encouraged their settlement by migrants from inner China and tried to restrict the rights of foreigners.

By the beginning of 1911 those efforts provoked a crisis which finally led to a Russian ultimatum. Petersburg demanded that China observe Russia's commercial rights in Mongolia and threatened to move troops into China if the Chinese interfered with Russian businessmen. The American and to a lesser degree the British press vociferously condemned Russia, and the oppositionists took up the cry and protested this "new Far Eastern adventure." Nevertheless, China unconditionally accepted the ultimatum and recognized Russia's economic preponderance in Mongolia.[16] When the Chinese Revolution began in the fall of 1911, Outer Mongolia drove out the Chinese authorities and proclaimed its independence under the protection of Russia.[17] In 1912 China recognized Outer Mongolia's autonomy and accepted the status of nominal sovereign over the region just as the Turks had retained nominal sovereignty over Bosnia in 1876.[18]

Thus, through the resurgence of Russian power and the emperor's consistent policy, Russia acquired a vast territory with great economic potential without the loss of blood. Although leftists up to and including Miliukov remained sharply critical of Russia's Asian policy, liberal organs like *Russkoe slovo*, which had no political ties, began to show some understanding of Russian national goals in Asia. The Octobrist newspaper *Golos Moskvy* wrote: "We must not only extend our system toward the deserts that separate us from China proper, but we must also occupy as much of them as possible so that they can be preserved, as they are now, as esplanades . . . . Northern Mongolia, like Turkestan and Jungaria, must be brought into closer relationship with Russia."[19]

POST REVOLUTIONARY PROGRESS

Two bumper crops in 1909 and 1910 gave the entire Russian economy a powerful thrust. Meanwhile land reorganization proceeded successfully. Stolypin, anxious to accelerate the reform, felt that the Peasant Land Bank, which came under the jurisdiction of the finance minister, was not responding adequately to the government's intentions and that its credit policy was too conservative. He moved to transfer the Peasant Bank to the main agricultural administration. Kokovtsov, however, resisted his scheme and threatened to resign if the bank were removed from his authority. The result was another long "dispute before the throne."[20]

Agricultural affairs, as Loubet had observed, constantly stood foremost among the emperor's concerns. On 22 September 1910 he wrote Stolypin from Germany: "A solid system of land tenure within Russia proper and an essentially comparable system for the settlers in Siberia are the two basic goals toward which the government must strive without fail. Of course, our other needs, such as schools, communications, and the like, must not be neglected, but questions of land tenure must take precedence."

The legislature forged ahead over a broad front with significant measures in a number of areas: the reform of local courts, expansion of public education, introduction of a sewerage system in St. Petersburg, regulations on a new system of food distribution,[21] and extensive financing of agricultural improvements (in which 9,000,000 rubles were appropriated to irrigate the "hungry steppe"). Meanwhile the number of repressive measures diminished: the death penalty was imposed 129 times in 1910 in comparison to 537 in 1909 and 697 in 1908. Administrative exile decreased in about the same proportion: about 3,000 in 1909 compared to 10,000 in 1908.

THE POLITICAL SPECTRUM

Popular interest in politics flagged perceptibly although, as in the past, an oppositionist tendency prevailed among the civic-minded. The 1909 by-elections for the Duma demonstrated the continued oppositionist mood of Petersburg, Moscow, and Odessa, where Kadet candidates won election. More significantly, a leftist trend began to appear in zemstvo and municipal elections in contrast to the conservative swing during the revolutionary period.

The rightist parties, which had the opportunity to function legally, presented a dismal spectacle of internecine strife. Purishkevich withdrew from the Union of Russian People and formed the Union of the Archangel Michael.[22] Even so, members of the old union continued to squabble. Its founder, A.I. Dubrovin, having been deposed, accused the new general council of wanting him dead: "Let them offer me a chalice filled with the wine of eternity, and I will calmly drain it to the dregs!"[23] Rightist groups frequently battled with provincial governors whom they accused of liberalism. To Stolypin's government they formed "an opposition on the right."

The Nationalists became the Duma fraction closest to the government. With 105 members they nearly equalled the strength of the 117 Octobrists who by 1910 remained in the League. The Nationalists, however, had practically no nation-wide organization. Basically they were moderate-rightist non-party deputies united only as members of the State Duma.

After the naval staffs crisis, the Octobrists increasingly expressed their displeasure at the government's failure to institute the "promised freedoms." At the opening of the session of 1909-1910 Guchkov declared that the assembly was beginning its work "under a cloud of uncertainty." In the debate on the budget of the ministry of interior the Octobrist leader (on 22 February 1910) observed: "We notice that calm has returned to the country, and to a considerable extent it is a durable calm." Therefore, he said, it was time for the government to abolish the regulations on administrative exile and revoke the governors' special authority over the press. "We are waiting, gentlemen," he concluded.

When Stolypin came before the Duma on 31 March 1910, he replied to Guchkov: "The government, of course, maintains and will continue to maintain order, and it will pay no heed to cries of reaction coming from places where [terrorists] bomb their way into banks and trains, where peaceful citizens are robbed in the name of social revolution." The prime minister assessed the state of the country in this way: "After the bitterness of the ordeal it has endured, Russia naturally cannot help being dissatisfied. She is dissatisfied not only with the government but also with the State Duma and the State Council. She is dissatisfied with parties of both left and right. She is dissatisfied with all these things because Russia is dissatisfied with herself. The dissatisfaction will pass when Russian national consciousness emerges from its amorphous condition and acquires form and strength—it will end once Russia again feels like Russia."

The influence of the left extremist parties was reduced practically to nil. The Socialist Revolutionaries had not recovered from the blow dealt by the Azef affair. A desperate internal struggle wracked the Social Democrats and gave rise to debilitating factionalism: the *"otzovisty"* or "recallers" demanded the recall of the SD fraction from the Duma; the "ultimatists" insisted on an ultimatum that the fraction adopt "more revolutionary tactics" (which hardly were practicable). In addition there were the "liquidators" who wanted to liquidate the party's old illegal conspiratorial organization and replace it with a workers' party in the West European mold. Their aim was to lean on the legal trade union movement which, though constantly exposed to constraints imposed by the police on revolutionary propaganda, managed nevertheless to make considerable headway.[24] Every Social Democratic tendency attempted to establish its own school: Maxim Gorky and Anatole Lunacharsky[25] founded a party school on the Isle of Capri in the fall of 1909; the *Vpered* [Forward] group, representing ultra-left Bolshevism [the otzovists], created one at Bologna in 1910; and the Leninists established still another outside Paris in 1911.

The only terrorist act during this period was the murder of the Okhrana chief Karpov, who was lured into a trap by a revolutionary who promised to deliver party secrets. Oppositionist deputies tried to paint the episode as another "provocation," but the Duma majority rejected their demand for an inquiry. V.A. Bobrinsky argued that "we have the responsibility to disperse those hyenas who flung themselves upon Karpov's corpse."

TOLSTOY'S DEATH AND ITS CONSEQUENCES

On 7 November 1910 Count Leo Tolstoy died in the railway station of Astapovo in Riazan province. He was 82. Ten days earlier, on 28 October, he had left his estate, Yasnaia Poliana, in order to end the dichotomy between his teachings and his personal life. The death of this great writer, especially under such unusual circumstances, was felt everywhere. Neither the government nor its opponents could claim him as one of their own, but in the eyes of many his excommunication for blasphemy crowned him with a revolutionary halo. All the same, at the moment of his death Tolstoy was unquestionably the most famous writer not only in Russia but in the world. He was the pride of Russian literature.

His death presented the government with an embarrassing

problem, namely, the attitude to take toward ceremonies in his honor. Ecclesiastics and rightist ideologues such as Lev Tikhomirov maintained that an Orthodox state had no right to honor posthumously a man under the ban of excommunication. Nevertheless, domestic and foreign opinion regarded Tolstoy's death as a grievous loss for Russia. Finally the emperor discovered the appropriate chord. In the official report of Tolstoy's death he wrote: "I sincerely regret the loss of this great writer who at the pinnacle of his career embodied in his works cherished images of one of the most glorious hours of Russian national life. May God be his Merciful Judge." No state official took part in Tolstoy's civil funeral, but neither did anyone interfere with it, even though it ran counter to established Orthodox custom. With several thousand people, mostly younger persons, in attendance, the great writer was laid to rest on a hill near Yasnaia Poliana.

Tolstoy's death had an unsettling effect on Russia's students. They gathered in their institutions of higher education to consider appropriate responses to the event. At some of those meetings leftists tried to push the highly-charged students into political action. Recalling Tolstoy's bitter essay against the death penalty ("I Cannot be Silent"), the revolutionary parties summoned the students to march "in memory of Tolstoy" under the slogan "Down with the Death Penalty". For the first time since 1905, St. Petersburg witnessed public demonstrations on the 8th, 9th, and 10th of November. Groups of workers joined the students, and the demonstrators stopped traffic on Nevsky Prospekt for several hours. On the 15th demonstrators carrying black flags took to the streets in Moscow. Some students refused to go along with the demonstrations and strikes. Professor Prince Eugene Trubetskoy spoke out against revolutionary agitators and for his pains was "censured" by a student rally.

"Is it not the beginning of a turning point?" asked Lenin in one of the foreign Social Democratic journals. The radicals found fresh fuel for their agitation in the news that Plehve's imprisoned assassin, Egor Sozonov, had committed suicide as an act of protest against the flogging of convicts. The turmoil in the universities flared anew. Moderate students reacted energetically. At Moscow University they organized a system of "door monitors" whereby bands of students blocked the entrances to lecture halls and prevented "wreckers" from entering. But the moderates were not always or everywhere able to cope with the situation. The councils of professors called on the police to restore order several times, and each police intervention gave new cause for a strike. Nevertheless, the disturbances were diminishing when the Christmas vacation arrived in mid-December.

Unfortunately, the new minister of public education, Lev Kasso (who succeeded Schwartz in September 1910), considered it necessary to take decisive steps to suppress all forms of agitation. On 11 January 1911 a decree of the council of ministers temporarily prohibited meetings of any kind within the walls of the institutions of higher learning. The measure applied not only to meetings approved by academic authorities but also to legal student organizations, which had to disband. Even moderate students objected to the order. When the schools reopened, the disruptions resumed with new vigor. Students held brief illegal meetings wherever they could—in corridors or in classrooms—and dispersed as soon as the police arrived. Nearly every higher institution in the capital proclaimed a strike for the entire spring semester.

Moscow University's council of professors protested the disregard of the police for the authorities of the university, and the rector, Professor Manuilov, and his assistant, Professor Menzbir, submitted their resignations. As a result they were dismissed from their posts and also suspended from their professorial duties. Thereupon several dozen Moscow professors and assistant professors resigned in protest. Kasso refused to compromise. He insisted that professors continue to lecture regardless of the number of students present. Police detachments were posted in the universities, and the officers had orders to arrest anyone who attempted to disrupt lectures. That made the strikers resort to the use of chemicals to obstruct classes.

The unyielding struggle went on into February. In some institutions, as in the Higher Woman's Courses, student attendance at lectures dropped to as few as two dozen people. Then slowly the numbers began to rise. Students in the technical institutes were the first to resume classes, and by the end of March the strike had ended practically everywhere.

In contrast to the 1908 student strike, which was ended from within the universities, the strike of 1911 had to be broken by force from the outside. Provincial institutions scarcely were affected, and the experience revealed that the strike was becoming an ineffective instrument of struggle. It also failed to arouse any public sympathy as strikes had in the past. "We must hope," wrote Izgoev in *Russkaia mysl*, "that this will be the last student strike, and that the students themselves will recognize both the moral inadmissability and the total inexpediency of this tactic, which can only destroy a university." But Kasso's handling of the strike also came under fire. The Octobrist M.Ya. Kapustin argued in the Duma that the strikes could have been prevented: "It was necessary, of course, to sweep up the litter, but when you want to tidy up your desk, you do not send for a janitor and a broom."

GUCHKOV'S DEFECTION

In March 1910 an event of great moment took place, although at the time it scarcely stirred St. Petersburg and passed almost unnoticed in the press. The event was the resignation of Nicholas Khomiakov as chairman of the Duma and the election of Alexander Guchkov, the leader of the Octobrists. Guchkov was poorly equipped for the position. Moreover, it meant that he had to abandon his responsible post as leader of the Duma center. Why, then, did he aspire to the title of Duma president? Apparently he hoped that the right to report personally to the emperor would enable him to influence Nicholas toward his own views.[26] His calculations proved to be dead wrong.

Nicholas suspected Guchkov's intentions and believed, moreover, that Guchkov sought to limit his power in some roundabout manner. At their first meeting on 9 March the tsar, deviating from his customary cordiality, greeted the new president of the Duma with studied coolness and plainly conveyed his distrust. Press reports of the interview told only that the audience lasted "more than half an hour." The usual expression, "a cordial reception," was missing. Although the tsar and Duma president later established correct, official relations, it never was possible to speak of Guchkov's influence on the emperor.

Guchkov was an extremely vain man—an endless succession of duels attested to that. He never forgave the emperor for the way he treated him. Gradually Guchkov came to perceive that Nicholas was the main obstacle to his own ambitions and to the type of Russian evolution that he strived to bring about. The combination of political and personal hostility toward the emperor made Guchkov a deadly and unyielding enemy. As leader of a moderate and strictly monarchist party and as president of the Duma, Guchkov could not openly vent his hostility, and that made him all the more dangerous. His inaugural address of 12 March 1910 contained a murky hint of his animosity: "I am a convinced proponent of constitutional monarchy, and my convictions were not formed only yesterday . . . . I cannot conceive of contemporary Russia's peaceful development outside the framework of a constitutional monarchy . . . . We frequently complain about the external forces that impede our efforts . . . we must not close our eyes to them: we will have to take them into consideration and, perhaps, we will have to reckon with them."

A MAN OF GOD FROM TOBOLSK

The year 1910 also marked the debut of "Starets Gregory" (Rasputin)[27] in the columns of the press. He was known to be a great favorite in certain court circles; at the same time his licentious behavior was becoming a common topic of gossip. *Moskovskie vedomosti* carried an expose titled "A Spiritual Quack" by a prominent churchman, [M.A.] Novoselov. When Hermogen, the bishop of Saratov, came to Petersburg in June, *Rech* attributed his visit to an effort to intercede in behalf of Rasputin. Hermogen replied: "Three years ago he impressed me as a man of lofty religious ideals; later however, I was informed of his scandalous conduct . . . . Church history reveals others who achieved the heights of spirituality and then fell into moral ruin."[28] The Kadet paper *Rech* continued to be intrigued by Rasputin, but the 10 June 1910 edition of *Novoe vremia* pointed to the insubstantial nature of the reports about him and concluded that "the whole campaign of accusations hardly can be interpreted as anything more than a dark and extremely dangerous gambit," which in itself implied "highly placed sources."

Rasputin and His "Court"

Rasputin, sprung from peasant roots in the province of Tobolsk, did indeed gain acceptance into the highest social realm. To many socialites he was a "prophet" or a "pastor of souls." He undoubtedly experienced moments of true religious inspiration, but he was equally capable of "deep and shameless sin." In the society of the imperial court he checked his passions in order to appear as a devout preacher, but once he moved into different surroundings he gave free rein to his basest instincts.

The emperor first met Rasputin in 1906 [1905][29] and noted the "strong impression" that he made. Nicholas once told Prince V.N. Orlov[30] that Rasputin was a man of "pure faith." The tsar also had an interest in the starets' views on problems confronting the state and sensed in his responses a genuine "tie with the land." Nevertheless, Rasputin's personal opinions carried no special weight with the emperor. Religious discussions with "Father" Gregory made a much deeper impression on the empress, but he owed his unique position to quite another quality. The testimony of several different witnesses attested to his ability to "charm away the blood," that is, to stop wounds from bleeding through hypnosis.[31]

Alexis Nikolaevich, the tsarevich, had inherited the potentially fatal disease of hemophilia, an affliction discovered early in his childhood. The characteristics of the disease are extremely fragile blood vessels and the low capacity of the blood to coagulate. As a result, the very slightest bruise could produce dangerous and painful bleeding, and an injury could lead to serious internal hemorrhaging. Although the heir's disease was considered a state secret, it was widely discussed. The constant need to protect the tsarevich from injuries and wounds required that he be raised under the most protective conditions. That was all the more difficult because the young prince was lively and energetic and did not take kindly to constraints. When it became clear that Rasputin's hypnotic powers controlled the bleeding more effectively than all the science of doctors and specialists, Father Gregory understandably found himself in an entirely different position. The empress saw him as the man on whom the life of her beloved son quite literally depended.

Unfortunately, when beyond the precincts of the palace, Rasputin continued his indecent behavior, and his indiscretions gave rise to embarrassing gossip. With a completely different view of this "holy man," the empress refused to believe anything evil said against him. In any event she could not yield to "slander" and part with the man whose voice could stem her son's affliction. Rasputin himself had no pretentions to political influence. That, however, did not prevent the emperor's enemies from making Rasputin the focal point of a skilfull campaign of slander which completely distorted the true state of affairs.[32]

LOFTIER DEVELOPMENTS

Aviation was developing rapidly everywhere, and Russia was no exception. Both Moscow and Petersburg staged "aviation weeks." Stolypin had an avid interest in flying and on 22 September 1910 he went up with the flyer Matsievich (who plunged to his death two days later).[33] His venture made Stolypin one of the first heads of government to ascend in an airplane.

On 6 January 1911 the emperor appeared unexpectedly at the Mariinsky Theater, where the opera *Boris Godunov* was being performed. At the close of the third act the curtain suddenly went up, and the entire "boyars" chorus, led by Feodor Chaliapin, fell to its knees and gave three renditions of "God Save the Tsar." The hymn was sung under the baton of the famous conductor Napravnik with the audience joining in. One person in attendance wrote that never since had he "heard such a singing of the hymn," and it was a long time before the leftists pardoned Chaliapin for such a display.

VARIATIONS ON A THEME OF NATIONALISM

Under the new order the "demophiles" began to outnumber the "aristocrats" in the councils of state.[34] The mood of the masses, especially those popular elements who remained loyal to the concept of the sovereign state, could hardly be neglected. In those areas of the empire with mixed populations, the majority of Russians aligned with the rightist movements. That was the pattern in Kiev, Odessa, all the cities of the western provinces, and to some extent in the Caucasus. Whereas in Moscow and St. Petersburg rightist candidates could garner no more than 5-10 percent of the vote, in western districts they received 40-50 percent. Leftists were elected only on the strength of non-Russian ballots.

Supported by the masses, right-wing leaders from the western provinces began to demand that the government redress the situation. Professor Pikhno, editor of the *Kievlianin*, introduced into the State Council a bill to revise the election of western provincial representatives to the upper chamber. He noted that nine Poles were elected in nine provinces even though Poles comprised only 2-3 percent of the population in some of those provinces. He demanded the creation of a separate Polish curia in order to ensure majority representation for Russians.

Pikhno's proposal violated the imperial principle of national equality. It was true that Poles did not form an actual majority, but most of the large landowners in the western provinces were of Polish descent. The State Council displayed little enthusiasm for Pikhno's bill. When the former director-general of the holy synod, Prince A.D. Obolensky, spoke on the issue, he restated the traditional "imperial" idea: "The foundation of our state rests on the principle that at the head of the Russian monarchy is a Russian Tsar[35] before whom all nations and clans are equal. The Sovereign Emperor stands above parties, nationalities, groups and classes. He can readily refer to 'My Poles, My Armenians, My Jews, My Finns,' for they all belong to him." To the surprise of many, however, prime minister Stolypin endorsed Pikhno's bill, which was then referred to committee. That moment in May 1909 marked Stolypin's departure on a new course—the redefinition of the principle of Russian nationalism.

An emphasis on nationalism, hitherto "shunned" by Russian society, began to emerge after 1905. *Slovo* ran a series of articles by Vasily Struve on "the national image." "The Russian intelligentsia, he wrote, "looses its identity by becoming an intelligentsia of *Russia* . . . . Just as we should not concern ourselves with russifying those who have no wish to become Russian, so we ourselves must not become an intelligentsia of the *Russians*. During the tribulations of the recent past, our national Russian consciousness has changed, becoming more complex and refined and yet also more mature and stronger. It would be unseemly for us to ignore that development and hide our faces."[36]

"The dominance of non-Russian elements in literature and art criticism" came under attack from the popular poet Andrei Bely, who set forth his views in the literary journal *Vesy* in 1909: "The leaders of national culture turn out to be persons alien to that culture . . . .   The pure strains of our native tongue are being corrupted by an impersonal Esperanto drawn from some international vocabulary . . . .   Instead of Gogol, a Sholom Ash is proclaimed; our intimate traditions are condemned to death, and a polyglot jargon is taking root . . . . Look at the staffs of Russia's newspapers and journals: who are the music and literary critics? You will find nothing but the names of Jews . . . who write in the gibberish of Esperanto and terrorize anyone who tries to deepen and enrich the Russian language."[37]   Articles of this type, quite uncharacteristic of the Russian intelligentsia, signaled a substantial deterioration of its mental state. There remained, nevertheless, a great distinction between the cultural nationalism of the intelligentsia and the Great Russian political nationalism of P.A. Stolypin.

STOLYPIN'S NATIONALISM: FINLAND

In the fall of 1909 Stolypin presented the council for affairs of the local economy[38] a proposal to introduce the zemstvo into the nine western provinces. His plan stipulated that the institution would have a Russian majority. Meanwhile the government also was backing the project of Bishop Evlogy to detach the Russian sections of Sedletsk and Lublin from Poland in order to form a separate province of Kholm (or Chelm). On another front the question of legislation of imperial concern reopened the dispute between the Russian government and Finland. Stolypin reverted to procedures followed in 1905 and by-passed the Finnish Diet in order to adopt a bill that regulated relations between Finland and the empire. Still another item in this cycle of nationalistic measures was a plan to restrict German colonization in the western provinces, where since 1905 German settlers had been buying up considerable amounts of landowners' property. The Duma generally supported all of these measures, although the opposition strenuously resisted them.

The legislation on Finland, introduced into the Duma on 14 March 1910, caused much protest abroad. In Finland various groups of prominent professors and lawyers published "manifestoes" contesting the right of the Russian government to legislate on Finnish affairs without the consent of the Diet. More than 400 French deputies and senators sent a protest to the State Duma. The Finnish Diet refused to consider the legislation, which it held to be in violation of the Fundamental Laws of the Grand Duchy of Finland.

In his defense of the project before the Duma Stolypin recognized the juridical arguments on both sides: "A mass of material, documents, and acts concerning Finland's relation to Russia make it possible to defend any thesis; any stack of material pulled out of the archives would suffice . . . and no special care would be necessary. All that is required is a certain preconception and a particular point of view." The legal question, he argued, was beside the point: the real issue was the interests of the Russian state. If the Duma rejected the bill, the Finns would interpret its action as a sign of weakness: "Gentlemen, destroy this dangerous apparition which goes beyond bitterness and hatred to contempt for our native land." When the majority voted to speed up the debate, the opposition stalked out of the chamber. The Octobrists attempted to introduce several amendments, but the rightists and nationalists formed a majority and approved the government's version without change.[39]

Despite some objections from both the left and the right, a substantial majority in the State Council also passed the bill, which then became law on 17 June 1910. The law permitted the Diet a consultative vote on all essential questions, imperial and domestic (press, assemblies, unions, public education, and police). All previous legislation remained in effect until superseded by the publication of new legislation. Actually then, no specific change occurred in Finland. Anti-Russianism mounted dramatically, however, as Finns concluded that the Russian government—now with the backing of Russia's national representatives—had violated Finland's autonomy for the second time.

STOLYPIN'S NATIONALISM: THE WESTERN ZEMSTVOS

Stolypin paid particular attention to the matter of the western zemstvos. He was a longtime resident of the region, owned an estate in Kovno province, and had served there as marshal of the nobility and governor. Eventually he decided to postpone the introduction of the zemstvo into the provinces of Kovno, Vilna, and Grodno, whose Russian population was too small. In the remaining six provinces of Vitebsk, Mogilev, Minsk, Kiev, Volynia, and Podolsk he moved to introduce the 1890 zemstvo with major modifications. Since Poles constituted almost all of the large landowners, the property qualification for Russians was cut in half [by the Duma]. The bill established separate curiae for Russians and Poles and guaranteed that a majority of elected representatives would be Russian. Other provisions assured the preponderance of Russians on the zemstvo boards and in the zemstvo administration.

The Duma's leftists bitterly attacked the bill's violation of the principle of equality for national minorities, and Stolypin vigorously defended his position: "We are striving to protect the rights of the economically weak Russian majority from the economically and culturally dominant Polish minority . . . . Is it worthy of the Russian government to take the position of a disinterested observer at the rail of history's race track, or that of the impartial judge at the finish line, and simply record the victory of one nationality or the other?" The government's objective, he concluded, was to "proclaim openly and without hypocrisy that the western region is and will remain a Russian region, always and forever!" It was during this debate that Stolypin made one of his more famous statements, which he addressed to the Poles who reproached him for vindictiveness: "In politics there is no such thing as revenge, but there are consequences."

The Duma passed the bill after making several amendments which tempered its anti-Polish character. It reduced the representation of the clergy, defeated the provision that required the chairman and a majority of the executive board to be Russian [while adding a clause that the official in charge of education should be Russian], but it retained the important principle of separate national curiae. In the third reading of the bill deputies of the left and right spoke against it. Bishop

Evlogy, who spoke for the nationalists, announced that they would vote for the bill, however distorted, though they would do so "with pain in their hearts." Finally the Duma approved the bill by a vote of 165-139. The State Council did not begin its deliberations for another eight months.

HERMOGEN AND ILIODOR

The province of Saratov was rent by dissension between the church and secular authorities. From his pulpit the influential Bishop Hermogen attacked the governor, Count S.S. Tatishchev, and openly criticized the government's policy. Meanwhile Iliodor, a recently confirmed monk with a rare gift for demagoguery, had attracted a large following in Tsaritsyn [later Stalingrad, now Volgograd] and was even less restrained in his denunciation of the government and certain individuals. He commonly referred to cabinet ministers as "kike-masons." The secular authorities finally managed to have Iliodor transferred to a different diocese, but he refused to go. Supported by a crowd of several thousand, he locked himself up in a monastery built by hand by his followers and defied both state and ecclesiastical superiors. He announced that "I will starve myself to death if they refuse to leave me in Tsaritsyn."

The emperor had no desire to employ force against a religiously motivated though unruly crowd [i.e. Black Hundreds]. Therefore he sent an aide-de-camp to Tsaritsyn to negotiate a solution. "The people should realize," he wrote Stolypin, "that their woes and joys are of concern to the tsar." Iliodor was persuaded to submit and soon afterward departed for a monastery in Tambov.[40]

The emperor was upset, however, with the spineless and clumsy handling of the affair by the director-general of the holy synod, General S.M. Lukianov. Therefore he decided to replace him with Pobedonostsev's former assistant, V.K. Sabler, whom the ecclesiastical authorities held in great esteem.[41] Stolypin came to Lukianov's defense: "I am exclusively responsible for the handling of the Iliodor affair," he wrote to the tsar on 26 February 1911. "If it becomes obvious that Lukianov was dismissed because of Iliodor, my conscience would torment me for having failed to defend him. For a statesman there is no greater sin, no greater fault than cowardice."

Nevertheless [on 2 May 1911] Nicholas appointed Sabler to head the holy synod.

STOLYPIN'S UNEXPECTED REBUFF

The State Council opened debate on the western zemstvo bill on the first of February 1911. It was clear from the start that most of the center and left opposed the project's main provision, the creation of separate national curiae. But the rightists stood apart from the center, and the government thought that it would have a secure majority. The right, however, also contained opponents of the bill. Some objected in the belief that to lower electoral qualifications would create an undesirable precedent for the other provinces. Others took their stand on the imperial principle of equality and considered it unwise to limit the rights of the conservative Polish nobility for the benefit of the Russian "semi-intelligentsia." Peter Durnovo, the chairman of the rightist group, sent the emperor a memorandum that set forth their objections.

Michael Akimov, the chairman of the State Council, informed the rightists that the emperor wished them to support the government in this matter. Akimov acted on instructions from the emperor who in turn was carrying out Stolypin's request. Many rightists regarded this as illegitimate pressure. One of the bill's opponents, V.F. Trepov,[42] obtained an audience with the tsar, expressed his reservations, and asked if the message conveyed by Akimov was to be understood as a direct order from the tsar. Nicholas answered that the members of the State Council were free, of course, "to vote according to their own consciences." Trepov reported the emperor's remark to his colleagues on the eve of the decisive vote on the national curiae. Stolypin, however, was not forewarned.

On 4 March 1911, after a brief debate, the State Council moved to a vote on the critical article and defeated it by a majority of 92-68. The results shocked the prime minister. Among the opposition were 28 rightists including Durnovo, Trepov, Shirinsky-Shikhmatov, and N.P. Balashov, the father of the leader of the Duma's Nationalist fraction.

Stolypin immediately left the Council's chambers He attached great importance to the western zemstvos, but probably even more significant to his mind was the fact that prominent rightists appointed by the tsar had voted against the government and had done so shortly after an audience with the sovereign. He concluded that he was the victim of an intrigue directed against him personally.

The evidence now available leads to the conclusion that there was no intrigue but that the Council's rightists simply had voted "according to their consciences."[43] Some, like Balashov for instance, saw the national curiae as a violation of the imperial principle, while others objected to the extension of the zemstvo into the new provinces. Although both points of view could be disputed, their legitimacy could not be denied. Moreover, Trepov's audience with the tsar was a reasonable response to Stolypin's effort to use the tsar to exert pressure on the right.

Stolypin's bitter reaction, on the other hand, was more than a mere display of anger and pride. The action of the Council convinced him that the upper chamber could interpose itself between the government and the Duma and that it could block reforms desired equally by the council of ministers and the elected representatives of the nation. Moreover, he concluded that the damage to his prestige destroyed his effectiveness.

On 5 March 1911 Stolypin went to make his report to the tsar and to inform him of his decision to resign.[44] Nicholas was stunned to learn that his prime minister desired to step down over such a personal matter. Stolypin maintained that he could not tolerate intrigues which undermined his authority, especially since his opponents claimed to be executing the emperor's will. Nicholas replied that he considered it impossible to part with Stolypin—"What will become of the government, which is responsible to me, if the ministers resign because today they have a fight with the Council and tomorrow with the Duma?" He urged Stolypin to come up with another solution.

Stolypin then suggested that both chambers be dissolved for a few days while the western zemstvo bill was put into effect by invoking Article 87. Nicholas asked: "And are you not concerned that the Duma itself will censure you for persuading me to take such a contrived step?" Stolypin told him that the Duma would be "dissatisfied in public but pleased in its soul."[45] Nicholas then said: "In order not to lose you, I am prepared to agree to such an unprecedented measure, but let me think it over." At that point the prime minister asked permission to raise another matter and then denounced the actions of Durnovo and Trepov. He "earnestly implored" the emperor not only to censure but also to punish them as an example to "dissuade others from the same course."

After hearing out this request, the emperor (as Stolypin himself told it) reflected for a long time and then, as though waking form a nap, asked: "What would you have me do, Peter Arkadeevich?" Stolypin's answer was that "those persons" should be requested to leave St. Petersburg and absent themselves from the work of the State Council for some period of time. The emperor made no response except to promise to consider everything Stolypin had said and to answer him "just as directly and sincerely."

On the following day Stolypin summoned his ministers to a private meeting and recounted his interview with the emperor. Most of the cabinet, observing Stolypin's mood, knew that it was useless to try to change his mind and therefore remained silent. A.V. Krivoshein and P.A. Kharitonov suggested that a more conciliatory solution with regard to Durnovo and Trepov would be desirable in order to preserve Stolypin's position. He retorted sharply: "Let those who value their positions seek compromises. I consider it more honest and honorable to step aside altogether than to go through what I have endured simply to maintain my position."

After the others had departed, Kokovtsov expressed his own doubts over the course that Stolypin intended to follow. He pointed out that the Duma hardly would be pleased; great violence would be done to the legislative order, and that would never be forgiven. It was even more questionable, he argued, to demand that the emperor punish those whom he himself had received in audience. Kokovtsov advised Stolypin to pass the bill through regular channels by reintroducing it into the legislature. Stolypin replied that he had "neither the skill nor the desire' to go through "such a long procedure; it is better to cut the knot right away than to face months of torment trying to unravel a tangle of intrigues."

THE WESTERN ZEMSTVO CRISIS

The tsar pondered his response for four days. During that period the press got wind of the crisis. "Reactionary intrigues" enraged the Duma circles. Tikhomirov telegraphed Stolypin: "I pay my deep respects to the defender of national interests who stands unflinching to the end." From the western region came bitter protests against the action of the State Council. The oppositionist press adopted a wait-and-see attitude. On 8 March the window of Datsiaro's, a fashionable Petersburg photographer, featured a portrait of Kokovtsov with the inscription: "Chairman of the Council of Ministers." The photo was removed the next day. Meanwhile, the Empress Maria Feodorovna and some of the grand dukes were convincing Nicholas to accede to all of Stolypin's conditions.

On 10 March 1911 Stolypin was summoned to Tsarskoe Selo. There the tsar signed an ukaz which recessed the legislature from the 12th to the 14th of March. At the same time he instructed Stolypin to inform Durnovo and Trepov that they were to leave the capital and absent themselves from the State Council until the end of the year.[46] Although he doubted the justice and legality of his actions, the tsar preferred that alternative to the loss of Stolypin. His decision clearly revealed how highly he valued Stolypin's abilities. "An unheard of triumph for Stolypin," recorded Count A.A. Bobrinsky in his diary on the 12th of March.[47]

The publication (on 12 March) of the ukaz recessing the legislature immediately precipitated a great hue and cry. A delegation of Octobrists called on the premier and emphatically announced that the arbitrary use of Article 87 was absolutely unacceptable to them. Stolypin admitted that, though he had "stretched the law," he would create the western zemstvos in the form approved by the Duma. Everything that had occurred, he assured them, represented a decisive victory over "the reactionary conspiracy;" the Duma had nothing to fear. With that Stolypin, confident of his victory, left in a cheerful mood to spend several days at his daughter's estate. When he returned, he discovered that the situation had changed completely.

An imperial decree established the western zemstvos on 14 March 1911. The general reaction was that "the law must not be trifled with in such a manner." That notion of procedure and legality overshadowed everything else. In protest Guchkov resigned his chairmanship of the Duma and went off to the Far East on a long vacation. Several Duma fractions submitted resolutions calling for inquiries into "the violation of the Fundamental Laws." The repressive measures against Durnovo and Trepov angered the rightists. A.A. Bobrinsky's diary for 14 March noted that "Petersburg's indignation knows no bounds," and as for Stolypin: "He was holding exceptionally strong cards, but he foolishly lost everything." Tikhomirov, who only recently had praised Stolypin when his resignation seemed quite imminent, now wrote: "Stolypin has decided to set a record for stupidity . . . . Some sort of conspiracy! The program of every monarchist organization calls for the reestablishment of absolutism—how could there be a conspiracy? Numerous persons, as individuals and in delegations, have urged the emperor to reverse the edicts of 1906. How devious! I never thought that Stolypin would stoop to such patently false accusations in the heat of battle."

Returning on 17 March, the Duma immediately took up the question of an interpellation into the government's use of Article 87. "A tempting proposition has been laid before us," said the Octobrist S.I. Shidlovsky. "But since we stand for legality, we must not desert the upper chamber . . . . It is both ridiculous and tragic that those in charge of Russian policy are so ill-informed as to think that they could possibly find support in the Duma for their crude infringement of the law." Miliukov ironically pointed to the confusion of the foreign press, "when they discover that state officials, members of the supreme chamber, are subjected not only to disciplinary action for expressing their opinions but also to punishment in a paternalistic manner like serfs . . . . For that we can thank our new Boris Godunov." At the conclusion of his speech, V.N. Lvov [the chairman of the center fraction] recalled that Karamzin once characterized Arakcheev as "a favorite who toyed with the sacred name of the monarch."[48]

N.E. Markov, the rightist, opposed an inquiry. The Duma, he said, could be dissolved "for an hour and in an hour." But Count A.A. Bobrinsky, a member of the same fraction, asking rhetorically whether Stolypin had acted properly toward Durnovo and Trepov, answered: "Oh, Your Excellency, improperly!"

Only the Nationalists defended Stolypin. V.V. Shulgin, one of the Duma's foremost orators, was one rightist who took Stolypin's side and joined the Nationalists on that issue. By an overwhelming majority, however, the Duma voted for an interpellation.

Although *Novoe vremia*'s editorials consistently supported the prime minister, its correspondent Menshikov, guided by the "attitude of the planets," asked regarding Durnovo: "If he had not found within himself a soldier's courage and a soldier's loyalty to the throne, do you think Stolypin could have built a career on him?"

STOLYPIN'S "FINAL AGONY"

The State Council also voted to interpellate the government. During the process, the prime minister was criticized by A.F. Koni, the Pole I.A. Shebeko, and Count D.A. Olsufiev. The latter observed that apparently it was "not service to the tsar but servility to the government which is demanded of members of the State Council." Stolypin had not expected such a violent reaction and he sensed the ground slipping from under him. The reaction confirmed the fears of Nicholas and Kokovtsov: Society was not afraid of a "reactionary conspiracy" but stood firmly opposed to "stretching the law."

On 1 April 1911 Stolypin responded to the Council's interpellation. He contended that "extraordinary circumstances" had warranted his use of Article 87. The circumstances were the Council's rejection of a measure so eagerly awaited by the citizens of the western provinces. "The government," he said, "cannot admit the infallibility of the State Council. It cannot concede the State Council the right to tie a dead knot that can be untied only from above. I do not know whether [government by decree] is good, but I do think that sometimes it is necessary, just as a tracheotomy is necessary when a patient is choking . . . ." By a vote of 99-53 the Council rejected Stolypin's explanation.

Stolypin appeared before the Duma on 27 April and made what proved to be his last public speech. He implied that the ukaz of 14 March established a precedent that was useful to the Duma.[49] The zemstvo project, he argued, was instituted in the form approved by the Duma. "However severely you may judge and even condemn the form of what has been done, I know, I believe, that many of you admit in your hearts that what happened on 14 March did not infringe but indeed strengthened the rights of Russia's young representative body."

During the debate, the speech that best elucidated the issue was made by V.A. Maklakov, who compared Stolypin to a herdsman: "When told that his cattle are in the oats, he replies: 'those are not my oats, they are my neighbors.' May God deliver us from such guardians! . . . The chairman of the council of ministers may still retain power: he will be kept there by fear of revolution—revolution which his own agents are fermenting; he will be kept there by the fear of creating a precedent. But this, gentlemen, is the final agony." Maklakov then addressed Stolypin with his own words: " 'In politics there is no such thing as revenge, but there are consequences.' These consequences have overtaken you and you will not avoid them now."[50]

Even Stolypin's supporters recognized that he had worked himself into a cul-de-sac. P.N. Balashov suggested that the Duma be dissolved and a new electoral law drafted. Only the supreme authority could have approved such a "dictatorial solution," and the emperor already had concluded that Stolypin had acted improperly. Nicholas regretted that he had given in to his minister's demands. The situation was worse than before, and the tsar had lost confidence in the political wisdom of his prime minister.

"Somehow Stolypin's prestige evaporated all at once. Clubs, especially those associated with court circles, literally breathed malice," Kokovtsov observed in his memoirs. "Stolypin became unrecognizable . . . something within him snapped, his former self-assurance vanished, and he seemed to feel that everyone around him, secretly or openly, was hostile to him." The Duma and State Council were dismissed two days before the deadline prescribed by Article 87 for the reintroduction of the western zemstvo bill into the legislature. Therefore the law technically remained in force, if only until fall. During the summer, zemstvo elections were held in the western provinces. Nationalists failed to win their expected victory, and most of the representatives were elected without party affiliations.

During the period of Stolypin's personal crisis, the monk Iliodor escaped from his place of exile and returned to Tsaritsyn. Once again a crowd of thousands gathered around his retreat, and this time Bishop Hermogen openly supported him. The newly-appointed Saratov governor, P.P. Stremoukhov, requested instructions from Petersburg. P.G. Kurlov, the assistant interior minister, told him to send police some night to break into Iliodor's cell and arrest him. But, fearing a blood-bath, Stremoukhov asked Stolypin himself for instructions, and on 23 March was told to "cease any actions against the Iliodor monastery." And so, Iliodor managed to remain in Tsaritsyn. Stolypin later told Stremoukhov: "What is so terrible is that Iliodor is right in his analysis, but the methods he uses and the lawlessness he creates ruin everything."

In a letter dated 9 July Tikhomirov urged Stolypin to initiate reform that would restore all legislative authority to the tsar, that is, to transform the Duma into a consultative institution. Stolypin wrote on the letter: "All this fine idealistic logic translated into action would be a deliberate provocation that would ignite another revolution."

Feeling "semi-retired," Stolypin vacationed for the entire summer at his estate near Kolnobrzhe and returned only briefly to Petersburg in July. During that period, Krivoshein and Kokovtsov, who was substituting for Stolypin, agreed to drop the project to transfer the Peasants Bank from the ministry of finance to agriculture. That was a reorganization that Stolypin strongly desired, and with bitterness he later told Kokovtsov: "You have betrayed me." Count Witte, whose statements must always be read with caution, wrote that Nicholas informed Stolypin after he had made one of his reports: "Peter Arkadeevich, I am preparing another assignment for you." Rumor had it that Stolypin would be sent to some other post, either an embassy or the viceroyalty of the Caucasus, or to a newly created post such as viceroy of the western provinces, and that he would be elevated to the rank of count.

THE AGADIR CRISIS

The Agadir incident marked the summer of 1911 in international affairs. Responding to disorders that threatened the lives of foreigners, France sent troops deep into Morocco. Thereupon Germany insisted on the right to protect its own citizens in that area and sent the gunboat *Panther* to the southern Moroccan port of Agadir. Paris regarded that move as a challenge, an invasion of the French sphere of influence. In a sensational speech at a banquet given by London's lord-mayor, David Lloyd George promised France the support of England. Excitement ran high on both sides, but Russia remained neutral. Nothing in their alliance required Russia to assist France in the Moroccan question. Because of the absence of Stolypin and the lengthy illness of Sazonov, the assistant foreign minister, A.A. Neratov, represented Russia during the crisis. In response to the German ambassador's inquiry, Neratov declared that Russia supported "all measures aimed at eliminating the Moroccan question as a source of friction in international politics." On 1/14 August at the very height of the Agadir crisis Russia and Germany concluded the agreement that defined their mutual interests in Persia.[51] Russia's decidedly pacifist stance aided French premier Joseph Caillaux in finding a compromise solution to the Moroccan crisis.[52]

A LIFE FOR THE TSAR

The unveiling of a monument to Alexander II was scheduled to take place in Kiev in late August. The emperor and other prominent dignitaries were to attend. Stolypin attached special importance to the ceremonies, for they also would mark the inauguration of expanded public activity in the southwest as a result of the introduction of the zemstvo. The participation of imperial personages and the highest officials was well publicized.

The prime minister arrived in Kiev on 25 August, four days before the imperial family. The festivities began with a tour of Kiev's holy places, including the Cathedral of St. Sophia and the Pechersky Monastery. The emperor received many delegations. On the 31st there was a huge military review and in the evening a concert in the lavishly illuminated Merchants Garden on the high bank of the Dnieper. Everything was staged with great enthusiasm. However, a number of elusive indications told Stolypin that his resignation was becoming more and more probable. He told his assistant Kurlov: "I am on leave at my own request until October 1st, but it is unlikely that I will return to St. Petersburg as chairman of the council of ministers . . . ."

On 1 September the emperor, much to his delight, reviewed the "poteshnie."[53] That evening the play *A Life for the Tsar* was performed in the municipal theater. The Kievan police had information that terrorists were planning an assassination, and during the first days of the festivities cordons of police and gendarmes were everywhere in evidence. They hindered the crowds that gathered to welcome the tsar, but he insisted that security be kept to a minimum. The people of Kiev were filled with genuine monarchist sympathies, and their exuberance pleased and touched the tsar.

The performance was nearing its end. Kokovtsov, who was departing for St. Petersburg, already had bid farewell to Stolypin. Then around 11:30 during the second intermission, an unknown young man dressed in a tailcoat walked rapidly up to the prime minister, who was standing in the first row of seats. The assailant shot him twice at almost point-blank range. Stolypin staggered but then straightened up. He turned toward the tsar's family and with his left hand made the sign of the cross. (One shot had passed through his right hand.) Then he slumped into a chair. Cries of horror shook the theater. In the confusion the assassin, who immediately made for an exit, nearly escaped but was seized at the door. To prevent panic the orchestra began to play the national anthem. The emperor moved to the rail of the imperial box and stood there for all to see, as if to assure everyone that he was still at his post. He remained—despite great concern over another attempt—until the last strains of the anthem were finished.

Professor Rein administered emergency treatment to Stolypin, who then was taken to the Makovsky Clinic. The doctors immediately discovered that one of the bullets had struck his liver and that his condition was very grave. As he was being carried from the theater, he asked that someone "inform the emperor that I am happy to die for him and for our motherland." For the first two or three days Stolypin's strong constitution prevailed. The papers reported that he probably would live. The emperor expressed the same hope. Throngs of people crowded the streets around the hospital. People in all parts of the country sent telegrams expressing their grief, horror, and good wishes. Kokovtsov, meanwhile, was delegated to act as chairman of the council of ministers.

BOGROV'S DOUBLE GAME

The identity of the assailant inspired rumors which heightened the shock of his attempt to slay Stolypin. The man who played such a fateful role in the history of Russia must be examined more closely. His name was Dmitry Bogrov—he used the name "Mordka" only after his arrest—and he was the son of a wealthy Jewish landlord who even belonged to the nobles club in Kiev. Bogrov was 24 at the time. Since his gymnasium days he had expressed the most extreme revolutionary beliefs. Although he called himself an "anarcho-communist," no party satisfied him. He offered his services to the Okhrana in Kiev to which he passed on a great deal of intelligence. (A subsequent investigation disclosed his information "to be of a completely indifferent nature."[54]) Bogrov never suffered from lack of funds, and there is reason to believe that he made contact with the Okhrana in the interests of the revolution. Although the police in Kiev trusted him, when Bogrov moved to Petersburg and tried to contact the Okhrana, the chief of the Petersburg bureau, Colonel von Kotten, clearly suspected him. Bogrov, therefore, broke with the Okhrana for two or three years; he graduated from the university and took a job.

In 1910 he contacted the prominent Socialist Revolutionary, E.E. Lazarev, and told him that he intended to kill Stolypin. "This is neither a joke nor insanity but a thoroughly conceived plan," he said. "A systematic revolutionary struggle against key figures is the only rational approach under Russian conditions." Bogrov asked that *after his execution* the Socialist Revolutionaries announce that the murder was committed with the party's knowledge and that it marked the beginning of a new wave of revolutionary terror. Lazarev regarded the whole thing as too fantastic and refused to make any promise.

About a year later, on the eve of the festivities in Kiev, Bogrov again approached the chief of the Kiev Okhrana, N.N. Kuliabko, for whom he had worked four years earlier. He gave Kuliabko the details of an assassination plot, for which two assassins were supposedly coming to Kiev. (Bogrov invented the entire story.) He presented everything in such a plausible manner that Kuliabko was completely taken in. For several days Bogrov "reported" on the progress of the "conspiracy." During that time he managed to instill such trust in his reliability that Kuliabko gave him a ticket for the concert in the Merchants Garden and then another for the municipal theater.[55]

Bogrov had a chance to kill the tsar in the Merchants Garden. He let it pass, because he feared that the murder of the tsar by a Jew would have unleashed massive pogroms against all Jews. Then, having killed Stolypin, he made no effort to conceal his ties with the Okhrana but, to the contrary, went to great lengths to stress them.

The facts about Bogrov published since the revolution (particularly the book by his brother) convincingly exposed the assassin's true intentions. His goal was not simply the removal of Stolypin: at the same time he wanted to spread discord and contention among the ranks of the government's forces, to sow mutual suspicion among them, and to force them to start shooting "their own people." In order to deliver the most telling blow to the hated system, Bogrov conscientiously sacrificed his "revolutionary honor." There is no doubt that he accomplished both goals.

From the moment it was learned that Bogrov had entered the theater with a ticket issued by the Okhrana, rumors proclaimed that Stolypin's murder was the work of reactionary "instigators" in the Okhrana. The most frequently mentioned suspect was Kurlov, the assistant minister of interior. The authorities became so suspect that representatives of several rightist organizations in Kiev demanded to be present at Bogrov's execution in order to confirm that he actually was hanged. The suspicion that Bogrov was the executioner in some "vendetta" of the Okhrana (which was absolutely without foundation) became so deeply rooted in the public mind that it completely destroyed public confidence in the government organizations directly engaged in the struggle against revolution.[56]

THE END OF THE STOLYPIN ERA

The emperor visited Dr. Makovsky's clinic on 3 September. On the 4th Madam Stolypin arrived from Kovno. By then Stolypin's condition was known to be hopeless, and on the following day, 5 September 1911 at 10:12 p.m., he died.

Suddenly the Russian people recognized the greatness of the statesman they had lost. The oppositionist press, adhering to the version of an "Okhrana-assassin," naturally proclaimed Stolypin "a victim of the system that he himself had created." Otherwise, Stolypin's death reconciled to him all those who had questioned his policies in the spring. Most striking, perhaps, was the reaction of Lev Tikhomirov who wrote:

On the shattered deck of a once great ship, with its machinery broken down and its plates full of holes, with its bottom leaking everywhere and its crew demoralized, under constant shelling from enemies of the state and nation—P.A. Stolypin—with his inexhaustible strength under dreadful strain, his tireless dedication to duty, and his rare talent for leadership—still was able to navigate and carry his passengers in relative security . . . . There have been statesmen with a more profound national philosophy, others of stronger character, some with a broader knowledge, and of course still others with a more definite world view. Nevertheless, I have never known a statesman who brought together such brilliant qualities just when they were needed, when one man had to take the place of scores—a statesman so selfless and so intensely devoted to Russia.

Tikhomirov recalled Stolypin's own words: "What I am I do not know. But I believe in God and know for certain that despite any obstacles I shall accomplish all that I am destined for; and I know that despite any contrivances I shall not accomplish what is not destined . . . . I believe in Russia. If I did not have such faith, I would not be able to accomplish anything."

P.B. Struve, writing in *Russkaia mysl*, referred to "an inexpressible natural aversion" caused by Stolypin's murder. "For the first time we have witnessed the assassination of a statesman known to so many as a living human being rather than as the abstract symbol of a political system . . . . As a revolutionary act, Stolypin's assassination was purely accidental." Having enumerated both his merits and faults, Struve summarized Stolypin's major traits as "the outstanding power of his spirit and the amazing strength and flexibility of his will."

In the *Kievlianin* V.V. Shulgin reminisced about the Second Duma and Stolypin's historic speech proclaiming that the government was "not afraid." "The monster was tamed. Within an hour people were congratulating one another on the streets of Petersburg. Russia could extinguish her Diogenes lantern: she had found her man. Now five years have passed, and the lantern must be lit again."

The emperor had journeyed to Chernigov to worship the relics of St. Feodosia Uglitsky, who had been canonized during his reign in 1896. On 6 September he returned to Kiev and prayed for a long time beside Stolypin's body. "You see, Your Majesty," said O.B. Stolypina, "Russia has not yet run out of Susanins."[57]

Stolypin was buried on September 9th at the Kiev Pechersky Monastery. He once had said, "Let me be buried wherever I am killed." He had lived for some time with a sense of impending doom: "When I go out into the street, I never know whether I will return or be brought back in a hearse."[58] There were several funeral orations, and many commemorative ceremonies were held throughout Russia. A subscription was started to build a memorial, and eventually three were erected: in Kiev, Saratov, and Grodno. On the monument in Kiev were inscribed his words: "You need great upheavals, but we need a great Russia." Time did not ease but rather increased the sense of his great loss, for indeed Stolypin's death was a numbing blow to the Russian nation. Even if he had resigned, so great a statesman would only have been placed "in reserve" to be recalled to duty when the need arose. The hand of the killer deprived Russia of the one man most capable of mastering the complexities of the Duma Monarchy.

CHAPTER SIXTEEN

The tragic loss of Stolypin did not alter Russian policy, for the emperor himself set the course. V.N. Kokovtsov, who had functioned for the prime minister during the last month of his life, became his successor. Kokovtsov quite possibly would have become prime minister even if Bogrov's bullets had not felled Stolypin. The new chairman of the council of ministers had great respect for his predecessor, and he came to power with the aim of continuing Stolypin's policy. As Stolypin's successor in the ministry of interior the emperor initially considered two conservative young governors, Alexis Khvostov and Nicholas Maklakov. (The emperor got to know Maklakov in September 1911, when he traveled from Kiev through the province of Chernigov.) Eventually, however, Nicholas agreed with Kokovtsov that it was better to appoint an older, more experienced official, State Secretary Alexander Makarov, one of Stolypin's former assistants.[1] Agriculture remained in the hands of Krivoshein, who continued the established agrarian policy. Credit facilities and measures to improve agricultural productivity received increasing attention. The success of these policies became more apparent with each passing year.

Kokovtsov was less avid than Stolypin in furthering the policy of Great Russian nationalism, which the former premier enunciated in 1908. Nevertheless, even in that area Kokovtsov did not depart completely from his predecessor's program. During his ministry, both legislative chambers approved the separation of the district of Kholmsk from the Kingdom of Poland. Russian Kholmsk, or the Kholmshchina, a predominantly Russian area, covered parts of the Polish provinces of Lublin and Sedlets. Pressure for the separation of the region from Poland came mainly from the Russian peasants and clergy led by Bishop Evlogy. In the Duma the Polish delegation vigorously fought another partition of Poland, and the oppositionists argued the purposelessness of the measure. However, on 1 September 1913, Kholmsk with its capital at Kholm became the 51st province of European Russia.

In his first appearance before the State Duma Kokovtsov emphasized the continuity of imperial policy toward Finland. The government obtained as imperial legislation the passage of two major bills. One provided for the disbursement of funds from the Finnish treasury for defense requirements; the other established civil equality for Russian citizens residing in Finland. The unanimous opposition of the local population forced the government to abandon a plan to detach and incorporate into the province of St. Petersburg the southern districts of the Finnish province of Vyborg. Thus the Russian government on the one hand affirmed the principle of all-imperial legislation but on the other hand refrained from disrupting the internal structure of the grand duchy.

As tranquility returned to the empire, the incidence of judicial and administrative repression—executions and exiles—continued to decline. The press enjoyed greater freedom. New socialist publications appeared. Beside monthly journals like *Russkoe bogatstvo*, *Sovremennyi mir*, *Obrazovaniia* [Educacation], and from 1912 *Zavetov* [Precepts] there were socialist weeklies (*Zvezda* [The Star]) and even dailies. Two newspapers were published in St. Petersburg: the independent socialist *Den* [Day] and the Bolshevik organ *Pravda* [Truth].[2]

Stolypin had been able to defend the government against public opinion by dint of his personal prestige and his authoritative, clever, and eloquent oratory. The new cabinet followed his policies (and in some cases even more "liberal" policies), but it ran into progressively stiffer conservative and liberal opposition. The government found itself incapable of countering those attacks. The reason was that the ministers not only lacked Stolypin's oratorical gifts but also were divided among themselves. The cabinet had its own "left" and "right," and at times its divisions were quite apparent, as when the ministers voted on opposite sides of matters before the State Council.

GUCHKOV'S ATTEMPT TO SMEAR THE OKHRANA

Kokovtsov's opposition came mainly from the right. He was reproved for the lukewarm militancy of his nationalism, and he was reproached for coolness toward the efforts of right-wing organizations. Stolypin had found it useful to subsidize many conservative and reactionary journals and papers, but Kokovtsov sharply reduced and in many cases terminated those gratuities. The left focused its attacks on the other ministers. Stolypin's opposition naturally observed no truce with his successors. The government's most dangerous antagonist was Guchkov, who skilfully exploited his prestige as a moderate leader and frequently hid behind the name of the murdered prime minister. At first Guchkov's campaign consisted of individual sallies and seemed to lack any general focus. It became evident, however, that his real target was the supreme authority, against which he invariably made broad, deliberately incomplete, and vague but weighty accusations.

The circumstances of Stolypin's assassination furnished congenial grounds for charges and innuendoes. Bogrov's efforts had not been in vain! Various parties demanded a Duma inquiry, and their resolutions reflected a common inclination to blame the government. Nationalists referred to "criminal inactivity," Octobrists to "the assassin and the persons who controlled him." Oppositionists advanced their favority theory of "provocation." In his speech to the Duma on 15 October 1911, Guchkov hinted at the Okhrana's involvement in the killing: "That gang is only concerned with its own careers and personal welfare . . . . They are big-time bandits with all the talents of swindlers. When they realized that they would be found out, that their tails would be stepped on, that their claws were about to be drawn, that their expense accounts were to be audited, they allowed events to take their course . . . . The government has become the prisoner of its own servants—and what servants!"

Guchkov's charges seemed impressive, but they lacked any real substance. No animosity had existed between Stolypin and the Okhrana, which was subordinate to him as minister of interior.[3] His murder offered no advantage to the Okhrana chiefs in Kiev. Indeed, the assassination had a directly negative effect on their careers. But Guchkov was careful not to accuse anyone directly—only "that gang." When Makarov, the

V.N. Kokovtsov

new interior minister, responded to the inquiries, he observed that the police authorities in Kiev had been remiss in only one respect, and at that they had deviated not from the law but from a ministerial directive: "Informers" such as Bogrov were not to be employed even indirectly in protective roles. Therefore Colonel Kuliabko had acted improperly in admitting Bogrov to the Merchants Garden and the theater.

The government instituted proceedings against Kuliabko and other police officials including assistant minister Kurlov, who was responsible for the security arrangements in Kiev. The judicial department of the State Council divided evenly on the question, although no one supported the allegations of official complicity in the crime. The chairman's vote broke the deadlock, and the matter was referred to the courts. The emperor, having examined the evidence, was convinced that the higher officials (who had no knowledge of Bogrov's presence in the theater) bore no substantive guilt. He found no evidence of criminal intent on the part of Kuliabko. Therefore, he refused to permit the prosecution and the matter came to an end. Kuliabko was dismissed; Kurlov resigned immediately after the assassination. The tsar's decision peremptorily halted "the shooting of their own people," which had been Bogrov's aim.

RASPUTIN AND THE SYNOD AT BAY

Guchkov made a far more serious attack on Rasputin. The starets, who made a pilgrimmage to the Holy Land in 1911, addressed several contrite letters to his admirers. Then, presumably having cleansed himself of his sins, he returned and was welcomed once again into the bosom of the court.[4] Meanwhile, Bishop Hermogen, a devout but extremely quarrelsome fanatic who long had struggled with local officials in his diocese, was invited to become a member of the holy synod. He immediately became engaged in a controversy with most of the hierarchy and with the director-general, V.K. Sabler. In a telegram to the emperor in Livadia Hermogen bitterly denounced the synod for consorting with heretics, for permitting prayers for the non-Orthodox, and for favoring the establishment of an order of deaconesses. The emperor perceived that Hermogen was ill-suited for the collegial work of the synod and on Sabler's recommendation ordered the bishop to return to his diocese in Saratov.[5]

At the same time Hermogen and Iliodor, who had accompanied him to the capital, attempted to establish their influence over Rasputin, with whom they previously had enjoyed the best of relations. There was an ugly scene. After a violent argument, Iliodor and one of his cronies began a fight with Rasputin in the presence of the bishop. They beat him and forced him to surrender letters that he had received from the imperial family. Rasputin barely was able to save himself, and he later insisted that they intended to maim him.[6] This episode did nothing to improve the tsar's attitude toward Hermogen, but that was not the reason for the order to return to Saratov. Nevertheless Hermogen, Iliodor, and their associates later blamed everything on "Rasputin's intrigues." Hermogen had no desire to return to Saratov, and he refused to submit to the emperor's will. In interviews with correspondents of the oppositionist press he lodged every possible accusation against his "unfriends." Faced with a case of blatant insubordination toward his imperial authority, the tsar waited two weeks. Finally he ordered Hermogen taken not to Saratov but to the Zhirovitsky Monastery in the province of Grodno and Iliodor to the Florishchevsky Monastery.[7]

The controversy then hit the newspapers. One of Hermogen's admirers, the religious layman M.A. Novoselov, published in Guchkov's *Golos Moskvy* a letter of unprecedented vindictiveness. He attacked the authorities of the church, St. Petersburg's Metropolitan Anthony, and Director-General Sabler, accusing them all of complacency toward "the sectarian Rasputin."[8] That issue of *Golos Moskvy* was confiscated. Then, at Guchkov's initiative and despite the objections of many moderate Octobrists, the demand for an interpellation was introduced into the Duma, and the text of the suppressed article was read into the record. On 26 January with scarcely an objection the Duma approved the interpellation.

At that point members of the government and court made a serious effort to get rid of Rasputin. Citing the starets' disgusting orgies, they tried to convince the emperor that Rasputin was a sectarian, a *khlyst*. On 26 February 1912 Nicholas charged the chairman of the Duma, Michael Rodzianko,[9] to investigate the allegations, especially the charge that

Rasputin was a heretic. The emperor himself considered that particular charge ill-founded; the empress regarded the entire affair as slanderous.

Those events coincided with the Duma's consideration of the state budget. On 9 March 1912 the holy synod's estimates came to the floor, and Guchkov seized the opportunity to deliver a bombastic assault: "One feels the need to speak out—nay, to shout—that the church is in danger, the state is in danger! . . . You all know the tortuous spectacle that is unfolding in Russia . . . and at the very center of that drama stands this mysterious tragicomic figure, like some shade from Hades or a vestige of the dark ages, an unnatural figure reincarnated in the twentieth century. How did this man acquire such a central position, how did he achieve such influence that even the supreme authorities of church and state bow before him? Just consider who it is that stands as master over all—think who is spinning the wheel that determines the course of policy and personnel, the rise of some and the fall of others?" Guchkov denounced "the monk's backers" who "prompt him on what to whisper next" and he concluded with a vicious attack on Sabler. The speech astounded the Duma, and only Markov had the courage to shout from his seat: "A pack of old wives' tales!"

Sabler, the director-general of the synod, took the rostrum and with great dignity responded to Guchkov: "When an individual ambiguously accuses the church and thereby joins the enemies of the church, I have the obligation to tell him straight out that he is in error. And the reason is very simple: the secret mysteries of concocted charges carry no weight in a serious debate. The director-general of the holy synod knows his duty. He is constantly aware of his responsibilities before the tsar, the holy church, and the motherland. He is never intimidated by vague and pernicious allegations."

Guchkov's speech completely frustrated all efforts to persuade the tsar to exclude Rasputin from the court. Nicholas knew better than anyone that he alone controlled "the course of policy and personnel." He always understood his own authority as a sacred duty, and he jealously preserved the tsar's conscience from the influence of outsiders. Consequently he could only conclude that the reports of Rasputin's influence in affairs of state were blatant lies intended as insults to him personally. Such careless disrespect for the truth made the tsar skeptical of any reports of Rasputin's personal vices. His skepticism was reinforced by the failure of every effort to link "the monk" with the *khlysty*.[10]

After Guchkov's performance, the emperor had no interest in receiving Rodzianko, whose report he had read and found wholly inconclusive.[11] "The Duma's conduct is exceedingly outrageous," he wrote on the report [?]. "Guchkov's speech on the holy synod's estimates was particularly repulsive. I shall be most gratified if those gentlemen learn of my displeasure. It shouldn't be necessary to bow and smile at them all the time." He told Kokovtsov: "I am simply stifling in this atmosphere of gossip, lies, and malice."

The campaign to besmirch Rasputin's name went beyond the political attacks in the Duma. Early in 1912, soon after the confrontation between Iliodor and Rasputin, hectographed copies of letters from the empress and her daughters began to circulate in both capitals. The authorities went to work and managed to obtain the originals, which dated back to 1908 or 1909.[12] At that time Rasputin had not yet become the target of ugly rumors. The letters contained protestations of fidelity and faith in "the man of God." That did not prevent someone from circulating them—distorted as they were in the copying—and smearing them with the filthiest insinuations. Although the purveyors of the letters implicated Guchkov, it was by no means proven that the former chairman of the Duma was the instigator of that vile campaign which disgusted and infuriated the tsar. The whole affair convinced the tsar more deeply than ever that the only honorable response to such slander was scorn.

GUCHKOV STRIKES AT SUKHOMLINOV

Guchkov launched another attack on 18 April 1912. His target this time was General Sukhomlinov, the minister of war. From friends in the war ministry Guchkov had obtained certain secret information on the basis of which he charged that Sukhomlinov had commissioned his friend S.N. Miasoedov,[13] a gendarme colonel, to spy on members of the officer corps. According to Guchkov, Miasoedov already was mixed up in the illicit smuggling of revolutionary literature for use in provocations.[14] When the charge reached the newspapers, Miasoedov challenged Guchkov to a duel. They fought on 22 April; neither was injured. The attitude of the press in this matter was not as one-sided as before, and rightist papers were not alone in their criticism of Guchkov. *Russkaia mysl* (edited by Peter Struve) warned that "Guchkov's speeches bear the stamp of a fatal lack of direction" and compared him to "Turgenev's duelist Luchkov, who with his coarse mustache strode into the political arena."

It was noteworthy that even the Octobrists, who once looked upon Guchkov as their unchallenged leader, did not approve the sharply oppositionist tack of his activities during the final session of the Third Duma. The division was most evident in connection with the navy. The emperor, of course, attached special importance to the naval construction pro-gram. Naval experts led by Captain A.V. Kolchak[15] argued before the Duma committee for a fleet of capital ships. Guchkov marshaled all of his prestige against that concept and stubbornly contended that Russia should restrict itself to a "defensive navy" of destroyers and submarines. However, leading Octobrists like Rodzianko, Savich, and Alekseenko opposed him on that, and in one of its final meetings the Duma by a vote of 228-71 approved 500,000,000 rubles for a new naval program. Even the Poles and Muslims joined the majority, and the opposition consisted only Kadets, the extreme left, and A.I. Guchkov.

The Third Duma completed its work in an atmosphere of political uncertainty and confusion. But despite Guchkov's realignment, the Duma adhered to a basic line of cooperation with the government and opposition to the revolution. On 8 June the emperor received members of the Duma at Tsarskoe Selo and told them: "I shall not pretend that in some matters you have not followed the course that I desired. I do not think that moderation has always characterized your debates, and yet the most important prerequisite for business is tranquility. Nevertheless, I am pleased to note that you devoted much time and effort to the solution of problems that are of major importance to me: a land tenure system for the peasants, protection and insurance for workers, public education, and matters of national defense." The emperor also stressed the need to provide credits for parish schools. On the

A.I. Guchkov

following day when that matter came up, opponents of the bill left the hall, the quorum was lost, and the question was unresolved. On that note the Third State Duma passed out of existence.

MASSACRE IN THE LENA GOLDFIELDS

In the spring of 1912 tragic events in the Lena goldfields of Eastern Siberia aroused all of Russia. Several thousand miners toiled in that region under desperate climatic and physical conditions. (The goldfields were cut off from the outside world for several months of each year.) Early in 1912, economic conditions precipitated a strike. Relations between the workers and administration grew tense as the strike dragged on. With their great numerical advantage the workers began to take control; the police force of 35 men found itself powerless. A military detachment was called in. Excitement reached feverish proportions, and finally on 4 April some 5,000 workers clashed with the army. About 200 workers were killed and more than 200 were wounded.

Reports of that bloody encounter shocked the country. The great number of victims, the brutal working conditions in the taiga, and the fact that the soldiers suffered no casualties—obviously there had been no armed resistance—all that sent a wave of indignation through the public mind. The Duma resounded with pointed questions. Even the extreme right joined in the protest: Markov in particular pointed to the Jewish management of the Lena gold company. On 11 April the interior minister, Makarov, declared that "when a mob under the influence of malicious agitators loses its mind and hurls itself upon troops, the troops have no choice but to fire. It was ever thus, and thus it will ever be."

The press immediately seized upon the expression, "It was ever thus . . ." and the public became all the more agitated. Strikes broke out in shops and factories all over Russia, and there were several attempts to stage public demonstrations.[16] After studying the local reports, S.I. Timashev, the minister of commerce, concluded that the contentions of the police were not beyond question. With Kokovtsov's approval, Timashev came before the Duma and in a conciliatory speech promised that a competent official would be sent to the goldfields to make an investigation. The emperor selected a former minister of justice [1905], S.S. Manukhin, a man who inspired general confidence.[17]

Gradually the strikes diminished. Manukhin's investigation and conclusions satisfied the public. He reported that the management of the Lena gold-mining company had demonstrated total indifference to the needs of the workers and had refused to improve living conditions in any way. (The entire administration resigned.) Manukhin also concluded that the local police had been too lax initially and then had abused its authority and thus was responsible for the loss of so many lives. The local police chief was prosecuted. Two years later, however, he was pardoned by a court, which ruled that he had been helpless in the face of a huge angry mob.

THE CHURCH VENTURES INTO POLITICS: THE 1912 ELECTIONS

By 1912 the Duma had become such a central institution in Russian life that the government felt compelled to take an active role in the new elections. At one point Stolypin had recommended massive support to moderate rightist organizations and especially to the nationalists. Kokovtsov, however, took the position that the government should meddle as little as possible in the electoral process. A.N. Kharuzin, as assistant minister of interior, was responsible for supervising the elections, and the local governors were responsible for the actual conduct of the elections. The Law of 3 June guaranteed that landowning electors would have the decisive voice. In districts without a large landowning class small landowners formed the majorities, and there the village clergy held the balance because they were classified as the owners of the property of the churches.

Through the bishops the director-general of the holy synod urged the clergy to work as actively as possible in the elections. The results were surprisingly effective: great numbers of priests were chosen as electors—over 90 percent of the electors in 20 provinces and 81 percent overall! The press sounded the alarm; it was estimated that as many as 200 priests would be elected to the new Duma. The great landowners also grew concerned. But on the whole the clergy was not really interested in politics. Reporting to the electoral assemblies as ordered by their diocesan superiors, the village priests formed no distinctive party. Nor did they invariably vote with the conservatives. The priests rejected only a few prominent Octobrists who had defended freedom of conscience in the Third Duma. Michael Rodzianko, the chairman of the Duma, won re-election only because he persuaded the government to separate the priests of his district into a special curia.

In a few provinces (Viatka, Nizhni Novgorod, and Chernigov) local authorities applied more direct pressure. They simply crossed off the electoral lists the names of some of the better known oppositionists. In doing so they reasoned that complaints against the illegal deprivation of voting rights would be investigated only after the elections were over. Authorities routinely deleted the names of Jews on the technicality that they enjoyed only "conditional" residence in a given locality. Those tactics were a great source of irritation and complaints, but generally speaking they had very little effect on the outcome of the elections of September and October 1912.

A definite leftist trend became apparent in both the first and second municipal curiae. In Moscow and Petersburg full slates of Kadets and Progressists were elected without difficulty.[18] The results were the same in every major city except Odessa where the exclusion of a large number of Jews gave rightists an unexpected victory. From the daily electoral results published by the official telegraph agency in Petersburg it became evident that rightists claimed about 57 percent of the electors, the opposition about 50 [30] percent, and the Octobrists about 10 percent. Everyone was prepared for a rightist Duma, and the oppositionist press derided the "electoral comedy."

The first official statistics on the composition of the new Duma seemed to confirm the electoral results: 146 rightists, 81 Nationalists, 80 Octobrists, and 130 oppositionists of all descriptions. As soon as the deputies assembled, however, an entirely different picture emerged. The telegraph agency had automatically identified almost all peasants and priests as rightists when in fact many were Octobrists and even Progressists. The rightist majority, which existed only on paper, quickly melted away. The Octobrists suffered some losses, but they still numbered about 100 deputies. Kadets and Progressists gained at their expense. The Nationalists split, and their "center group" deserted to the left. In the final analysis the right wing gained only slightly.[19]

Even more critical in this election was the fact that the election of Octobrists generally ran counter to the wishes of the government. Results which in 1907 represented a victory for the government became in 1912 a victory for the opposition. The reversal was reflected immediately in the selection of the Duma's presidium when the Octobrists looked to the left for support. Thus Michael Rodzianko was re-elected chairman over the opposition of the Nationalists and rightists, and a Progressist, Prince D.D. Urusov (later succeeded by N.N. Lvov), was elected vice-chairman. Even so, the new Duma possessed neither a solid majority nor an inclination to engage the government in a systematic struggle. That became quite clear late in 1912 when international complications pushed domestic squabbles into the background.

THE ITALO-TURKISH WAR AND RUSSIA'S BALKAN POLICY

On 15/28 September 1911, only a few days after Stolypin's death, the international balance in the Near East was upset by the intrusion of a power which had remained passive for more than fifteen years. On that date Italy decided to begin the partition of the Ottoman Empire. The move was well-timed. The Franco-German confrontation over Morocco had not yet been resolved. The Triple Entente—that term was already being applied to England, France, and Russia—was maneuvering to draw Italy into its camp. Despite German sympathy for Turkey, the Germanic allies could not overtly oppose their partner. Italy in other words was able to march without fear of opposition from any quarter.

Under the pretext of Turkish mistreatment of Italian citizens in the ports of Ottoman Africa, Italy presented an ultimatum which demanded the right to occupy Tripoli, Bengazi, and other North African ports. The Turks rejected this extraordinary demand, and on 16/29 September 1911 Rome declared war. Italy ran little risk, either diplomatic or military. Turkey was practically without a navy, and "neutral" (actually British) Egypt separated the mother country from its North African possessions. Difficult natural conditions and the belligerence of a few Arab tribes inhabiting Tripolitania could only postpone the inevitable outcome. Nevertheless the Italo-Turkish War dragged on for a whole year.[20] Although the great powers tried every way possible to ignore it, the war raised the general question of the disposition of the Ottoman Empire.

M eanwhile in the fall of 1911 Russian diplomacy sought to take advantage of Italy's violation of the status quo by persuading Turkey to open the Straits to the Russian fleet. Petersburg approached Berlin, and Bethmann Hollweg, desirous of affirming the spirit of Potsdam, responded positively. The kaiser, however, wanted Vienna's opinion, and Aerenthal replied that Austro-Russian relations had deteriorated substantially since 1908 so that now Austria would have to demand "compensation" for the opening of the Straits. Sazonov, who had just recovered from his long illness, traveled from Davos to Paris only to learn that neither England nor France sympathized with Russia's aim. Therefore he did not press the matter.[21]

Although it was obvious that the fall of Turkey's African possessions was only a question of time, the fighting in Tripoli raged on. Meanwhile the domestic enemies of the Young Turks were raising their heads. Albania was in open rebellion [May 1912]. At that point the Balkan states, whose chief interest was the partition of European Turkey, concluded that the moment had arrived to take matters into their own hands. Deep-seated rivalries between Bulgaria and Serbia and Bulgaria and Greece always had prevented those countries from coming together. But on 29 February 1912 Bulgaria and Serbia signed a secret treaty of alliance against Turkey, and soon afterward Greece and Montenegro joined the pact.[22]

Russian diplomacy followed a rather complex course. St. Petersburg's overriding goal was to secure for Russia those "twenty years of peace" that Stolypin had sought. The Balkan nations were well aware, however, that regardless of the restraint that Russia urged on them, Russia would save them from disaster and never would allow the Turks to encroach upon their territories. That confidence gave them the courage to push ahead on their own.

FRANCOPHILIA AND GERMANOPHOBIA

The Agadir crisis had left a deep scar on France. Patriotic fears refused to die and instead grew more intense. The Caillaux government which had concluded the Moroccan agreement with Germany was driven from power. A new government led by Raymond Pioncaré took charge with a pledge to restore national unity. Poincaré's cabinet initiated an active foreign policy and moved to reinforce its relations with Russia.

Late in July 1912 the tsar and kaiser met at Port Baltic, but nothing of a practical nature issued from their visit. The official communique made it clear that no realignment of the European powers was to be expected from this meeting. The German chancellor thanked the imperial government for its moderating influence in the Moroccan crisis, and Sazonov declared that as long as Russia and Germany remained on good terms nothing untoward would befall them.[23] The chancellor remained in Russia for several days, met with Kokovtsov, and paid a visit to Moscow. At about the same time Russia and France agreed on a naval convention to supplement the alliance.[24] Then about a month after the Russo-German meeting at Port Baltic, Poincaré arrived in Petersburg on a visit that left no doubt about the cordiality of Franco-Russian relations.[25]

The attitude of the Russian public was mainly responsible for his enthusiastic reception. Partly for domestic reasons and partly because of the Bosnian crisis, the Russian public—and not only the intelligentsia but also military and court officials—were hostile toward Germany. In May 1912 *Russkaia mysl* made passing reference to a well established fact: "In foreign affairs we must not preach lightly that form of active Germanophobia, which in our country sometimes passes for evidence of progressive thought." Another great social occasion occurred with the arrival of a British parliamentary delegation early in 1912 (reciprocating the earlier visit of Russian legislators to England). Descriptions of banquets and speeches as well as photos of the delegates filled the papers. No one stressed the government's obvious restraint: Sukhomlinov, the war minister, was the only official to attend any banquet. In contrast the newspapers scarcely mentioned Chancellor Bethmann Hollweg's visits to St. Petersburg and Moscow.

RUSSIA FRETS WHILE THE BALKANS BURN

Russia continued to work for the maintenance of peace in Europe. The emperor, the late prime minister, Stolypin, his successor Kokovtsov, and foreign minister Sazonov were all committed to that end. Because the partition of the Ottoman Empire could easily ignite a European conflagration, Russia in 1912 assumed the unfamiliar role of champion of Turkish integrity, at least until a more fortuitous occasion should present itself. The Balkan states had assured St. Petersburg that they would not move without Russia's blessing, but after a time they concluded that Turkey was so weak and the risk so small that they could attack without outside assistance. In this calculation Bulgaria counted to a degree on Austria's goodwill.

The Italo-Turkish war was winding down. Turkish resistance in Tripoli was collapsing. Italy easily occupied several islands in the Aegean Sea and threatened further conquests. In July 1912 a bloodless coup in Constantinople drove the Young Turks from power. Their successors agreed to sue for peace. The Balkan nations had to hurry lest they miss their chance.

In response to a bombing by Macedonian terrorists, Turkish troops massacred the Bulgarian residents of the village of Kočana [19 July/1 August]. The entire Balkan press erupted in a campaign of denunciation. The great powers tried to stem the course of events. Russia took the initiative[26] and with the support of France, England, Germany, and Austria warned the Balkan League and the Turks that "the great powers will not permit any alteration of the territorial status quo of European Turkey as a result of war." This demarche was presented in the Balkan capitals on 25 September/8 October. On the same day Montenegro declared war on Turkey and began operations.

The Balkan League assumed that the warning of the great powers was not to be taken seriously. The kaiser understood their position and even condoned it. "Why wait until Russia is ready?" he wrote. "Let the war come. Let the Balkan states prove themselves. If they beat the Turks decisively, that will prove that they were right and deserve their rewards. If they're defeated, they'll shut up and sit still for a good long time." Sazonov, on the other hand, was greatly agitated. When they concluded their alliances, the Balkan states had promised to consider Russia's interests. Instead, they were launching a war at a moment most inconvenient for Russia. In conversations with French statesmen Sazonov went so far as to declare that he would regard the defeat of the Balkan League, especially Bulgaria, a lesser evil since it then would be easier to insist on the status quo.

Events moved rapidly. On 8 October Montenegro declared war; on the 18th Italy and Turkey signed a peace treaty; on the same day Bulgaria, Serbia, and Greece entered the conflict.[27] The war was immensely popular in the Balkans, and general jubilation attended the mobilization of troops in Sofia, Belgrade, and Athens. The Turks never had a chance. They were completely routed at Kirk-Kilissa and then at Lüle Burgas by the Bulgarians and at Kumanovo by the Serbs. Within a month the allies had driven the Turks back into the lines around Chatalja only 40 kilometers from Constantinople. Except for the besieged fortresses of Adrianople, Yanina, and Scutari, nothing remained of Turkey's European possessions. On 22 October/4 November Turkey requested the mediation of the great powers.[28]

THE SLAV TIDE AND RUSSIA

Russians generally greeted the victories of the Balkan Slavs with jubilant approval; domestic problems suddenly seemed unimportant. After the allied victory, any thought of preserving the status quo was out of the question of course. What Sazonov had tried to avert became a reality: Russia would have to enter into the partition of the Ottoman Empire under disadvantageous conditions. Therefore, Petersburg proposed that the great powers jointly declare their disinterest in a partition. France and England willingly associated themselves with the proposal, and Germany raised no objection. Austria and Italy were less enthusiastic. They agreed between themselves to create a new state, Albania, out of the Turkish provinces along the Adriatic Sea. Though demanding nothing for themselves, they demanded a great deal for Albania.[29]

In order to avoid a general European conflict, the great powers agreed to cooperate in a common effort to liquidate the Balkan war. But Austria immediately announced its resolve to prevent Serbian access to the Adriatic. The Dual Monarchy ordered a partial mobilization and began to concentrate its forces along the Russian frontier. In response Russia extended the service of an entire levy whose military term had expired.[30] For a moment in November 1912 war threatened Europe.

On 4/17 December 1912 a conference of the great powers' ambassadors convened in London. The frontiers of Albania presented the most difficult question. At England's insistence Russia yielded on its demand for a Serbian port on the Adriatic. France also warned that it had little desire to see that issue become the cause of a war. Serbia itself finally agreed to give up its demand.

When Turkish obstinacy impeded the peace conference of the belligerents [which also began on 17 December in London], the great powers delivered threatening notes which advised the need for concessions and reminded Turkey of the possibility of further complications in its Asiatic possessions. The Turkish government summoned the Council of Notables and was prepared to yield, but at that point [23 January 1913] the Young Turks staged another revolt, seized power, and refused to sign the proposed treaty of peace. The armistice expired, and the war was resumed. Adrianople was besieged and held out for several weeks. Finally Serbian troops joined the Bulgarians, and on 13 March 1913 the ancient Turkish citadel capitulated.

Russians, rejoicing at the fall of the fortress, paraded through the streets in celebration of the victory of the Balkan Slavs. The police, as usual, dispersed the demonstrators but were reprimanded by the authorities, even though the government had little sympathy for the demonstrations. Throughout the war the great powers tried to maintain a common front, but a significant segment of the Russian public pressed for active support of the Balkan Slavs and even for direct action against Turkey. One of the slogans carried by marchers on the Nevsky Prospekt read: "A Cross for St. Sophia." Rodzianko's memoirs related how in February 1913 he urged the emperor to intervene in the war![31] These incidents indicate the light-hearted attitude of some circles toward the possibility of a European conflict. Russian intervention in the Balkans in the spring of 1913 would have meant war with the Triple Alliance, including Italy (which had aligned itself with Austria's Balkan policy), and perhaps with Rumania. Moreover, England's position was uncertain. The emperor, of course, could not give serious consideration to such dangerous advice. His policy produced great dissatisfaction in certain circles, and the "Slavonic banquets" often rang with anti-dynastic speeches which embarrassed many listeners.

THE BALKAN WARS, ROUND TWO

The final challenge to European peace arose over the question of Scutari. The great powers agreed to transfer the city to Albania, but the Montenegrins continued to besiege it. In Russia agitation mounted in behalf of "Scutari to Montenegro," but the government adhered faithfully to the agreement of the powers. A display of [international] naval power off the coast of Montenegro finally persuaded the king to yield in return for certain compensations territorial and financial.

On 17/30 May 1913 Turkey and the Balkan League concluded the Treaty of London, but the victorious allies immediately fell into bitter disagreement. The secret treaties of 1912 promised Serbia an outlet on the Adriatic; Greece was to receive Epirus [along the Adriatic], and most of Macedonia including Saloniki was to go to Bulgaria.[32] But the great powers reduced the Ottoman Empire and created Albania out of territories destined [by the Balkan alliances] for Greece and Serbia. The Bulgarians insisted on their share of the spoils as agreed. They contended that they were not to blame that Albania was carved out of the shares of their allies. Serbia and Greece countered that they too had fought on the Bulgarian front and therefore had earned a redivision of the former Turkish territory. Russian diplomacy attempted to intervene in the dispute as mediator and arbitrator in accord with the Serbo-Bulgarian treaty.[33] The tsar appealed personally to the Balkan monarchs but to no avail. Confident of its army and of Austria's enmity for Serbia, Sofia refused to back down.

During the night of 17/30 June 1913, the Bulgarians attacked the Serbs and Greeks in an effort to drive them out of Macedonia. The Second Balkan War was underway. It proved, however, to be brief, for the Bulgarians had grievously miscalculated. They failed to smash the Greco-Serbian front, the Rumanians attacked them from the rear, and without a formal declaration of war the Turks advanced on Adrianople. That

The Tsar and Grand Duchesses on Tour

fortress, only recently won with fearful casualties, fell without a struggle. In just ten days Bulgaria was forced to capitulate.[34]

The victors dictated a harsh peace at Bucharest. Bulgaria had to surrender all of its recent acquisitions except for a small area around Enos and in addition it ceded to Rumania the southern Dobrudja. The great powers raised no objection to the treaty, although Russia and Austria agreed unexpectedly in their desire to see the port of Kavalla [on the Aegean Sea] reserved to Bulgaria. The other four powers, however, insisted that Kavalla should go to Greece. Austria also wanted to reduce Serbia's gains, but neither Italy nor Germany would support Vienna on that issue. Bulgaria also had to accept the loss of Adrianople.[35] The Treaty of Bucharest was signed on 28 July/10 August 1913. *Revue des deux Mondes* commented that "after ten months of hard labor, Europe has taken a vacation."

THE ROMANOV TERCENTENARY (1613-1913)

February 21, 1913, marked the 300th anniversary of the accession of Michael Feodorovich Romanov to the throne of Russia, and great ceremony attended the dynasty's tercentenary.[36] An imperial manifesto issued on the anniversary recalled that "the Russian State was created and grew strong through the combined efforts of Our crowned predecessors and all the faithful sons of Russia. Time and again Our Fatherland faced stern tests, but each time the Russian people stood firm in their Orthodox Faith, their staunch devotion to Russia, and their selfless loyalty to their sovereigns, and they emerged renewed and strengthened from each adversity. Muscovite Rus expanded beyond its narrow frontiers, until today the Russian Empire stands among the principal powers of the world."

Following established custom, the tsar granted numerous favors: the forgiveness of debts, contributions to charities, and the reduction of penalties. In the Winter Palace he received the empire's highest officials and accepted their congratulations. Rodzianko made an eloquent speech in behalf of the Duma and presented the tsar an icon of Christ the Savior. On the following day there was a religious procession in Moscow, and Russia's most revered icon, The Mother of God of Vladimir,

Iversk and Kazan, was displayed. That was followed by a great military review on Red Square in front of the Moscow Kremlin. The anniversary was commemorated by postage stamps which, for the first time, bore the images of all the Russian sovereigns from Tsar Michael Feodorovich to Emperor Nicholas II. At first some postal officials, fearful of "desecrating the tsar's portrait," did not dare to cancel the stamps.

The emperor wanted to extend the festivities beyond the capitals, and so with the coming of spring he decided to travel through the old regions to Suzdal and Muscovy, where Rus was nurtured and developed and where the ancestral lands of the boyars Romanov were located. On 15 May, despite the illness of the empress and the tsarevich, Nicholas set out from Tsarskoe Selo with his family. They passed through Moscow on their way to Vladimir. From there they went by car to Suzdal and visited the village of Bogoliubovo. At Nizhni Novgorod they boarded the Volga steamer *Mezhen* which carried them to Kostroma and Yaroslavl. Swarms of peasants hoping to catch a glimpse of the tsar covered both banks of the Volga. Flags and greenery decorated piers and houses along the river banks.

The reception at Kostroma on 19-20 May was particularly heartwarming. The entire population of the city and its outlying districts turned out to meet the imperial family, and their numbers were swelled by grand dukes and duchesses, clergy and officials—all assembled to welcome the tsar to the ancestral home of the Romanovs. At the Ipatievsky Monastery, where emissaries of the Zemsky Sobor entreated the nun Martha to bless her son before his ascent to the throne, Tikhon, the archbishop of Kostroma, greeted the emperor: "If a chronicler were to witness this grand occasion, to see this regal advent, to hear the pealing bells and the cheers of boundless devotion, he would undoubtedly write of this day: 'And it came to pass that there was great joy in the Ipatievsky Monastery and through all of Kostroma.' " In the presence of the imperial family the foundation of a memorial to the 300th anniversary of the house of Romanov was laid on the edge of a high bluff overlooking the Volga. As the emperor left Kostroma, a throng accompanied him along the river bank for some distance, and many waded after him until the water reached their waists. The emperor was delighted and moved by his reception at Kostroma.[37]

From Kostroma the emperor continued on to Yaroslavl and Rostov, and on 25 May he returned to Moscow. His ten-day journey through central Russia made a lasting impression. He witnessed his subjects' loyalty but also acquired a picture of their poverty and need as he motored through their villages.

DISINTEGRATION OF THE OCTOBRISTS

The Balkan wars and the Romanov celebrations dominated the first half of 1913, but politics reasserted itself in the fall. Soon after the unsatisfactory election of the Fourth Duma, the governor of Chernigov, Nicholas Maklakov, replaced Alexander Makarov as minister of interior. Nicholas had wanted to appoint Maklakov earlier, for he valued him as person whose views on state affairs were close to his own. The same could not be said for most of the other ministers. The Duma had little regard for Maklakov, partly because he used administrative pressure in his province in order to defeat several prominent left-Octobrists.

The State Council gained ascendancy partly through the infusion of newly elected noblemen and landowners but mainly through the appointment of retired conservative officials who gradually filled the vacancies in the chamber. The Council's majority stood farther to the right than the government. It either rejected or radically amended almost every major bill that came out of the Duma: the introduction of zemstvos into Siberia and Arkhangel, the creation of the volost zemstvo, and a bill for the reform of local courts. By a vote of 94-74 the Council amended a bill establishing municipal self-government in Poland; it added a clause requiring the exclusive use of the Russian language in all sessions and work of the municipal dumas, councils, and secretariats. It adopted this amendment against Kokovtsov's insistence to the contrary, but after the western zemstvo crisis, the government no longer attempted to bring pressure on the State Council.

In the Moscow municipal elections held late in 1912 the ballots were divided almost equally between left and right [Octobrists]. Prince George Lvov and Alexander Guchkov vied for the post of mayor, but the latter withdrew after receiving fewer votes. The emperor was reluctant to confirm a member of the opposition as mayor of Russia's first capital, and the mayor's office remained vacant during all of 1913. Maklakov recommended B.V. Stürmer, a prominent rightist in the State Council, but Kokovtsov convinced the emperor that all of Moscow would oppose that move. Consequently, the premier's assistant, V.D. Briansky, continued to perform the mayoral functions in Moscow.

All of these developments irritated the left and also the Octobrists. After his electoral defeat Guchkov spent nearly a year in the Balkans. In the fall of 1913 he journeyed to Kiev to attend a municipal congress on urban economics, and on 21 September he delivered a sharp oppositionist speech "from behind the curtain." He declared that "overall the work of the congress is marked by dejection and a lack of confidence that our efforts will bear any fruit." He said that "the paralysis of the entire state organism, the stagnation of the legislature, and the confusion of the executive" were quite obvious. Therefore he called upon the congress to adopt a political resolution. Although the chairman of the congress, the mayor of Kiev, refused to put it to a vote, the delegates gathered in a corridor and just as in student meetings approved the resolution by a show of hands.

The press observed a "leftward trend" throughout the country. From the spring of 1912 on, and especially after the Lena goldfield massacre and the start of the newspaper *Pravda*, the number of political strikes staged by workers increased sharply. In most instances the strikes were protest demonstrations that lasted only a day.[38]

On 8 November Guchkov addressed a conference of Octobrists in St. Petersburg. His speech offered a detailed justification of his reorientation. "Octobrism," he said, "was a silent but solemn agreement between the historical power and Russian society. The Manifesto of 17 October was an act of trust on the part of the supreme power in the people. Octobrism became an act of trust in the supreme power by the people." But then, he contended, "the reaction set in, and strange new figures began to operate." He pointed to the role of the right wing in the State Council and to the United Nobility; he recalled the efforts to control the Duma elections and noted the rumors of imminent changes in the Fundamental Laws.[39] "The agreement has been violated and torn to shreds by the government," he concluded. "We are forced to defend the monarchy against those who are the natural defenders of monarchy, the church against the hierarchy of the church, and the army against its leaders."

Guchkov's dangerous double-entendre seemingly justified any violation of discipline, but no one objected and the conference unanimously approved his remarks. When the question of joining the opposition was put to the Duma delegation, however, only 22 of the 100 members favored it. The delegation split into three groups. A majority of about two-thirds of the members including Rodzianko, Savich, Kovalevsky, and other fraction leaders formed the "Zemstvo-Octobrist" group.[40]

OFFICIAL ANTI-SEMITISM: THE BEILIS AFFAIR

From 24 September to 28 October 1913 the Kiev district court was the scene of a trial that attracted hundreds of foreign correspondents and observers. This was the famous Beilis Trial.

In March 1911 a twelve-year-old boy, Andrei Yushchinsky, was found murdered in Kiev. His body had been stabbed 47 times and was drained almost completely of blood. It was rumored immediately that Jews had killed the boy and drained his blood for use in some secret ritual.[41] Some members of the judiciary, in particular the district prosecutor Chaplinsky, took it upon themselves to prove that allegation. The investigation by the local police pointed to an entirely different explanation, for the evidence indicated that a band of thieves had murdered the youth. The supporters of "ritualistic murder" contended that the Jews had bribed the police. In May 1911 a resolution for an inquiry into that charge was introduced into the Duma.

Ignoring the agents of the police criminal investigation division, who disbelieved the theory of a ritual murder, the prosecutor finally uncovered witnesses willing to testify that one Mendel Beilis, a [Jewish] brickmaker, had kidnapped Yushchinsky and together with unknown accomplices had murdered him. Beilis was arrested in August 1911. In violation of the Russian code the official investigation continued for over two years and only in the fall of 1913 was the case brought to court.

The Russian and foreign press took a great interest in the affair. Noted Russian writers and publicists of liberal persuasion denounced the "bloody slander" of Jews. Some of Russia's finest lawyers joined forces to defend Beilis: N.P. Karabchevsky, V.A. Maklakov, A.S. Zagrudny, and O.O. Gruzenberg. The right-wing press, led by *Novoe vremia*, generally endorsed the ritualistic version of the murder. G.G. Zamyslovsky, a member of the Duma, and the prominent Moscow attorney A.S. Shmakov, author of several anti-semitic tracts, offered their services as "civil plaintiffs to assist the prosecutor."

The weakness of the prosecution's case was evident from the first day of the trial. An article by V.V. Shulgin on 27 September in the old rightist paper *Kievlianin* created a great sensation. Shulgin wrote that he had sworn on the casket of the late editor, D.I. Pikhno, to print only the truth. He reported in the words of police officers how they had been ordered by their superiors to "find a Yid" whatever it took. He quoted the prosecutor himself that the issue was not whether Beilis was guilty but to prove that Jews practiced ritual murder. "You yourselves are sacrificing a human being," he wrote. "You are treating Beilis like a rabbit stretched out on a vivisection table." For the first time since its founding, the authorities confiscated an issue of the *Kievlianin*. The Nationalist fraction mildly rebuked Shulgin, and he later joined the Centrists.

In their reports to St. Petersburg the police repeatedly stressed the weakness of the testimony of the witnesses for the prosecution and the persuasiveness of the experts for the defense. Among the experts assembled by the prosecution were several prominent professors of forensic medicine, but they could testify only to the fact that the blood had been drained intentionally from the body. Their testimony could not prove a ritualistic motive.

The composition of the jury was said to be "grey"—peasants, lower middle class city dwellers, and one postal official. The leftist press accused the government of trying to exploit "the ignorance of the people," and Korolenko wrote that such jurors could not be competent. But those simple Russian folk took their responsibility seriously. "How can we judge Beilis when they do not mention him in court?" they asked themselves, according to reports of the gendarmes.

The prosecutor's speeches offered them little assistance. He spoke at length about ritual murder in general and about how "the Jews would destroy Russia," but he said practically nothing about the defendant himself. On 28 October the jurors found Beilis not guilty. As to whether the murder had been committed in the brickyard belonging to the Jew Zaitsev and whether the body had been drained of blood, they answered affirmatively. Although *Novoe vremia* attached great significance to those findings, two days later an article by Menshikov in that same paper admitted that "Russia has suffered a defeat." The joy of the leftist press was understandable, but the outcome was in itself proof of the freedom and independence of a Russian jury and a refutation of official pressure on the court.[42]

THE FATALISTIC KAISER AND THE HOPEFUL TSAR

Although the great powers had found a way to liquidate the Balkan wars without setting off a general European conflict, international tension remained high. In the spring of 1913 the German Reichstag adopted a military budget of one billion marks. Then France restored the three-year term of service and thereby increased the size of its peacetime army by 50 percent. The German chancellor defended the new budget before the Reichstag by rather unexpectedly warning that "the Slav tide is running." He was alluding to the victory of the Balkan Slavs, but at that he was only repeating an idea frequently repeated by the kaiser from 1913 on in his marginal notes on the reports of German diplomats. During the fall of 1912, Emperor William had reacted rather favorably to the victory of the Balkan League over Turkey, but after that he began to imagine the inevitability of "the struggle of Slavs and Germans."

The tsar had an entirely different attitude. In May 1913 he travelled to Germany to attend the wedding of the kaiser's daughter to the Prince of Cumberland. He went with the intention of finding the basis for some durable improvement in Russo-German relations.[43] The emperor expressed his own satisfaction with the state of affairs in the Balkans. He was prepared to renounce Russia's long-standing interest in Constantinople and the Straits, leaving Turkey to continue as "doorkeeper," if Germany would agree to restrain Austrian expansionism and leave the Balkan states to work out their own destinies by themselves. That visit marked the final meeting of the Russian and German emperors. Although it passed in a cordial atmosphere, it led to no lasting improvement of relations. The kaiser grew ever more fatalistically resigned to the inevitability of war.

Fresh reports of William's changed attitude reached Nicholas when Kokovtsov returned from abroad in November 1913. The kaiser had received the Russian prime minister in a rather friendly manner, but in a conversation with the director of the credit chancellery, L.F. Davydov, he complained about the tone of the Russian press which he said was leading to a catastrophe. The kaiser foresaw "an approaching conflict between the two races, Romano-Slavic and Germanic." War, he said, "may become simply unavoidable" and "it makes absolutely no difference who starts it."[44]

Kokovtsov made his report to the tsar, including his conversation with the kaiser, in Livadia around the middle of November. Nicholas remained silent for some time. "He was gazing out the window at the boundless sea in the distance," wrote Kokovtsov.[45] "Then finally, as if waking from a reverie, he said: 'In all things is the will of God.' "

Yet in one instance the German government still demonstrated its willingness to defer to Russia's wishes. In the fall of 1913 the German general Otto Liman von Sanders was appointed commander of the Turkish forces in Constantinople. German officers had served previously as advisors to the Turkish army, but this case was different for General Liman was to assume a command position and that in the region of the Straits. The Russian press protested vigorously. During his visit to Berlin, Kokovtsov had warned the Germans that Russia would find Liman's appointment unacceptable. The kaiser was indignant, but eventually he yielded. Since the appointment already had occurred, it was revoked in a most unusual manner: The kaiser promoted Liman to general of cavalry, and the sultan made him a marshal. With those ranks he was too exalted to be a mere corps commander, and so he was replaced by a Turkish general.[46]

That solution pleased the emperor very much. "Now I have only friendly smiles for Germany," he half-jokingly told ambassador Pourtales at a dinner on 14 January 1914. The kaiser, however, made an angry notation on the ambassador's report: "That is quite enough! That is all we ever get from him!"

Ostensible calm settled over the international scene during the winter of 1913-1914, but a curious psychological transformation was overcoming all national leaders. Very few consciously and openly desired war, and of that minority only Austria's Field Marshal Franz Conrad von Hötzendorf frankly set forth his views in writing.[47] Nevertheless, many if not most of the statesmen in responsible positions were slipping from consideration of the possibility of war to the fatalistic resignation that war was inevitable. In that frame of mind they began to formulate their assumptions and plans for the future.

Only a few remained firm in the faith that war could be avoided if one remained steadfast in the desire to avert it. The Russian emperor was one of them. Kokovtsov, the chairman of the council of ministers, shared that point of view. But other members of the Russian government were succumbing to the inevitability of war. War minister Sukhomlinov, who stood out as a rather foolhardy optimist; agriculture minister Krivoshein; and after the summer of 1913, foreign minister Sazonov—all of them betrayed their conviction that war was practically unavoidable. At the end of 1913 Kokovtsov chaired a special ministerial conference which considered Russia's prospects in the event of war.[48] The conferees included Sazonov, Sukhomlinov, Admiral Ivan Grigorovich, the naval minister, and the chief of the general staff, General Jacob Zhilinsky. They concluded that the support of England and France was prerequisite to Russia's success, but of all the participants only Kokovtsov stressed the great disaster that would befall Russia as a result of war.[49]

VODKA AND BUDGETS–KOKOVTSOV'S FAREWELL

Russia's rapid economic development—so obvious that no one could ignore it—attracted critics to its negative impact on individuals. Tax receipts increased each year without an increase in rates. Despite rising military expenditures and larger annual appropriations for education, the budget escaped any deficit spending. But the greater part of the state's revenues was produced by the liquor monopoly. (Estimates for 1914 reflected total revenues of about 3.5 billion rubles, an increase of about 1 billion rubles.) The circulation of more money in the villages led to an increase in drunkenness, and from 1911 to 1913 the consumption of vodka increased by 16,000,000 *vedra* [about 5,000,000 gallons] or 17 percent in two years. Reports of "hooliganism" in villages and towns filled the newspapers.

As a result, temperance societies spread through the country. Reformers discovered that state liquor stores were the source of the evil, even though private pubs were no less and perhaps more responsible for the rise of alcoholism. Despite the fact that all countries had taxed alcohol from time immemorial, audiences were impressed by speakers who denounced "the alcoholic budget" and berated the treasury for "turning the people into drunks." The popular condemnation of the state reflected in the temperance movement pained the emperor, who felt that this reproach contained some degree of moral justification.

The political parties began to take note of the teetotallers. The Union of 17 October organized several large temperance rallies. At one of the meetings (14 May 1913) Professor I.M. Gromoglasov and a prominent member of the Third Duma, P.V. Kamensky, voiced their regret that Stolypin, "who was responsive to popular movements such as this," was not in power now. Apparently even Rasputin, who had extensive personal experience with the "temptations of the bottle," often remarked that it was "not good for people to get the habit of hard drinking." Through the efforts of a temperance crusader, the Samaran millionaire "of the people" Chelyshev, the Third Duma adopted a bill to step up efforts to combat national alcoholism. The main thrust of the measure was to grant municipal dumas and zemstvo assemblies the right to prohibit the establishment and demand the closing of liquor stores in certain localities. When the bill reached the State Council in the winter of 1913-1914, it set off a furious debate. Kokovtsov had little confidence in the effectiveness of prohibitive legislation against drunkenness, and his main concern was to see that such measures did not disrupt the state's finances. That was the substance of his collision in the State Council with a coalition of the most diverse interests.[50]

The emperor had been wavering, apparently for some time, for he was reluctant to part with Kokovtsov. He highly valued his minister's work, deeply respected his quiet firmness, and completely shared his conviction of the absolute necessity to maintain peace. The campaign against Kokovtsov came from several quarters: Meshchersky's *Grazhdanin* assaulted him;[51] his ministerial colleagues, Sukhomlinov, Maklakov, and Krivoshein, frequently disagreed with him; Guchkov attacked him as "Stolypin's successor." But the emperor proved—and not for the first time—that he would stand by his ministers under the most difficult conditions, as long as he himself agreed with them. Therefore, in the final analysis there is every reason to believe that Kokovtsov's resignation came about because of the emperor's conviction that his leadership was incapable of producing a basic reorientation in the struggle against national alcoholism.

Rumors of Kokovtsov's imminent retirement were abroad by the middle of January 1914. On the 28th the emperor received his report and spoke with him at length about current projects and especially a revised trade agreement with Germany. However, the next morning a courier brought Kokovtsov a letter written by the emperor himself:

No feeling of displeasure but a long-standing and deep realization of state requirements now compels me to tell you that we have to part. I do this in writing, because it is easier to choose the right words when setting them down on paper than during an unsettling conversation.

The events of the past eight years have convinced me beyond any doubt that it is both awkward and improper for a country such as Russia to combine in one person the duties of chairman of the council of ministers and those of minister of finance or interior.

Moreover, both the swift tempo of our domestic life and the striking development of our nation's economic forces demand the application of the most exact and serious measures, and that is a responsibility best entrusted to a man fresh for the task.

The emperor also observed that he had "not always approved of the policy of the ministry of finance," but he thanked Kokovtsov for his "great service in achieving a remarkable improvement in Russia's state credit." He regretted, he said, the need to part with his assistant of so many years.[52]

A special rescript published in the official *Pravitelstvennyi vestnik* expressed the emperor's gratitude for Kokovtsov's services. It also explained that "poor health" prompted his resignation and announced that he had been granted the title of count. When he received his former minister, the tsar could not hold back his tears: he was painfully grieved that a distinguished official and man whom he respected had to experience such bitterness and resentment. He granted Kokovtsov's request to appoint to the State Council three assistant finance ministers who had resigned because of his dismissal, even though the emperor did not appreciate such pointed gestures. He offered the former minister a lump sum of 300,000 rubles to settle some private debts, but with characteristic scrupulousness Kokovtsov requested the emperor not to make the gift. His attitude contrasted sharply with that of Witte, whose memoirs repeatedly criticize Nicholas and Kokovtsov but who, nevertheless, appealed to the emperor through Kokovtsov for a grant of 200,000 rubles, which he received (in July 1912) in return for past services.

Ivan Goremykin became Kokovtsov's successor. Krivoshein was mentioned as a possible candidate, but he was quite ill at the time and went abroad for a cure. The emperor valued Goremykin very much for his exceptional loyalty and his ability to follow instructions to the letter without ducking difficult assignments. The new prime minister compared himself to "an old fur coat taken out of mothballs."[53] Actually Goremykin who was 74 at the time possessed a keen, alert mind.

The reasons for the reorganization of the government were given in a rescript addressed to Peter Bark[54] who became the new minister of finance. The emperor wrote that during his journey through the Great Russian provinces he had witnessed "encouraging evidence of gifted creativity and strength at work. But beside that I was greatly saddened to observe heartrending scenes of the people's infirmities, of poverty-stricken families and neglected homes—the inevitable consequences of besotted lives. I also saw what happens to the people's efforts when in a moment of desperate need they are deprived of financial assistance arranged through an appropriate and accessible system of credit. Since that time I have pondered the situation continuously and checked my impressions until finally I am firmly convinced that I have an obligation to God and to Russia to introduce without delay certain basic changes in financial management for the benefit of my beloved people. The health of the treasury must not be based on the destruction of the spiritual and economic vitality of my loyal subjects." Those words heralded the approach of an extensive reform, a war against alcoholism, such as never before had been attempted in any large country.

RUSSIA ADRIFT

The report of Kokovtsov's retirement was received by the State Council on 29 January 1914. The news caused a great deal of excitement, and that perhaps was the reason that the chairman, M.G. Akimov, did not interrupt the speaker, who departed from the agenda and the topic of alcoholism to address a more general subject. The speaker was the ambassador to Tokyo, Baron R.R. Rosen, who declared: "I do not share in any way the placid indifference or the complacent optimism toward the present situation domestic or foreign. I do not share this optimism because I firmly believe in causal relationships and in the inexorable logic of events . . . . You are well aware that for the past two decades Europe has existed under the regime of two alliances into which two implacably hostile powers have managed to draw the rest . . . . This situation must result either in the elimination of that fundamental antagonism, which is totally alien to Russian interests, or in an armed conflict which Russia, always faithful to its obligations, cannot avoid. . . . No one can foretell the future, but so unprecedented a measure as a billion in taxes for armaments testifies to the fact that the crisis is not far ahead. In any event, one thing is certain: The hour will come when we least expect it. "

Moving to domestic affairs, Baron Rosen continued: "The Russian people still revere the cult of the tsar and the power of the tsar and, as history has taught us, only in that faith has Russia found salvation in time of crisis. But the discord between the government and the public becomes increasingly aggravated . . . . There is hardly a reasoning man in Russia who does not sense instinctively that we are, to use a nautical expression, adrift—being swept along by wind and tide toward a treacherous coast which threatens to smash our ship of state, unless we decide in good time to seize the helm and steer a clear and definite course."

CHAPTER SEVENTEEN

MORAL CONFUSION, MATERIAL PROGRESS

In *Vestnik evropy*'s New Year's survey V.D. Kuzmin-Karavaev, a well-known political liberal, wrote that it did not take "a prophet to see that the year 1914 promises nothing outstanding in our socio-political life." And indeed, the attitude of Russian society gave no visible evidence of any appreciable change. Russia, as Stolypin had put it, remained "dissatisfied with herself." Oppositionist tendencies reappeared in the zemstvo and municipal circles which dominated the Duma. It was widely rumored that limitations on the rights of popular government were imminent; sharp criticism was levelled against the activities of several ministers, particularly Maklakov, Shcheglovitov, Kasso, and Sabler. Confusion reigned among the rightists, and the various right-wing organizations such as Purishkevich's Union of the Archangel Michael were far more interested in settling scores with each other than in the "struggle against the revolution."

A kind of grayness, an undefined, blind opposition without clear slogans or goals, settled over political life. In *Moskovskie vedomosti*'s New Year's edition Lev Tikhomirov observed that "current attitudes reflect a most alarming inertness. We are living quietly, perhaps, but our quietude is lifeless. Not only do we fail to perceive any passion for greatness, for some all-embracing national ideal, but even the belief that something of this sort can be realized has evaporated."

Although the Russian political situation may have seemed unsatisfactory and even tense, the country was enjoying a full life that bore little resemblance to the denunciations broadcast by oppositionist politicians. During his trip abroad in the fall of 1913, Kokovtsov in an interview with the editor of the *Berliner Tageblatt* remarked that domestic discontent "may be the case in the large cities, but a hundred kilometers from the provincial capitals the people know nothing of such politics." The Russian press ridiculed that statement, but it very close to the truth.

The twentieth year of the reign of Emperor Nicholas II saw Russia at the highest level of material prosperity in its history. Only five years had passed since Stolypin had said, "Give us twenty years of peace, domestic and foreign, and you will not recognize contemporary Russia," and already the transformation was beginning to be felt. With bumper harvests in 1912 and 1913 the biennium between the summers of 1912 and 1914 saw the Russian economy soar to new heights. In twenty years the empire's population had grown by 50,000,000, a 40 percent increase and a growth rate of more than 3,000,000 persons per year.

During those two decades the standard of living rose appreciably for most citizens; the increasing population testified to the nation's vitality and to the existence of conditions that made it possible to feed a growing number of people. During those twenty years, the Russian market's consumption of domestic and foreign goods more than doubled. Sugar consumption, for example, rose from 450,000 tons or 8 pounds per person in 1894 to 1,440,000 tons or 18 pounds per person in 1913. Despite the failure of the sugar beet crop in 1911-1912 and a significant rise in sugar prices, demand remained steady because to most people sugar had become a necessity. Growing receipts from the liquor monopoly (which gave rise to some criticism on moral grounds) also testified to a rising standard of living. Beer production doubled and the consumption of spirits was on the rise. The consumption of tea increased from 40 million kilograms in 1890 to 75 million kilograms in 1913.

Because of the expansion of agricultural production, the development of communications, and the prudent management of food reserves, the "famine years" that had marked the beginning of the twentieth century became a thing of the past. Crop failures no longer meant famine, for a poor harvest in certain localities was supplemented by the production of other districts. The production of bread-grains (rye, wheat, and barley), which averaged something under 36 million tons at the beginning of the emperor's reign, expanded to more than 72 million tons in 1913-1914. The nature of the crop changed somewhat: the production of wheat and barley doubled, and wheat nearly equalled rye, whereas formerly rye alone had accounted for nearly half of the total output. Considering both the growth of exports (Russia exported about a quarter of its grain) and the population increase, the per capita domestic consumption clearly was rising. In the cities the consumption of white bread began to rival that of black bread.

The per capita consumption of manufactured goods also doubled. Russian textile production increased by 100 percent, but textile imports rose by several hundred percent. Deposits in state savings banks grew from 300 million rubles in 1894 to two billion rubles in 1913. The volume of mail increased from 400 million letters to two billion, while the number of telegrams rose from 60 million to about 200 million.[1]

Industry expanded alongside agriculture, and industrial growth kept pace with the high rate that marked the first half of the reign. The reduction of the growth rate during the first years of the new century gave way in 1909 to a new industrial surge. Coal mining increased continuously. The Donets Basin, which produced less than 5,400,000 tons of coal in 1894, yielded more than 27 million tons in 1913. The later years saw the exploitation of the mighty deposits of the Kuznets Basin in Western Siberia. In the empire as a whole coal production increased more than 400 percent in twenty years.

Oil production in the old Baku fields never recovered its former level after the fires of 1905, but new oil deposits in the Apsheron Peninsula [in the Caspian Sea near Baku] and elsewhere (Grozny and Emba) almost made up for that loss. By 1913 Russia was producing nearly 11 million tons per year, an increase of two-thirds over the beginning of the reign. Industrial growth steadily increased the demand for fuel. The exploitation of peat deposits augmented the consumption of petroleum, coal, and wood. The latter, the oldest form of natural energy, remained the chief fuel in northern and northeastern Russia. Research was conducted on other combustible shales.

With the opening of rich deposits of iron ore at Krivoy Rog in southern Russia and of manganese at Nikopol and Chiaturi in Transcaucasia, the metallurgical industry expanded rapidly. Pig iron production nearly quadrupled in twenty years, while copper production increased almost fivefold. The extraction

of manganese ore, most of which was exported, also increased fivefold.

Although Russia continued to import certain types of machinery, especially machine tools, mainly from Germany,[2] locomotives, railroad cars, and rails all were produced domestically. But even machine production experienced rapid growth after the turn of the century. In the three-year period 1911-1914, the capital value of the Russian machine-tool industry increased from 120 million to 220 million rubles.

The brisk development of the textile industry barely kept pace with the even more rapid surge of demand. Cotton production, which stood at nearly 260 million tons in 1894, doubled by 1911 and continued to expand. Russia was becoming less and less dependent on imported raw cotton. By 1913 Turkestan supplied half of the requirements of Russia's cotton mills, and since the beginning of the reign the output of Turkestani cotton had increased sixfold. The production of linen, wool, and silk rose by 75-80 percent. In two decades the number of workers employed by the textile industry doubled (from 500,000 to 1,000,000), and the total industrial work force expanded from 2,000,000 to 5,000,000.[3]

Russia's economic surge was explosive and multi-faceted. So powerful was agricultural expansion and the development of the empire's enormous domestic market during the emperor's second decade that Russian industry was completely unaffected by the industrial recession of 1911-1912, which struck Europe and America with such intensity. Russian economic expansion continued unabated, and even the crop failure of 1911 could not check it. The demand for agricultural equipment, household utensils, and decorative items placed Russian manufacturers in competition with foreigners (principally the Germans), who poured growing amounts of cheap goods into the Russian market. The availability of inexpensive foreign manufactures in rural Russia made possible the rapid improvement of the peasants' standard of living.

Revenues of the state treasury reflected Russia's vigorous economic development. The state's income increased from 1.2 billion rubles at the beginning of the reign to 3.5 billion rubles.[4] The liquor monopoly and the state-owned railroads accounted for more than half of the government's receipts. Year after year revenues outstripped expenditures and produced a ready cash surplus. In the decade 1904-1913 income exceeded expenses by more than two billion rubles. The gold reserve increased from 648 million rubles in 1894 to 1,604,000,000 rubles in 1914. Reflecting the growth of the national economy, the state budget expanded without the aid of new taxes or increases in the old ones. Rising traffic over the state railway system, expanding receipts from the liquor trade, from sales taxes on tobacco and sugar, from industrial taxes and customs revenues—all this enabled national income to outpace national expenditures. The length of both the rail and telegraph systems doubled since 1894, as did the size of the river transport fleet, which was the world's largest.[5]

MILITARY PREPAREDNESS

The size of the Russian army increased roughly in proportion to the population and in 1914 consisted of 37 corps (not counting Cossacks and irregular formations) with a peacetime strength of over 1,300,000 men. After the Russo-Japanese War the army underwent a thorough reorganization. In a report of 24 February 1914 to the German secretary of state for foreign affairs, Gottlieb von Jagow, the chief of the German general staff, General Helmuth von Moltke, provided the following appraisal of Russia's military reform between 1907 and 1913: "Russia's military preparedness since the Russo-Japanese War has been completely and exceptionally successful and now surpasses any previous state of readiness. Accordingly, one should note some of the particular respects in which Russia excels in military preparedness over the other powers, including Germany. These include: the policy of keeping draftees under colors until the recruits are trained completely; a policy which eliminates the military weakness that prevailed earlier during the winter season; the frequent inspection of the entire mobilization system by means of practice mobilizations; and the possibility of an unusually rapid mobilization aided by the "period preparatory to war" [premobilization].

General Moltke also observed that the redeployment of several corps from the western frontiers deep into the interior (a measure which, as we have seen, created some anxiety in France in 1910) gave Russia greater freedom of maneuver: "Formerly, the combat forces intended for operations against

Austria and Germany were predetermined; that meant that the center of gravity could be shifted from one front to the other only with great difficulty. Now a central army has been formed with troops from the Moscow and Kazan districts, and that force can be deployed wherever it is needed."

The Russian navy, mortally wounded in the Russo-Japanese War, was completely revitalized, largely through the efforts of the emperor who twice overcame the stubborn resistance of the Duma. In the Baltic four dreadnoughts[6] were almost ready for service, and four super-dreadnoughts were under construction in the Black Sea, one of which was nearing completion.[7] Older ships-of-the-line were represented by eight battleships and armored cruisers in the Baltic and seven battleships in the Black Sea. Several light cruisers, destroyers, and submarines also were under construction. Except for a few smaller vessels, all the ships of the new Russian navy were being built in Russian shipyards at Petersburg and Nikolaev.

HIGH MARKS FROM FOREIGNERS

The transformation taking place in Russia attracted the attention of foreigners. Toward the end of 1913, two French ministries commissioned Edmund Théry, editor of the *Economist Europien*, to investigate the Russian economy. Struck by Russia's startling success in all areas, Théry concluded: "If the nations of Europe continue from 1912 to 1950 the course they have followed from 1900 to 1912, then by the middle of the present century Russia will dominate Europe politically, economically, and financially."[8]

In an analysis of the agrarian reform the Dutchman Vit-Knudsen (in 1913) and the German W.D. Preyer (in March 1914) noted the achievements of the Law of 9 November—"a revolution as significant as the emancipation of the serfs." "It was a bold undertaking," wrote Preyer, "a leap into the unknown. It involved no less than a rejection of the old foundation and its replacement by something untried and uncertain. Stolypin tackled this momentous question with resolution and courage, and the results indicate that he was right."[9]

Maurice Baring, the well-known English writer who had spent several years in Russia and knew the country well, wrote in *The Mainsprings of Russia* in the spring of 1914: "There has perhaps never been a period when Russia was more materially prosperous than at the present moment, or when the great majority of the people seemed to have so little obvious cause for discontent." In commenting on society's oppositionist mood, he noted that "the casual observer, glancing at the subject for the first time, will be tempted to ask, 'What more can the Russian people want?' " Baring, who conscientiously presented the viewpoint of the intelligentsia, observed that it was mainly the upper classes that displayed widespread discontent, while "the population on the whole are prosperous at the present moment, and their grievances are neither sharp nor strong enough, nor sufficiently abundant, to make the temperature of their discontent rise to the boiling point."

VIGOROUS EXPANSION OF PUBLIC EDUCATION

The material side of Russian life received the most attention because advances there were so obvious. But perhaps of even greater significance was the progress made in public education. Writing in November 1913, the Trudovik Zhilkin, a former member of the First Duma, asserted that "one portentous feature looms ever more prominently, and that is the mighty development of public education. Unheard, almost unnoticed (mainly because of the rumble of superficial events that today annoy, irritate, and whet our hopes—events that tomorrow will become boring, meaningless, and easily forgotten), an awesome transformation is taking place: Russia is passing from illiteracy to literacy. The whole expanse of Russia seems to have opened up and received the seeds of education. Instantaneously green young sprouts shoot forth from every furrow and begin to rustle."

The following figures illustrate the growth of public education: In 1914 the central government, zemstvos, and municipalities spent about 300 million rubles[10] on education, compared to about 40 million in 1894. E.P. Kovalevsky, *rapporteur* to the Duma on the budget of the ministry of public education, declared on 6 June 1914 that 51 districts [*uezdy*] would have comprehensive systems of education by 1 January 1915, and that by 1920 they would exist in 218 of Russia's 800 districts. As of 1 January 1912 more than eight million[11] of Russia's school-age population of fourteen million[12] were

Strikers Shot at the Lena Gold Mines, 1912

enrolled in schools. According to Kovalevsky's data,[13] institutions of higher education enrolled 80,000 students, with 40,000 in the universities proper. High schools enrolled more than 700,000, and trade or lower technical schools about 50,000. The Third Duma initiated the policy of increasing the budget for education by about 20 million rubles per year (half for new schools, and half for school maintenance). In 1912 Russia had 122 teachers' colleges with about 20,000 students.

Without regard to the danger of the political consequences, the government was extending sizable "credits" to the intelligentsia in matters of education. The authorities retained some supervision in order to prevent the open dissemination of revolutionary propaganda in the schools. At the same time, however, the government supported the efforts of the Duma, the zemstvos, and the municipalities to establish a system of universal education in Russia.[14]

THE FIRST ALL-RUSSIAN CONGRESS OF TEACHERS

On Christmas Day, 1913, the first All-Russian Congress of Teachers opened in St. Petersburg. The oppositionist press was unanimous in predicting that the government would prohibit the convention or that it would disband it almost immediately. Public school teachers long had been considered politically unreliable. The leftists could not understand how Kasso and Maklakov, the ministers of education and interior, could permit such an assembly. Nevertheless, about 7,000 delegates attended the congress, which was held in the House of the People, Petersburg's largest theatrical hall. According to *Vestnik evropy*, "An impressive and unprecedented spectacle stunned St. Petersburg at Christmastide when a genuine living province poured into the capital. The responsiveness of the teachers signifies that the province is neither apathetic nor dead . . . . Finally Russia, too, is setting out along the only true and dependable course toward national cultural strength."

The congress met for ten days. There were many sections, and hundreds of papers were delivered on varied problems affecting the pedagogical profession. The delegates adopted about two hundred resolutions. The leaders of the congress, fearful that it might be closed, strived tirelessly to avoid politics. But the teachers, much to the surprise of the capital press, showed not the slightest inclination to engage in politics. Purishkevich's pamphlet, "Educators Preparing for the Second Russian Revolution," proved quite inopportune. A note of disappointment could be detected in the comment of the Kadet *Rech*: "Instead of being closed, the congress demonstrated attentiveness, cooperation, and tolerance . . . instead of two hundred resolutions, ten resolutions of more substance and weight would have been preferable." The official newspaper *Rossiia* made this evaluation of the congress: "Clannishness strained for recognition at every turn, but the great majority of teachers ignored it and went their own way . . . . Russian life is growing more complex. The demands upon the schools are increasing just as they are upon the teachers. But in any case clannishness, despite all the power at its disposal, is not dragging the teachers down that road."

The only negative signal from the congress was the indication that cultural separatism was spreading among the non-Russian nationalities. The section on problems facing national schools resounded with sharply worded protests against the policy of russification, and the teachers—Ukrainians, Tatars, Poles, and others—generally objected to the compulsory teaching of Russian language and literature. Ill-wishers of the congress—rightists as well as leftists restless over the "absence of politics" in the other sections—paid special attention to the national section. "Those attitudes," wrote Ekaterina Kuskova in *Sovremennyi mir*, "give reason to expect all sorts of opportunities to arise during great national misery and upheavals."

The Petersburg congress was an instructive experience. Most of the teachers adhered, naturally, to a socialist outlook, but they proved that they could work realistically within the framework of the existing system. The system itself was growing more diverse and vital. In an election the teachers would have voted for Left-Kadets, but working business-like in the congress they were prepared to cooperate with Maklakov and Kasso. The congress logically concluded its work by sending a telegram of greetings to the emperor. With very few exceptions this theoretically leftist body turned out to be far less actively oppositionist than Duma progressives, Moscow industrialists, or Guchkov's group, all of whom were considered far more conservative.

Public school teachers received modest salaries, even less than workers in some branches of industry. However, an organization that sponsored foreign tours for teachers came into existence in Moscow in 1909 through the private initiative of Countess V.N. Bobrinskaia. In just a few years the organization enabled several thousand teachers to travel abroad.[15] At only a modest cost to themselves they were able to visit Germany, Switzerland, Italy, France and other countries, though by far the most appealing was the Italian tour. The Russian government lent its assistance by suspending the fees for passports and by providing the excursionists with railway passes.

THE ZEMSTVO'S GOLDEN JUBILEE

January 1914 marked the fiftieth anniversary of the Russian zemstvo. Despite its on-going dissatisfaction with some zemstvoists, the imperial government participated fully in the celebration. It did so in order to emphasize its appreciation of the contributions of local citizens to the improvement of economic conditions, to the establishment of an excellent system of medical assistance, to local school systems, and to road construction. The festivities began on 7 January with a requiem for Emperor Alexander II in the Cathedral of Sts. Peter and Paul and a mass in the Kazan Cathedral. On 8 January, which was the anniversary of the promulgation of the regulations on provincial and district zemstvo institutions, zemstvo representatives from all parts of Russia were introduced to the emperor in the Winter Palace. The chairman of the Moscow provincial zemstvo board addressed the emperor: "We bow low before you, Sire, and beg you to accept our Russian bread and salt [a traditional form of greeting]. We hope that you will be pleased to present to the tsarevich, who is the hope of all loyal Russia, this humble gift, which symbolizes the work of the zemstvos." Thereupon members of the delegation presented "a model of a village of *khutors*" fashioned by craftsmen of the Moscow zemstvo.

The emperor thanked the zemstvo delegation and, concluding his address, said: "It is my firm conviction that the zemstvos working in close unity with my government will be imbued and inspired with boundless concern for the innumerable needs and welfare of the local citizenry. The reasonable satisfaction of local needs is the principal guarantee of the development and enhancement of the prosperity of the entire state. I envision a contented, healthy, and powerful Russia, true to its historical destiny, joyous at the love of its grateful sons, and proud of their absolute devotion to our throne.'' On 9 January the minister of internal affairs gave a large reception that was attended by numerous zemstvo figures, including even the most liberal of them. On the following day the emperor attended a grand reception for the nobles' assemblies. To commemorate the golden anniversary of the zemstvo the emperor ordered that a special medal be struck.

In their home districts members of the zemstvos often sided with leftists against their governors and sometimes took decisions that clearly were unacceptable to the authorities. But in the capital those same zemstvo officials demonstrated true statesmanship and a willingness to cooperate in a positive relationship with the conservative ministers. The best example of that was their work in the periodic meetings of the council on affairs of the local economy. In that body, a feature of government since Stolypin's ministry, members of the zemstvos and officials of the ministry of interior deliberated measures prepared by various departments on the most crucial aspects of local affairs. Thus the celebration of the zemstvo's anniversary, like the congress of teachers, provided an extraordinary demonstration of that higher sense of responsibility.

RUSSIA'S EXTRAORDINARY COOPERATIVE MOVEMENT

The spontaneous economic activity of the masses was evident in the unparalleled speed with which cooperatives developed. Until 1897 Russia had only about a hundred consumer cooperatives with an insignificant membership and a few hundred small savings and loan associations. Then in 1897 the government issued standard regulations governing consumer cooperatives and enabling them to be formed simply with the consent of local authorities. In that year the first credit associations with government or zemstvo participation were formed. By 1904 Russians had established about a thousand consumer cooperatives and some 1,500 credit associations. However, the cooperative movement really began to flourish only after 1906. Consumer cooperatives and small credit institutions spread from the cities into the countryside, and by 1 January 1912 there were nearly 7,000 consumer cooperatives. That represented a sixfold increase in just five years, and the number of rural cooperatives, which made up two-thirds of the total, had increased twelve times over.

Certain cooperatives (the Trans-Baikal Railway Employees Association, for example) had an annual cash flow of several million rubles. In 1914 some 800 cooperatives merged into the Union of Moscow Consumers Associations which, with an annual turnover of 10,500,000 rubles, was the fifth largest cooperative association in Europe. By 1914 the capital assets of Russia's credit institutions had increased seven times over assets in 1905, and their membership stood at nearly 9,000,000. Credit associations provided 85 percent of the capital of the Moscow People's Cooperative Bank whose opening in 1912 gave fresh impetus to the development of co-ops.

The growth of cooperatives created opportunities for the employment of semi-intellectuals. Thus was formed a new social stratum similar to public teachers in its "narodnik-socialist" theoretical outlook. Theory, however, had little effect on their routine activities in the cooperatives, and by and large they shunned "pure politics." In fact they developed a unique ideology which attributed universal significance to the cooperative movement. The cooperatives, they maintained, would alter all economic relations, abolish "exploitation," and form the basis of a people's economy rooted in an all-embracing humanitarianism.

Not only did the government not impede the development of cooperatives (as sometimes was claimed when a cooperative employee was arrested for spreading revolutionary propaganda) but indeed, the government's extensive financial backing stood behind the rapid growth of credit cooperatives. Small credit institutions obtained hundreds of millions of rubles in loans from the State Bank. As a prominent cooperative worker later observed, "In no other country, with the possible exception of India, did credit cooperatives enjoy such official support as in Russia."[16]

Russia was changing. Political orators still brandished terms like "reaction," "stagnation," and "paralysis of the state organism," but the facts contradicted their rhetoric, and foreigners were not alone in recognizing the discrepancy. Toward the end of 1913, Prince Eugene Trubetskoy published in *Russkaia mysl* an article on "The New Zemstvo Russia." "Two new facts in particular strike the observer of Russia's villages in recent years," he wrote. "One is the improved standard of living, and the other is the amazingly rapid growth of a new social order." Advanced technology, higher wages, the appearance of urban accoutrements (from "tortoise-shell combs to galoshes and umbrellas") among the peasants—all parallel the extraordinary expansion of rural cooperatives. And this growth took place not in opposition to the state but with its direct material support: "The government did not spare funds when it came to assisting the zemstvos in every program designed to improve the welfare of the peasantry . . . . What seemed impossible in 1905 was brought to fruition . . . . The cooperative movement proceeds on the basis of the cultural 'organic' work of the intelligentsia and masses combined, and it functions with the benevolent assistance of the government which funds it. The peasants become genuinely accustomed to prosperity and property. They acquire something to cherish and defend." As a result, concluded Trubetskoy, the old "Pugachev" socialism has been left behind, and Russia has acquired the foundation for a "bourgeois democracy" based on peasant landowners.

"Yes," replied I.I. Bunakov, a prominent Populist publicist,[17] "the betterment of the peasantry, associated with improved agricultural technology and the development of peasant society mainly through cooperative institutions, does represent a deep social transformation of rural Russia. And, much to their shame, our urban intelligentsia scarcely noticed it . . . . During the years of 'reaction' and 'stagnation' so-called, rural Russia—and therefore the basic mass of the Russian social order—has witnessed progress which bears enormous significance for the future of our county . . . ." Bunakov acknowledged the error of the "narodniks" who in 1905 had predicted the "decay of the villages" unless a land reform program (presumably their own) was carried out. "The land reform did not pass but neither did the decay materialize. On the contrary, the villages entered the road of agricultural progress, and there is no reason to believe that they soon may leave it."

Unlike Trubetskoy, however, Bunakov still doubted whether peasant "psychology and ideology" could adapt to such rapid change. "Only a few years ago they treated property with such contempt . . . . Does history tolerate such metamorphoses?" he asked. Even though he was skeptical of the durability of the new trend in the countryside, Bunakov at least did not deny its existence, and he examined it with care.

THE SPIRITUAL CRISIS OF THE INTELLIGENTSIA

The rank and file of the intelligentsia generally refused to see any progress. They clung to their notion that Russian reality consisted of "oppression," "arbitrariness," "poverty," and the "suppression of all spontaneity." Peter Struve dealt with that attitude in March 1914 in an article in *Russkaia mysl* titled "Why Has Our Spiritual Life Stagnated?" In the past, he said, the thought of the intelligentsia had forged ahead of Russian reality, but now "life, steadily and with elemental force, moves forward, while ideological work lags hopelessly behind, producing nothing, marking time."

What caused this phenomenon? The intelligentsia had lost confidence in its former ideals. Materialism had become suspect, as had the ideals of the eighteenth and nineteenth centuries. No longer did the intelligentsia trust in the all-redeeming power of revolution, but they dared not admit it to themselves. Meanwhile, the roots of their disillusionment ran deep. The younger generation reflected it—students, even youths just beginning to be conscious of life. "The authority of the older generation carries even less weight with youth than is customary among fathers and children," wrote Professor V.I. Vernadsky in the 1914 annual edition of the Kadet newspaper *Rech.* "It has been a long time since authority has ebbed as low in Russia as it has during these recent years of political and moral turmoil."

As the old tenets of the intelligentsia decayed, an epidemic of suicide broke out among young people around 1910. Then the rash of self-destruction began to recede and it gave way to a search for religion. In institutions of higher learning, where politics were on ice (less because of Kasso's repressive measures than the students' change of mood), various religious groups (an unprecedented phenomenon) began to appear. In

1913 Russian students participated for the first time in the world congress of Christian youth held in the United States. "The spread of religious circles among Russian students is indicative of personal liberation," wrote Professor Vernadsky in the article cited above. "Until recently Russian youth suppressed any religious feelings, and membership in a religious organization was unthinkable . . . . The goal used to be the welfare of the masses; the struggle for economic and political liberation stood foremost and it stifled every other consideration."

An entirely new and different development was the burgeoning interest in physical activity of all types. In the past Russia's sober youth had regarded athletics as a "non-intelligentsia" pastime. Then suddenly soccer and tennis clubs began to spring up everywhere, and gymnastic programs for children and young people spread all across the land. One organization, called the *poteshnie* after the youthful comrades of Peter the Great, concentrated on a kind of preservice military training. Another, the Sokol, was a Slavic sports organization that was most highly developed among the Czechs. Then there were the Boy Scouts patterned after the English organization founded by Colonel Baden-Powell.

Nicholas II had an avid interest in the development of these organizations, especially the *poteshnie*. From discretionary funds at his disposal he contributed 10 million rubles and proposed the creation of a special government department of physical education. Kokovtsov maintained, however, that the Duma would be poorly disposed to fund the new agency. On that question, as on the establishment of a special ministry of health, the Duma trailed far behind the initiative of the government. Young Russians also were becoming sports-minded, and that too was a new phenomenon which occasionally inspired the radical journals to mock the youthful concern for "biceps" and "records."

Newspapers and journals continued to propound the timeworn formulas. Only a few writers, like the contributors to *Vekhi*, had the courage to discuss openly the need to re-examine the world view of the intelligentsia. But throughout the entire cultural strata of the intelligentsia only the youth reached a profound ideological crossroad, and they alone embarked on a new quest for solutions to their disillusionment.

Russian society was departing from its well-trod path. The intelligentsia's espousal of the doctrines of atheism, materialism, and socialism no longer had the ring of fanatical certitude. But this uncertainty had not yet penetrated the ranks of the semi-intelligentsia, where indeed the seeds of the nineteenth century were only beginning to take root. Thus shopworn dogmas, unquestioned, still flourished within the substrata of the intelligentsia, and they spread like weeds among the masses as literacy spread through the nation.

The villages were prospering. Hunger was becoming a thing of the past. Literacy was increasing rapidly. But at the same time village youths were turning their backs on their age-old religious traditions. I.A. Rodionov's novel *Our Crime* (*Nashe prestuplenie*) presented a disturbing picture, for with vivid but unembellished accuracy it described the spread of unthinking brutality and hooliganism in the villages. Every part of the country reported the decline of religion among the peasantry and especially among the younger generation.

In his article on "The New Zemstvo Russia" Prince Trubetskoy noted that "no discernible spiritual regeneration as yet has accompanied the obvious and striking spread of material comforts. One hardly can be gratified by the spiritual constitution of our petty bourgeoisie . . . . A mighty organism of some sort is taking shape: in time it will give birth—to what? To human greatness or to some powerful, hulking, but witless monster? . . . If we have any reason to be confident of Russia's future greatness, our confidence looks more to the past than the present." Trubetskoy's fears essentially mirrored the concerns expressed by Stolypin in his letter to the emperor on Siberia's "crude democracy." The same issue of *Russkaia mysl* that carried Trubetskoy's essay also carried a response by Feodor Shcherbina who asserted that "the cooperative movement and the religious movement go hand in hand. The improved well-being of the masses is the essential precondition that enables them to worry about their souls and to ponder the loftiest ideals."

CHURCH REFORM AT AN IMPASSE

Religious stirrings among the intelligentsia and the erosion of faith among the masses coincided with a deep crisis within the

Russian Orthodox Church. The church council (*Sobor*) scheduled for 1905 never took place. The first pre-conciliar conference finished its work on 15 December 1906,[18] and a second conference was held in 1911. The latter, considerably narrower in composition, consisted almost exclusively of clergymen. Nothing was done to convene a similar conference of the landed gentry even though many churchmen favored one.

Paradoxical as it may seem at first glance, the basic obstacle to the convening of a church council stemmed from the existence of a legislative establishment. The Fundamental Laws made no provision for special legislation on ecclesiastical affairs. Leading religious circles, moreover, were hesitant to see the internal affairs of the Russian Orthodox Church decided by the votes of atheists and adherents of other faiths. The emperor shared their concern. Meanwhile the State Duma harbored a jealous interest in asserting its jurisdiction over an entire aspect of national life. Consequently, how to handle church reform remained an open question.

Beyond that, the religious community itself was divided on matters of ecclesiastical organization and especially on whether to re-establish the patriarchate. As a result, the church stood by passively while all types of sectarianism, both mystical and rationalistic (the Baptists), spread across the land.

The Religious-Philosophical Society, which early in the century had attempted to discover a common language for the intelligentsia and the church, was drifting into politics. It became involved in the agitation generated by society over the Beilis affair and took steps to expel so famous a writer as Vasily Rozanov for admitting the possibility of ritualistic murder. Peter Struve blasted the society's campaign as ridiculous and resigned from its council.[19]

A VOICE IN THE WILDERNESS

During the winter of 1913-1914, A.M. Rykachev's essay "On Some of Our Prejudices," which appeared in *Russkaia mysl*, attracted great interest and touched off a lively debate. The author, a young scholar, contended that Russia's vigorous economic progress was accompanied by "organizational frailty and a lack of the enthusiasm and joy of creation among the public." He saw the reason for this in society's powerful antipathy for business activity. Influenced by Marxist theory, the intelligentsia looks upon all employers as "exploiters," he wrote. Members of the intelligentsia are willing to work for employers and to take their pay which at times is very generous, but they shrink from becoming employers themselves. "They consider it more honorable to hire themselves out as agronomists to a landowners' zemstvo than to become landowners themselves, to become statisticians in the employ of industrialists but not industrialists themselves. Society's cultural poverty, the humility of its personalities emerges as a preference to take a back seat, to tremble at the thought of new careers, and to reject the courageous and forthright use of power!"

Rykachev insisted that "people can in fact become successful and influential entrepreneurs without sacrificing their political convictions or their personal moral standards . . . . Does this alternative not afford a marvelous application for the energies of those who feel dissatisfied with their present circumstances? . . . To the children and grandchildren of those who once went 'to the people,' one wants to shout: Go to trade and industry!" Although socialist critics caustically disdained Rykachev's advice, the younger members of the higher intelligentsia found his ideas intriguing.

THE ARTS IN FLUX

The world of Russian fiction more than any other sphere reflected the deep spiritual crisis of the intelligentsia. The more prominent writers, who in any case tended to avoid cliches, displayed less of this disillusionment than did the "literary masses"—the rank-and-file contributors to the various "thick journals." The earlier critical tales with their positive characters portrayed as "fighters for the people" began to give way to "modern" novels and disillusioned heroes. Personal interest gained the edge over "public" interest.

Tolstoy's death deprived Russia of any writer of world renown. Maxim Gorky and Leonid Andreev became noticeably less popular with the intelligentsia in general (although Gorky produced several semi-biographical novels during this period). Ivan Bunin and Alexander Kuprin and among the newer writers, Boris Zaitsev[20] and Count A.N. Tolstoy,[21] enjoyed the greatest popularity. By then Merezhkovsky and Hippius were making the transition from literature to political-religious journalism.

In poetry the symbolists—Balmont, Briussov, Blok (the most popular), and Bely—had attained general recognition. The clear personal lyricism of Anna Akhmatova and Maria Tsvetaeva[22] won them distinction among the newer poets. The acmeists, forming around Nicholas Gumilyov, sought to instill new vitality into poetry.[23] Innokenty Annensky achieved in death the recognition that had eluded him in life.[24] Amid the galaxies of poets that illuminated the early twentieth century there glittered the bright stars of Vladislav Khodasevich, Osip Mandelshtam, and Boris Sadovsky.[25]

Poetic innovation ran to extremes. The works of Victor Khlebnikov and David Burliuk offered nothing but sound in a senseless void.[26] Igor Severianin attempted to create a new vocabulary and especially new word endings, and his works were the most successful with the reading public.[27] The futurists attempted to blend the odd combination of poetry and carnival buffoonery, but one futurist with an undeniable talent was Vladimir Mayakovsky.[28]

It was impossible to detect in any of the writers of the period the comprehensiveness of the intelligentsia *Weltanschauung* that prevailed in the 1890s and emerged so clearly for the last time in the plays of Anton Chekov. V.G. Korolenko, one of the last of the old school, had abandoned pure literature in order to write his autobiography, *The History of My Contemporary (Istoriia moego sovremennika)*.

In the field of art the *peredvizhniki*[29] and the champions of utilitarianism lost any influence, as tendentious and didactic canvases came to be regarded as examples of bad taste. Just as the symbolists came to dominate poetry, so in art the representatives of *Mir iskusstvo* [and the principle of art for its own sake] occupied the central position. The posthumous exhibit of the works of V.A. Serov early in 1914 confirmed how great an artist Russia had lost. The principal artists of the period were Somov, Shukhaev, Serebriakova, Grigoriev, Benois, and the designers Bakst and Dobuzhinsky.[30]

Sculpture contributed little of distinction. Of the numerous monuments erected on the streets and squares of Russia's cities only the monument to Emperor Alexander II on the square before St. Petersburg's Nikolaevsk railway station claimed distinction for its extraordinary power.

Architecture likewise produced little that was new or original. The more notable buildings of the period were: the Emperor Alexander III Museum of Fine Arts in Moscow; the Church of the Saviour on the Water and the Church of the Romanov Jubilee in Petersburg, both in the classical style; and the Feodor Cathedral, built at Tsarskoe Selo in the old Russian tradition. Less successful was the Church of the Saviour on the Blood erected in Petersburg on the spot where Alexander II was assassinated and patterned after St. Basil's [or the Kazan] Cathedral in Moscow.

In 1913 Moscow was the setting for the Romanov Church-Archeological Exhibit and also for an exhibition of old Russian art sponsored by the Imperial Archeological Institute. Together the exhibits gave numerous Russians an opportunity to acquaint themselves with native art of the fourteenth-seventeenth centuries, which the emperor treasured so highly. For the first time the artistic significance of Russian iconography received the recognition that it deserved. The annual edition of the Kadets' *Rech* called the exhibits "the greatest event in the life of Russian art in recent memory."

Russian drama also set out in new directions. The Moscow Art Theater, long the standard of perfection achieved through hundreds of rehearsals, ceased to be the "last word." "Stylization" became the vogue. At Kommisharzhevskaia's theater Vsevolod Meyerhold produced plays which featured simplified sets and stressed acting in accord with his theory of "conditional" theater.[31] There developed a unique and witty theater of parodies, known as the "crooked mirror," the likes of which could not be found in Western Europe. The "ancient theater" attempted to resurrect medieval mystery plays and the works of playwrights such as Cervantes, Lopé de Vega [Vega Carpio], and Calderon. The theater of artistic miniatures enjoyed tremendous success most notably with Baliev's "The Bat." In "poets pubs" the miniatures often were performed in conjunction with poetry readings and interpretive dances.[32]

It was during this period that the Imperial Russian ballet became world famous. Its performances abroad were true artistic sensations. Its impresario, Sergei Diaghilev, and company—Anna Pavlova, Vaslav Nijinsky, Michel Fokine [and numerous others]—acquired fame far beyond the borders of Russia.[33]

THE MONARCHY, RUSSIA'S BEST HOPE

The Russia of 1914 was much less poisoned by politics than the Russia of 1904. Political parties had very little significance. The Kadets remained the party of the intelligentsia. The Octobrists had become the party of the zemstvoists, for the industrialists recently had transferred their allegiance to the Progressists. The more extreme right represented no particular social stratum, except perhaps the landed gentry, but it found many adherents among the Russian masses and especially among townsmen in the western provinces. The Marxian socialists, the Social Democrats, exercised a significant influence over the workers and probably were the best organized party even though they did not exist "legally." The Populist socialists (the Socialist Revolutionaries, Trudoviks, and Popular Socialists) claimed many members among the semi-intelligentsia of the villages. However, with the possible exception of the Social Democrats not one of the parties conducted a general and concerted nationwide campaign of propaganda.

Neither the intelligentsia, stripped of its confidence in its old faith and bereft of any new one, nor the primitive-socialist semi-intelligentsia possessed either political experience or a comprehensive statesmanlike perspective. Amidst this formless "public" only tsarist authority had the strong tradition, the extended governing experience, and the tested cadres to implement policy—only tsarist authority was capable of directing the life of this complex country. Only the authority which stood outside and above the interests of the country's separate groups and strata could carry out basic reforms. The Law of 9 November [1906—the agrarian reform] proved that. Legislative institutions could serve the government not so much as the foundation but as an occasional *brake* and also as an instrument to measure the "temperature" or the "barometric pressure" of the nation.

"Tsarist authority," wrote the former deputy Baron A.F. Meyendorf (as though repeating Pushkin's famous letter to Chaadaev), "seems to me the most European of all Russian institutions, perhaps the only European one . . . Russia was a land of whimsical dreams in which imperial rule was the least eccentric center."[34] Noting the unimportance of lineage in the appointment of Russia's highest officials, Meyendorf concluded that "the Russian Empire was the most democratic monarchy in Europe." Nearly half a century earlier, Constantine Leontiev had expressed his concern over the fundamental instability of all Russian foundations and systems. Despite the expansion of national wealth and education, his words still had the ring of truth.

In February 1914, Peter Durnovo warned: "Especially fertile soil for social upheavals is to be found in Russia, where the masses unconsciously profess the principles of socialism. But despite the opposition of Russian society, a stance as unconscious as the socialism of the broad masses of the population, a political revolution is not possible in Russia. Any revolutionary movement must degenerate inevitably into a socialist movement, for the opponents of the government do not have the support of the people." Durnovo went on to point out that the government's worst mistake in the face of new disorders would be to make concessions to the intelligentsia. Such a response, he explained, would weaken the government's effort to combat the socialist elements. "Although it may sound like a paradox, the fact is that in Russia an agreement with the opposition positively weakens the government. . . . It is more than strange, under these circumstances, that the government should be asked to reckon seriously with the opposition and that to do so it should renounce its role of social relationships . . . ."[35]

The emperor undoubtedly agreed with that assessment. He had no intention, except in a dire national emergency, to retreat from the Fundamental Laws which he himself had granted. Persistent rumors to the contrary lacked any substantive basis. After 3 June 1907 the emperor permitted only one deviation, not from the letter but from the spirit of the code, and that was to allow Stolypin to use Article 87 to push through the western zemstvo bill. But at this time [1914] the emperor did not see how it was possible to increase the influence of "the public" in the conduct of affairs of state: He did not perceive in the Duma or in Russian society in general those elements to which his imperial authority *would have the right to delegate the destiny of Russia.*

REWARDS OF THE EMPEROR'S ASIAN POLICY

Since the very first year of his reign, and indeed even since his days as tsarevich, Nicholas II had taken an extraordinary interest in Russia's Asiatic mission. Asian affairs were important ingredients of Russian foreign and domestic policies. Behind the mighty development of the Russian Empire stood its emerging Asiatic possessions. Lomonosov's prophecy[36] —Russia's might would develop through Siberia and the Arctic Ocean—was coming to pass. Of course, northern Siberia with its vast expanse of tundra and permafrost held little promise; its three and a half million square miles continued to hold about half a million people, two-thirds of whom were Yakuts and other nomadic northern tribes.[37] But to the south between latitudes 55° and 58° and stretching from the Urals to the Pacific was a broad belt several hundred miles wide with an area of nearly two million square miles. Its mountainous topography and remoteness from the sea gave the region a climate that was far more rigorous than Europe's. The area more closely resembled Canada than the United States; the soil was fertile, and the region abounded with vast, virtually untapped natural resources. Farther south across an expanse of deserts lay Central Asia, a region rather densely populated by diverse peoples and studded with cotton fields, orchards, and vineyards. The vassal states of Khiva and Bukhara formed a kind of transitional zone leading to areas within the Russian sphere of influence—Northern Manchuria and Mongolia, where Russian preponderance already was recognized formally, and Chinese Turkestan, where Russians had begun to sink roots.

In his book *Toward a Knowledge of Russia (K poznaniiu Rossii* [1906] D.I. Mendeleyev had observed that Russia's economic center was shifting eastward to an axis running approximately from Samara to Saratov. The growth of Russia's Asiatic possessions confirmed the great scientist's prediction. In twenty years the population of Asiatic Russia had grown from 12 million to 21 million persons. During the same period the population of the central belt rose from 4 million to 10 million. In the colonized areas of Western Siberia[38] the population increased from slightly under three million to seven million.

West Siberian colonization centered on the Altai region which, as the personal property of the reigning emperor, was administered by His Imperial Majesty's Cabinet. In 1899 Nicholas II had ordered these lands opened to colonization by Russian peasants and other national minorities who inhabited the region. Then in 1906 the emperor's Ukaz of 16 September transferred all of the region's unoccupied lands to the resettlement administration for distribution to the landless and land-hungry peasants of European Russia. Those two decrees placed in the hands of peasants, both local inhabitants and colonists, some 25 million of the 41 million desiatins administered by the cabinet.[39] By 1914 the population of the Altai exceeded three million—a density of more than ten persons per square verst [about five per square mile]. Altaic cities grew at a remarkable pace: Novo-Nikolaevsk, founded in 1895, had 100,000 inhabitants in 1914; Slavgorod, where in 1909 a wooden cross had been erected on a bare spot of ground, by 1913 had 7,000 residents and commerce valued at six million rubles a year.

In the space of two decades some four million settlers from the interior of Russia found homes in Siberia. More than three million settled in the central belt, about 500,000 moved into the maritime provinces of the Far East, and about 100,000 took up land in Turkestan. The budget of the resettlement administration, which handled this colonization, reached 30 million rubles in 1914 (up from less than 500,000 rubles in 1894).

The Great Siberian Railway, completed in 1905 in the heat of the Russo-Japanese War, already was inadequate to serve the region's growing needs. The Amur Railway, under construction since 1908 and scheduled for completion in 1916, traversed almost uninhabited territory. Therefore, in order to serve the major settled areas, plans were laid for a South Siberian line to run parallel to and about 200 miles south of the Great Siberian. Its terminals were to be Orsk and Semipalatinsk. Three branch lines were to serve the Altai region, including one from Novo-Nikolaevsk [now Novosibirsk] to Semipalatinsk via Barnaul and another into the Kuznetsk coal basin. Another branch was to run northward from Minusinsk

to Achinsk [on the Great Siberian] and still another south-
ward through the Transbaikal [from Ulan-Ude] to Kiakhta on
the Chinese frontier. Construction of the new routes in the
Altai region began in 1913. In the same year the Tiumen-Omsk
line was completed, greatly reducing the route from Petersburg to Siberia. In the summer of 1914 contracts for the construction of the South Siberian line were awarded to a joint-
stock company headed by the former state councillor, V.F.
Trepov.

The completion in 1906 of the Orenburg-Tashkent Railway
linked Central Asia with the Russian rail network, and work
then began on the necessary regional subsidiary lines in Turkestan. Meanwhile planning was underway to link Turkestan
with Siberia by means of a railway to the Semireche [Balkash
region] at Verny and Pishpek.

The Siberian river system had one major drawback in that
all the great rivers except the Amur flowed on parallel courses
from south to north. In 1909 the government created a special
commission in the ministry of ways of communication to develop a long-range plan for a Siberian waterway between the
Urals and Vladivostok. The system, more than 6,000 miles
long, was to connect with the Kama and Volga Rivers by
means of canals and locks constructed in the southern Ural
region.

Beginning in 1910 the government launched extensive efforts to establish a regular system of communication with Siberia by way of the Arctic Ocean. Expeditions from Vladivostok reached the mouths of the Kolyma and Lena Rivers.
In 1913 Captain B.A. Vilkitsky led a very successful expedition which discovered a huge uncharted island which he named
Nicholas II Land. In the same year the Norwegian steamship
Korrekt under the famous polar explorer Fridtjof Nansen
sailed from the west to the Yenesei and then proceeded nearly
200 miles up-river. There it met the Russian steamer *Turuk-
hansk* and transferred 1,800 tons of cargo. In the summer of
1913 the first radio station went into service on West Siberian
coast of the Arctic Ocean.

Siberia was producing a grain surplus of as much as
1,800,000 tons a year. (The area under cultivation totalled
12 million [desiatins-?] and the annual yield stood at 7-8
million tons.) Even so, Siberia's chief contribution to Russian

exports was butter, produced mainly in the Altai and shipped primarily to England. Butter production soared dramatically, from practically nil in 1894 to exports valued at 70 million rubles in 1913.[40]

The Siberian peasantry was noticeably better off than the peasants of European Russia. Although the Siberian population was twelve times less numerous than that of western Russia, Siberians possessed half as many horse-drawn rakes, threshing machines, and mowing machines. Since the turn of the century, Siberians had purchased more than 150 million rubles during the first five years of the century and later more than 20 million rubles a year.[41]

The hot, dry climate of Turkestan posed different problems, for there the main deficiency was water. The emperor's estate at Murgab demonstrated how much could be done through proper irrigation techniques. The estate of 104,000 desiatins was located in a part of the steppe that once produced only nettles. However, reservoirs were built to collect the spring runoff from the River Murgab. In fifteen years (1895-1910) the estate was transformed into a cotton plantation of 25,000 desiatins. It included orchards and also settlements lighted by electricity generated from dammed waters. In 1913 the Romanov irrigation canal was opened in the hungry steppe of Samarkand. This single canal was designed to irrigate some 45,000 desiatins by 1915. The general hydrographic plan of the ministry of agriculture called for the irrigation of an additional 35,000 desiatins in Central Asia also by 1915.

To commemorate the Romanov tercentenary the Duma voted to release one billion rubles for irrigation and other land reclamation projects. (The Russian railway network had cost around six billion rubles.) Plans for the use of the first part of that appropriation, some 150 million rubles, already were completed and ready to be carried out. These efforts provide a truly remarkable example of how land reform, resettlement, personal liberation, and industrial development combined to infuse new life into Russian technology, brilliantly enlivening whole areas that until then had lain dormant.

PETER DURNOVO, PROPHET OF DOOM

In February 1914, shortly after Kokovtsov's retirement, Peter Durnovo prepared and submitted to the emperor a memorandum which expressed his fear for the future of Russia should it continue to adhere to the established course of its foreign policy.[42] Durnovo contended that a purely defensive alliance with France was useful: "The alliance with Russia guaranteed France against an attack by Germany; the latter was safe—thanks to Russia's proven pacifism and friendship—from French revanchist ambitions; and Russia was secured—thanks to Germany's need to maintain amicable relations with us—against excessive intrigues by Austria-Hungary in the Balkan peninsula."

However, the Anglo-Russian rapprochement destroyed that equilibrium. During the Russo-Japanese War and the Revolution of 1905, Austria would have found it very easy "to realize its cherished ambitions in the Balkans. But at that time Russia had not yet linked its destinies with England, and Austria-Hungary was compelled to forsake an opportunity most auspicious for its purposes. No sooner had we taken the course of closer accord with England than immediately there followed the annexation of Bosnia and Herzegovina . . . . In short, the Anglo-Russian accord has brought us nothing of practical value so far, while as for the future, it threatens us with the inevitability of armed conflict with Germany."

Durnovo warned that even a victory over Germany would produce no benefits for Russia: "Poznan? East Prussia? What need have we for those territories, densely populated as they are by Poles, when we already have our hands full with our own Russian Poles?" Galicia? That region is a turbulent nest of dangerous Ukrainian separatists. "The conclusion of a commercial treaty with Germany, entirely acceptable to us, by no means requires that Germany first must be crushed . . . . Germany's defeat would undoubtedly end in a peace dictated from the viewpoint of England's economic interests. The British will exploit to the limit any success that comes their way, while in a ruined Germany deprived of its maritime commerce, we merely stand to lose a market which, after all, is valuable to us for our otherwise unmarketable products." Moreover, Russia will have fallen into "financial bondage" to its creditor-allies. Nor does Germany itself need a war from which it could seize from Russia only the densely populated regions of Poland and the eastern Baltic, both of which are of dubious value. "The German colonization movement diminishes steadily, and the day is not far off when the *Drang nach Osten* will become no more than a chapter in history."

Durnovo went on to forecast the course of events "in the coming war." Russia, France, and England will be arrayed on one side with Germany, Austria, and Turkey on the other. "Italy, if it has any conception of its real interests, will not join the German side . . . . and it is not out of the question that Italy would join the anti-German coalition, if the scale of war should incline in its favor." Rumania, too, "will remain neutral until the scales of fortune favor one side or the other . . . . The participation of other powers will be incidental." America and Japan are hostile to Germany and in any case will not enter the war on the German side.

The main burden of the war undoubtedly will fall on us . . . . Ours will be the role of a battering ram to breach the very heart of the German defenses . . . . This war is fraught with enormous difficulties for us, and it cannot lead to a mere triumphal march on Berlin. Both military disasters—partial ones, let us hope—and all kinds of shortcomings in supply are inevitable. Given the excessive nervousness and oppositionist mood of society, the importance of these events will be exaggerated and all the blame will be laid on the government . . . . The legislative institutions will unleash a bitter campaign against the regime, and throughout the empire revolutionary agitation will follow . . . . Having lost its most reliable men and swept along on the tide of the peasants' primitive desire for land, the defeated army will find itself too demoralized to serve as the bulwark of law and order. The legislature and the opposition parties of the intelligentsia, lacking real authority in the eyes of the people, will be powerless to stem the popular tide, which they themselves have generated. Russia will be plunged into hopeless anarchy, the outcome of which cannot be foreseen.

Having displayed this desperate panorama, Durnovo then concluded: "The Triple Entente is an artificial combination . . . which holds no promise. The future lies in the close and incomparably more vital rapprochement of Russia, Germany, France (reconciled with Germany), and Japan (allied with Russia in a strictly defensive alignment) . . . . It goes without

P.N. Durnovo

saying that for its part Germany must respond to our desires . . . and elaborate in closest agreement with us" the conditions for our mutual existence.

WAR CLOUDS RISING

There is no record of the emperor's reaction to the Durnovo
memorandum. Perhaps it never reached him. At any rate Germany gave no indication of any desire for accomodation, and
the Germans themselves became convinced of Russia's unap-
peasable enmity. The Russian press bore some responsibility
for that (although German ambassadors had complained about
the press ever since the reign of Alexander III). The chauvin-
istic attitude of the press in connection with the renewal of
the Russo-German trade agreement particularly irritated the
Germans.

The trade agreement of 1904, due to expire in 1916, was
far less advantageous to Russia than the earlier treaty of 1894,
which placed much lower tariffs on Russian agricultural com-
modities. Although Germany was Russia's chief supplier, it
was also Russia's best customer. Exports to Germany exceeded
half a billion rubles, and Russia consistently enjoyed a favorable balance of trade with Germany.[43] In his memoirs Kokovtsov recorded that Krivoshein prepared for those negotiations by sending to all zemstvos and chambers of commerce a
circular urging them to instigate an anti-German campaign.
Perhaps as a bargaining point such a tactic made some sense,
since an alleged need to satisfy public opinion might have won
certain concessions. In the tense atmosphere of 1914, however, that ploy simply reinforced German opinion that "our
cause in Russia is lost; all that remains for us is to arm ourselves and then, trusting in God, to wait till they attack us."[44]
But waiting for an invasion was only one step removed from
launching a pre-emptive attack.

The notion that Russia was preparing to attack was kept
simmering in Germany by sensationalist reports of a French
loan early in 1914 for the construction of strategic railroads.[45]
Other reports vaguely warned that several unnamed "grand
dukes" were members of a "war party" that had formed within the Russian court. These spurious rumors colored the attitudes of the German ruling circles including, no less, the kaiser

himself. Only Bethmann Hollweg, the chancellor, and a few diplomats including the ambassador to St. Petersburg, Count Pourtales, seem not to have shared that anti-Russian bias. As for the German press, on questions of foreign policy it was traditionally more "obedient" to instructions "from above" than its Russian counterpart, which was oppositionist as a matter of principle.

The Russian side also contained several individuals who poured oil on the fire. Russians and foreigners alike were well aware of Guchkov's anti-Germanism. *Novoe vremia* pursued a hostile editorial policy with tirades such as this: "We do not oppose friendship with Germany . . . but we believe that it must be based exclusively on Germany's acknowledgement of our strength." The left also rallied to the attack: during budget hearings in February 1914 the Kadet Shingarev contended that Germany was creating foreign difficulties for Russia in order to compel the government to conclude a disadvantageous trade agreement. Foreign minister Sazonov denied that, but the press quoted him in a manner that implied his agreement with Shingarev.

When the German ambassador protested, he was promised that a correction would appear in the press. But instead, on 27 February the evening edition of *Birzhevie vedomosti* carried the banner headline: "Russia Wants Peace But Is Prepared for War." Its lead article declared: "We can say with pride that the time when foreigners could threaten Russia has passed. Saber-rattling does not intimidate Russia. The Russian public has been correct in its equinanimous attitude toward the war scares fomented abroad during the past few days: We have no cause for concern. Russia is ready! The Russian army—which always has been victorious and which usually has waged war on the enemy's soil—will ignore completely the idea of 'defense' . . . Russian opinion cherishes the awareness that our motherland stands prepared for any eventuality, but prepared solely in the interests of peace." The "saber-rattling" referred to a story filed by the St. Petersburg correspondent of the *Kölnische Zeitung* (17 February /2 March) which maintained that Russia was preparing for war and would be ready by the fall of 1917. The *Birzhevie vedomosti* article, generally attributed (and as it turned out, correctly) to Minister of War

Sukhomlinov, elicited boisterous approval from the French press but ominous silence from the Germans.

After that exchange, reassurances published in the semi-official *Rossiia* and *Norddeutsche Allgemeine Zeitung* had little effect. Equally unsuccessful were the speeches of the diplomatic representatives, Jagow and Sazonov—the one in the Reichstag on 1 May and the other in the Duma on 10 May. Both statesmen stressed the invariability of firm friendly relations between Russia and Germany, and both deplored the harm caused by unrestrained polemics in the newspapers of the two countries. "There is a discrepancy in Germany between the government, which is full of sensible intentions and public opinion, which is seized by fits of passion," wrote an analyst for the *Revue des deux Mondes* (15 May 1914).

GOREMYKIN AND THE DUMA

Soon after his appointment to the post of prime minister, Goremykin informed Rodzianko, the chairman of the State Duma, of his desire "to move legislation from a standstill." On 1 March 1914 the chairmen of all parties except the extreme left met to discuss a major new military program. But the Duma was cautious and wary. The deputies were concerned about their parliamentary immunity, since one of their members, Nicholas Chkeidze, had been arrested for insulting the emperor in a speech to the Duma.[46] An editorial change in the title of a bill adopted by the assembly also produced consternation. Then Goremykin caused a sensation by asserting that questions could be addressed only to individual ministers and not to the chairman of the council of ministers. (No one, however, denied the premier's legal right to refuse to be questioned.)

In March 1914 women employees in several rubber factories in Riga and Petersburg (and later in other factories) succumbed to a wave of illness which produced nausea, convulsions, and fainting spells. The Triangle Works experienced over 300 cases in six days, a tobacco factory reported more than 150 cases, although nowhere was there a fatal case. The press sounded the alarm. Inquiries flooded the Duma. A storm erupted among the duputies when rightists suggested that the revolutionaries had resorted to "chemical warfare." The sickness soon disappeared completely. The first cases appear to have stemmed from a combination of stale air and rubber vapors and then to have spread through psychological contagion. Nevertheless, the "epidemic" gave rise to numerous strikes of protest.[47] The number of strikes was increasing in general. The Petersburg workers walked out because the assistant minister of interior made a speech on the Lena affair which they did not like. They struck when the government confiscated an issue of *Pravda*. And they shut down nearly every factory on the first of May [May Day].

Pravda celebrated its second anniversary on 22 April 1914. (It was closed several times but immediately reappeared under a different title.[48]) To mark the event collections were held in the factories for the "fund of the workers' press." On the same day the Duma's extreme leftists staged an obstruction to protest Goremykin's opening address. About twenty deputies began to shout and pound on their desks, and the demonstration ceased only after twenty deputies had been expelled for fifteen sessions. Among them were the Menshevik leader Chkeidze and the young lawyer Alexander Kerensky, the leader of the Trudoviks. Thereafter Goremykin returned to the Duma to deliver a brief but conciliatory speech: "My position is very simple. It consists of a desire to work cooperatively and amicably with you . . . in order that each of us might dedicate his energies to the service of our country within the limits of our duties as prescribed by law."

The deputies remained reserved in their attitude toward the new prime minister, but when the minister of interior appeared to defend the budget for his department, the Duma for the first time demonstratively refused to approve any funds. The deputies' rejection of any increase in the ministry's budget, meant, according to the law, that the previous year's estimates remained in effect. The new budget, however, contained a request for funds for the "rent and maintenance of offices in provincial cities." The Right-Octobrist Tantsov noted that omission of those funds would put a strain on the zemstvo budgets. The Zemstvo-Octobrist Stempkovsky admitted that but also insisted that to reject the budget would "force the minister of interior to start thinking." In the end the Duma rejected the ministry's budget by a vote of 159-147. Later, when a motion was made to remove from the budget funds for land reform in the Polish provinces, the Poles joined with the rightists to save the appropriation. Thus even in the Fourth Duma the Poles were able to play a decisive role.

Among the deputies expelled for obstructing the Duma was Roman Malinovsky, a Social Democrat who since 1910 had been in the pay of the secret police. Malinovsky enjoyed Lenin's complete confidence, served on the Bolshevik central committee, and as a result was able to keep the ministry of interior well informed of the Bolsheviks' plans. However, his inflammatory speeches in the Duma infuriated the new assistant minister of interior, Vladimir Junkovsky, who decided to sever relations with him. Malinovsky had no choice but to resign from the Duma and go abroad. Junkovsky then revealed Malinovsky's true identity to Rodzianko. Lenin long refused to admit that Malinovsky was a police spy. *Pravda* attributed his flight to nervous exhaustion and chastized him for his lack of endurance. Meanwhile the Mensheviks gloated over the Bolsheviks' misfortune. With Malinovsky's resignation, however, the government lost its chief source of information on the privy affairs of the Bolsheviks.[49]

The government had embarked on a temperance campaign, but society treated it as a joke. The Duma rejected the government's request for 300,000 rubles to subsidize temperance societies. "If you want temperance," Feodor Rodichev advised, "grant freedom!" As an experiment the government closed the liquor stores in Petersburg on the second and third days of the Easter holiday. Workers in several factories went on strike because "they were deprived of spending the holidays in the manner to which they were accustomed." Nevertheless, in April 1914 finance minister Bark could report that since the campaign began, 416 village assemblies had voted to close the local grog shops. The villages responded to the war on alcoholism quite differently than the cities.

With its constantly shifting political alignments, the Duma was unable to produce a stable majority. After a sharp encounter between the Octobrist N.P. Shubinsky and Paul Miliukov, the Duma voted to expel [temporarily] the Kadet leader, but it failed by three votes to obtain Shubinsky's expulsion. The Progressist A.I. Konovalov resigned from the presidium; he was replaced as vice-chairman of the Duma (by a vote of 303-11) by the Octobrist A.D. Protopopov.

In one of its final sessions, held behind closed doors, the Duma fully approved the new military program. The emperor responded by charging Rodzianko "to convey to the State Duma My sincere expression of pleasure at the Duma's patriotic resolution in releasing the credits for the defense of our country."

Although Goremykin followed Kokovtsov's policy and defended the use of the Polish language in municipal government affairs in the Kingdom of Poland, the State Council rejected the bill for a second time. The Council also rejected a proposal to establish the zemstvo at the district level. The conflicting moods of the two chambers made it ever more difficult to obtain new legislation. The assistant minister of education, Baron Taube, told the Duma that "ours is truly a time of transition which makes it quite inadvisable to draft organic statutes . . . . Regardless of the composition of the government, given the present combination and constellation of forces in the State Duma and State Council, this law cannot pass." (Voices on the left replied: "Thank you for the admission. That is correct.") *Novoe vremia* recalled Stolypin's last speeches on the "magic spell" that had been cast over legislation and the need for a tracheotomy.

The Duma completed its session on 14 June. In departing it adopted "until a time certain" the so-called Godnev amendment which, appended to the government's instructions, forbade the various ministers to use their own discretion in disbursing any unexpended funds in their budgets. When the State Council rejected the amendment, the leftist press insisted that the budget therefore had been rejected. However, the instructions were published without the Duma's amendment, and there the matter ended. The State Council recessed on 30 June 1914.

ON THE EVE

The first half of 1914 passed rather quietly on the international front. Much was written about the misadventures of Prince William of Wied, who was designated Prince of Albania but who failed to win the support of the Albanians themselves.[50] Parliamentary elections in France were fought on the issue of the three-year term of military service, and the socialists enjoyed great success. Nevertheless, President Poincaré refused to empower the opponents of the new military law. After an unsuccessful experiment with the Ribot government (which was overthrown on the same day that it faced the Chamber of Deputies), Poincaré appointed as prime minister the Independent Socialist René Viviani. A diplomatic politician, Viviani satisfied the left by promising to study the ways to replace the three-year conscription, and in the interim the law remained in effect. Caillaux, the potential leader of the left majority, was eclipsed temporarily. His wife was on trial for murdering the editor of *Figaro* because he had printed some personal letters that her husband had sent her. The Irish question hung ominously over England. Irish home rule was scheduled to take effect in the spring of 1914, but the Ulster Protestants were preparing for armed resistance. The British officer corps was openly resentful at the thought of marching against the "loyal" subjects of Ulster in behalf of the "Irish separatists."

Meanwhile Austro-Russian relations remained strained. Early in 1914 Austrian authorities began an investigation of pro-Russian propaganda in Marmarosh-Siget (in the Carpathian Rus) and Lvov. Count V.A. Bobrinsky, a member of the State Duma, went to Marmarosh-Siget to appear as a defense witness. (Some of the accused were acquitted.) Ukrainians in Austrian Galicia officially celebrated the centenary of the birth of the great national poet Taras Shevchenko, while in Russia they attempted to turn the celebration into a protest against Russian rule. Newspapers in St. Petersburg reported that Ukrainian separatists—Mazeppists[51] as they were called by their opponents—had even demonstrated with banners proclaiming "Long Live Austria." However, the governor of Kiev, N.I. Sukovkin, denied those reports.

On the 2nd of June the emperor and the entire imperial family journeyed to Constanza where they were the guests of the Rumanian royal family. (Crown Prince Ferdinand, his wife, and son had visited Russia in March.) Rumors persisted that an engagement was in the offing between Grand Duchess Olga Nikolaevna and Rumania's young Prince Karol.

On 15/28 June 1914 in the Bosnian capital of Sarajevo terrorists assassinated the heir to the Austrian throne, Archduke Franz Ferdinand. The archduke was regarded as one who

avored the transformation of the Danubian monarchy into a
rialistic (Germano-Hungarian-Slavic) state, a policy that depended on Austria's continued expansion into the Balkans,
even at Russia's expense. German and especially Hungarian
nationalists had little regard for him. "Russian opinion did not
number the late archduke among the friends of Russia," wrote
Novoe vremia, "but it can feel nothing but deep sorrow over
his tragic end and bitter indignation for the assassins whose
blind fanaticism leads them to spread death left and right."

The emperor sent his condolences to the aged Emperor
Franz Joseph, and grand dukes, ministers, and other prominent officials paid their respects to the Austrian minister [to
Bucharest], Count Czernin. As early as 18 June, however,
Novoe vremia warned of the outbreak of a "very dangerous
campaign" against Serbia. Even though both of the appre-
hended assassins were Austrian subjects, the Austro-Hungarian
press accused Serbia of having organized the crime. Serbs living in Bosnia were arrested, demonstrations were staged, and
Serbian shops were looted by mobs. Those efforts to use passions inflamed by the archduke's murder in support of Austrian aims in the Balkans were greatly resented in Russia.

During those troubled days, Nicholas Hartwig, the Russian
minister to Belgrade, died suddenly (28 June/11 July) in the
office of the Austrian minister to Serbia. His death was a great
blow to the Serbs, who rightly considered him their ardent
champion. Meanwhile, the Serbian government moved very
cautiously, even to the point of prohibiting demonstrations
against the Bosnian pogroms against Serbs. Meanwhile Petersburg clung to the hope that Germany would exert a restrain-
ing influence on Austria.

THE GREAT STRIKE OF JULY 1914

By the beginning of July the "evil of the day" in Russia was
the labor unrest that was reaching threatening proportions. A
strike in the Baku oil fields had been in progress for about a
month. The Social Democratic press in the capital called on
the workers to support their comrades in Baku. On 3 July a
demonstration took place outside the Putilov Works. The police dispersed the assembly, but several policemen were injured by stones, and nine workers were wounded. Protest

demonstrations began on the following day. Both the Social
Democrats and the Socialist Revolutionaries issued proclama
tions summoning the workers to battle. The 6th of July was a
Sunday; on the 7th the strike continued and grew even more
militant. Over 100,000 workers were striking in St. Peters
burg, and the movement was spreading to Moscow and Reval
In the workers' quarters in Petersburg trolley service came to
a halt; the demonstrators tore up streets and used the stones
to bombard the police from windows. Those events coincided
with the arrival of the French president and, as Poincaré noted
in his memoirs, Grand Duke Nicholas Nikolaevich told him
that he supposed that the Germans had organized the strike
in order to spoil the Franco-Russian meeting.

Throughout the 8th of July the rioters attacked street cars
200 of the 500 cars in the city were damaged. Only the govern
ment-owned factories were operating, and on the 9th they too
came to a halt. Workers felled telegraph poles along the Pri
morsky Railway and threw them across the tracks. Only 40
street cars were running. But then during the night of the 9th
the police arrested a group of strike leaders in the offices of
Pravda. The [Bolshevik] newspaper, *Trudovaia pravda*, was
closed, the printing presses sealed, and from that moment the
movement began to break up.

The foreign press made the disturbances appear worse than
they really were: Franco-Russian celebrations went on in the
center of the city unhindered by the chaos in the outskirts
(President Poincaré visited the capital on the 8th.) On the
10th the government decreed a lock-out at all factories be
cause of the strikes. Then street car traffic was restored every
where except in the workers' residential areas. The strikes con
tinued to spread through the provinces, nonetheless, and espe
cially to Riga and Nikolaev.

President Poincaré remained in Russia from the 7th to the
10th of July. The emperor met him at Kronstadt, and he
stayed in the Alexander Palace at Peterhof as a guest of the
imperial family. Military reviews were staged at Krasnoe Selo
on 9 and 10 July. In keeping with tradition the leaders ex
changed speeches testifying to their mutual friendship and
dedication to the cause of peace. On the evening of 10/23 Ju
ly the French squadron put to sea.

On that same evening Prince V.P. Meshchersky died at Tsarskoe Selo. Although he was 75 years old, he had remained active to the very end. In June he had his last lengthy conversation with the emperor, who always listened to Meshchersky's views even though he often disagreed with him.

On the following morning, 11/24 July, the foreign ministry received a cable from Belgrade: During the previous evening, the Austrian minister had presented the Serbian government with an ultimatum containing demands that were clearly unacceptable to a sovereign state.

CHAPTER THIRTEEN

1. *Russkaia mysl*, April 1908. (Oldenburg's note)
Dmitry Dmitrievich Protopopov (1856-) was active in zemstvo affairs in the province of Samara; he joined the Kadet Party, was elected to the First Duma and subsequently was barred from elective office for signing the Vyborg manifesto.

2. For example, the agenda of the plenary session of the State Duma on 1 January 1908 included bills on the management of the Church of Christ's Resurrection in St. Petersburg, the establishment of an instructorship in Lettish at the Veiversk Teachers Academy, the redesignation of the military governor's title in the districts of Akmolinsk and Semipalatinsk, and other similar measures. (Oldenburg's note)

3. For instance, if the norm for a given district were established at 300 desiatins, all owners of land in excess of that voted directly for their electors. All landowners with less than 300 desiatins gathered in an electoral assembly. Thus, 500 small landowners whose holdings totaled 3,000 desiatins would elect 10 representatives [to the provincial electoral assembly]. (Oldenburg's note)

4. *Nasha zhizn* [Our Life] was the title of two papers published during the revolutionary period: a left-wing Kadet daily published in St. Petersburg from November 1904 to July 1906, and the daily published by the Bolshevik central committee in Petersburg from October to December 1905. *Tovarishch* had no formal party affiliation but usually expressed the line of the Left Kadets and frequently carried articles by Mensheviks; it appeared daily in St. Petersburg from March 1906 to January 1908. *Pravda*, a Menshevik monthly dealing with art, literature, and social questions, was published in Moscow in 1904-1906. With the relaxation of censorship dozens of new publications appeared, some in only a few editions before disappearing. *Dni*, apparently, was one of those.

5. The provincial boards consisted of the governor and vice-governor, the provincial marshal of the nobility, the provincial manager of the state treasury, the state prosecutor, the chief of the provincial capital, the chairman of the provincial zemstvo council, and one of the electors of the provincial zemstvo. (Oldenburg's note)

6. The order of the original text, Vol. II, p. 9, is revised slightly to form this paragraph.

7. General Michael Hasenkampf, garrison commander of the St. Petersburg military district, protested to Stolypin that "the execution of petty thieves among the scum of the streets not only weakens the dreadful impact of the death penalty but also implies that the government answers terror only with terror." But Stolypin replied (10 November 1908): "I cannot agree with you. The robberies and violence which all revolutionary parties countenanced in 1905 now have become general

degenerate acts and must be extirpated without mercy." (Oldenburg's note)

Soviet historians usually refer to Stolypin's ministry as "the years of reaction." According to Soviet figures, between 1907 and 1909 tsarist courts imprisoned 26,000 political offenders and condemned 5,086 to death. *Sovetskaia istoricheskaia entsiklopediia*, 13:564.

8. "Sedition will be uprooted," Klingenberg added, "only when the revolutionary labor organizations are opposed by counter-revolutionary workers organizations, whatever their mottoes." (Oldenburg's note)

9. The political composition of the delegates was: 33 rightists, 34 moderates, 44 Octobrists, 4 Peaceful Reconstructionists, and 10 Kadets. (Oldenburg's note)

10. A professor of legal history and philosophy, Prince Eugene Nikolaevich Trubetskoy (1863-1920) deserted the Kadet Party in 1906 to help found the Party of Peaceful Reconstruction. *Slovo* was the official organ of that party.

11. In Moscow in the first curia Octobrists received 2,100 votes, Kadets 1,800, and rightists 400; in the second curia the Kadets received 16,000 votes, Octobrists 6,000, leftists around 3,000, and rightists 2,000.

In St. Petersburg the Octobrists received 1,000, the Kadets 800, and rightists 300 votes in the first curia; in the second curia the Kadets led with 20,000 votes, followed by the Octobrists with 9,000, the left with 8,000, and the right with 4,500. (Oldenburg's note)

For a detailed description of the election see Alfred Levin, *The Third Duma: Election and Profile* (Archon, 1973).

12. The following is the original composition of the Third Duma by political affiliation:

Rightists	51	(11%)
[Russian] Nationalists	26	(6%)
Moderate Rightists	70	(16%)
Octobrists	154	(35%)
Progressists	28	(6%)
Kadets	54	(11%)
Polish Kolo	11	(2%)
Polish-Lithuanians	7	(2%)
Muslims	8	(2%)
Trudoviks	14	(3%)
Social Democrats	19	(4%)

Thus there were 147 rightists, 154 centrists, and 141 leftists in a total of 442 deputies. Later, some changes occurred, especially among the Octobrists whose numbers decreased. (Oldenburg's note. Adapted to tabular form)

13. Representatives of the workers parties chose their electors in conventions. The Social Democrats commanded majorities in each of these conventions. Since the law required the election of one deputy from this curia and since all of the worker-electors, except those appointed by the party, refused to be candidates for the Duma, even the conservative provincial assemblies had no choice but to elect Social Democrats to the Duma. (Oldenburg's note)

14. For bibliographic references to the proceedings of the Third State Duma see above Volume 2, Chapter 12, note 10.

15. Nicholas Alekseevich Khomiakov (1850-1925) was the son of A.S. Khomiakov (1804-1860), a famous Slavophile ideologist, philosopher, and theologian. N.A. Khomiakov served in the ministry of agriculture and was active in the zemstvo movement. He was elected to the State Council in 1906 and then, as an Octobrist, was elected to the Second, Third, and Fourth Dumas. He served in the Red Cross with Denikin's forces during the Russian civil war and died in Yugoslavia.

16. The presidium of the Third Duma consisted of N.A. Khomiakov (chairman), Prince V.M. Volkonsky and Baron A.F. Meyendorf (vice-chairmen), Professor I.P. Sozonovich (secretary), and G.G. Zamyslovsky (senior assistant to the secretary). (Oldenburg's note)

17. Personal correspondence exchanged by Nicholas and Stolypin between 1906 and 1911 is reproduced in the *Krasnyi arkhiv*, 5: 102-28 and 30: 80-88.

18. Stolypin advised Guchkov that his remarks might better have been made privately to the emperor. Guchkov's publicity-seeking speech offended Nicholas and the imperial family, inspired their distrust and contempt, and reduced his political effectiveness. On the other hand, Guchkov probably was expressing widespread civilian and military dissatisfaction over the organization of the armed forces. Cf. Hosking, *Constitutional Experiment*, p. 79.

19. On 20 May 1908 an imperial ukaz subordinated the Finnish administration to the council of ministers, and the government began to consider other measures to revise the legislative relations between Finland and the empire. The Octobrists and the right worked hand in glove with Stolypin and the government to destroy Finnish autonomy. Nationalism and constitutionalism motivated the Octobrists. They regarded the empire as an indivisible union and could not tolerate Finland's semi-autonomous status. Furthermore, they wanted to subject the Finnish administration and legislature to the council of ministers and the Russian legislature. Before these revisions took place, Finland's administration and Diet were subject to the crown, because of the personal union in which the Russian emperor was the grand duke of Finland. Ibid., pp. 108-11; J.H. Hodgson, "Finland's Position in the Russian Empire, 1905-10," *Journal of Central European Affairs*, 20 (1960), 158-73.

20. The author is mistaken, for the government did obtain the credits necessary to begin the naval construction program. The State Council approved the credits rejected by the Duma. Therefore, when the previous year's budget came into force (in accord with the Fundamental Laws), funds were reallocated within the naval budget to provide for new ship construction. The Duma refused the credits because it questioned the naval administration's ability to use the money effectively and because it doubted whether the navy had developed a coordinated strategic plan. The Duma was right on both points, and the navy stumbled into and bungled its way through World War I.

21. For the disposition of the others see above, Volume 2, Chapter IX, note 53.

22. The ministry subsequently permitted women already admitted as auditors to complete their courses. Admission quotas for Jews were restored in the fall of 1907. (Oldenburg's note)

23. *Golos Moskvy*, published daily in Moscow, was the official organ of the Union of October 17 from December 1906 to June 1915.

24. Michael Lermontov (1814-1841) ranks second to Pushkin as Russia's finest lyric poet, and his dramas and prose greatly affected the development of modern Russian literature. In 1837 Lermontov published *The Death of a Poet*, a poem inspired by Pushkin's death following a duel. The poem was an indictment of the bureaucratic empire and its courtiers, and it led to his arrest and exile.

Alexander Pushkin (1799-1837), Russia's greatest poet and master of prose fiction and drama, was a romantic rebel. His works satirized the pillars of the old regime—serfdom, autocracy, censorship—and its highest officials, including Tsar Alexander I. Banished from the capital in 1824, Pushkin was pardoned in 1826, and Tsar Nicholas I offered to serve as his personal censor. Under this arrangement Pushkin composed a few "straight" pieces, but his rebelliousness no less than his genius was irrepressible.

25. Oldenburg describes this conference, held in 1902, in Volume 2, p. 52.

26. Symbolism and its initial lack of acceptance are discussed in Volume 1, pp. 142 and 217-18, notes 3-4.

27. Percy Pinkerton has translated *Sanin* into English; modern readers probably will wonder what all the fuss was about.

Michael Artsybashev (1878-1927) was the most sensational representative of the revolutionary realist tradition. *Sanin* was followed in 1911-12 by *At the Brink*. They were widely read, avidly discussed, and roundly condemned as immoral works without literary merit. Artsybashev preached the artificiality of civilization and the reality of sex and death. His message: Live your own life. After the revolution, Bolshevik censors, far more prudish than their predecessors, proscribed his works, and in 1923 the Soviet government expelled him from the USSR.

28. HMS *Dreadnought*, the first of a new class of warships, was commissioned at Portsmouth, England in December 1906. The dreadnought concept was that of a ship bearing all big guns—a swift platform for the heaviest naval artillery, superior to anything then afloat. Thus the launching of *Dreadnought* also launched a revolution in naval technology, and since every nation was starting from scratch, England's historic naval superiority was threatened. A fully illustrated survey covering all nations is *Dreadnought: A History of the Modern Battleship* by Richard Hough (Macmillan, 1964, 1975).

29. Sir Arthur Nicolson (1849-1928) entered the British foreign service in 1870 and held various junior positions abroad until 1895. In that year he was appointed minister to Tangier and in 1904-1905 served as British ambassador in Madrid. He was England's delegate to the Algeçiras Conference in 1905. He held the post of ambassador to Russia from 1906 to 1910 and then served as under-secretary of state for foreign affairs until his retirement in 1916. Nicolson and the British foreign minister, Sir Edward Grey, believed that Russia, though weak, was essential in a partnership to contain German ambitions.

30. The British prime minister made this remark in French on the occasion of the 1906 congress in London of the International World Union

of Parliamentarians. Sir Henry Campbell-Bannerman (1836-1908) first entered parliament in 1868 and became the recognized leader of the Liberal Party shortly after the turn of the century. He was elected prime minister in 1905 and died in office.

31. Besides the three major diplomatic collections—*Documents diplomatiques française, Die Grosse Politik,* and the *British Documents on the Origins of the War*—the basic published documentation on the Anglo-Russian rapprochement includes: S. Pashukanis, ed., "K istorii anglorusskogo soglashenia 1907 g." [On the History of the Anglo-Russian Agreement of 1907], *Krasnyi arkhiv,* 69-70 (1935), 3-39; I. Reisner, ed., "Anglo-russkaia konventsiia 1907 g. i razdel Aftanistana," [The Anglo-Russian Convention of 1907 and the Partition of Afghanistan], ibid. 10 (1925), 54-66; A.P. Izvolsky, *Au service de la Russie . . . Correspondance diplomatique, 1906-1911,* 2 vols. (Paris, 1937); *Graf Benckendorffs diplomatischer Schriftwechsel* [Count Benckendorff's Diplomatic Correspondence], ed. B. de Siebert, 3 vols., revised edition (Berlin, Leipzig, 1928); Baron de Taube, *La politique russe*; Viscount Grey of Fallodon [Sir Edward Grey], *Twenty-five Years, 1892-1916,* 2 vols. (London, 1925); G.M. Trevelyan, *Grey of Fallodon* (London, 1937); and Harold Nicolson, *Portrait of a Diplomatist: Being the Life of Sir Arthur Nicolson, First Lord Carnock* (London, 1930).

The major special studies include: Briton Cooper Busch, *Britain and the Persian Gulf, 1894-1914* (University of California Press, 1967); William L. Langer, "Russia, the Straits Question, and the European Powers, 1904-1908," *English Historical Review,* 44 (1929), 59-85; John B. Wolf, *The Diplomatic History of the Bagdad Railroad* (University of Missouri Press, 1936); and two previously cited monographs, Monger, *The End of Isolation* and Kazemzadeh, *Russia and Britain in Persia.*

32. In March 1907 the French government helped the Japanese float a large loan in France. Paris made the arrangements when the Russians indicated that their own discussions with Tokyo were proceeding satisfactorily. On 10 June 1907 France and Japan concluded an agreement that extended most-favored-nation treatment to their nationals in Japan and Indochina. They mutually pledged to respect China's independence and integrity and the open door. Finally, they pledged their mutual support to assure peace and security in areas under their sovereignty, protection, or occupation. The text of the agreement can be found in the *DDF,* ser. 2, XI, no. 24.

33. The Russo-Japanese agreement consisted of four conventions, one secret, concluded in June and July 1907. One regulated the Manchurian railway, the second dealt with fisheries, and the third was a treaty of commerce and navigation. On 30 July 1907 representatives of the two governments signed a secret political convention that established their spheres of influence in northeastern Asia. They defined their spheres of interest in Manchuria; Russia promised Japan a free hand in Korea and in return Japan recognized Russia's special interest in Outer Mongolia and promised not to interfere there. The texts of these agreements are reproduced in Victor A. Yakontoff, *Russia and the Soviet Union in the Far East* (New York, 1931), pp. 374-76.

34. For the text of the "Anglo-Russian Convention relating to Persia, Afghanistan, and Thibet, 1907" see the *British Documents*, III, pp. 618-20. The specific "Agreements" are given on pages 352 (Tibet), 502-4 (Afghanistan).

35. *Russkaia mysl*, January 1908. (Oldenburg's note)

36. Sir Edward Grey (1862-1933) served as British foreign minister from December 1905 until December 1916. He was a strong advocate of cooperation with Russia as a check on Germany and thus was a key figure in the formation and strengthening of the ties of the Triple Entente.

CHAPTER FOURTEEN

1. The Ukaz or Law of 9 November 1906 is discussed above in text and notes, Volume 2, pp. 225-26.

2. Article 87 of the Fundamental Laws empowered the government to enact emergency legislation when the Duma and State Council were not in session. Such enactments had to be submitted to the consideration of the legislature at its next session. The Law of 9 November was on the agenda of the Second Duma, but that turbulent assembly was prorogued before the law reached the floor. Therefore approval of Stolypin's agrarian reform was postponed to the Third Duma. The text of Article 87 is given above, Volume 2, p. 311, note 41.

3. The land settlement commissions (land commissions) were created by the Ukaz of 4 March 1906 (*Polnoe sobranie zakonov*, 3rd ser., No. 26,871). Basic studies on the conception and implementation of the Stolypin reform include: Launcelot Owen, *The Russian Peasant Movement, 1906-1917* (London, 1937); G.P. Pavlovsky, *Agricultural Russia on the Eve of the Revolution* (London, 1930); Lazar Volin, *A Century of Russian Agriculture: From Alexander II to Khrushchev* (Harvard University Press, 1970); W.E. Mosse, "Stolypin's Villages," *Slavonic and East European Review*, 43 (1964-1965), 257-74; George L. Yanet, "The Concept of the Stolypin Land Reform," *Slavic Review*, 23 (1964), 275-93; Robinson, *Rural Russia*, and Gurko, *Features and Figures of the Past.*

4. Each commission consisted of the marshal of the nobility and the chairman of the district board, indispensable members of the agricultural ministry, a member of the district court, the local zemskii nachalnik, and a representative from the obshchina being reorganized by the commission. (Oldenburg's note)

Yaney's investigation confirmed that the land commissioners generally approached their task with energy, initiative, and pragmatism. "Stolypin Land Reform," 292-93.

5. By the beginning of 1911 the land commissions employed 770 chief surveyors, 1,660 surveyors, and 2,670 assistant surveyors. (Oldenburg's note)

6. No new applications were accepted after the war broke out, and only the reorganizations then in progress continued. By 1 May 1916 the strips of 1,358,000 households had been consolidated—some 13,833,000

desiatins, representing eight percent of the total area in peasant hands. (Oldenburg's note)

7. Sergei Illiodorovich Shidlovsky (1861-1922) was a prominent landowner, liberal zemstvo leader, and since 1905 a Left-Octobrist. He was a board member of the Peasant Bank from 1899 to 1905 and served briefly in 1905 as the director of a department in the main agricultural administration. S.I. Shidlovsky (not to be confused with N.V. Shidlovsky, the state councillor) subsequently led the Progressive Bloc in the Fourth Duma. He was a member of the original Provisional Government and the Pre-Parliament of 1917. He abandoned Russia in 1920 and died in Berlin in 1922, leaving an important memoir that was published posthumously—*Vospominaniia* (2 vols., Berlin [1923]). See also by Shidlovsky, "The Imperial Duma and Land Settlement," *Russian Review*, 1 (1912), 18-26.

8. *Zaria* was a Social-Democratic scientific-political monthly published in Stuttgart in 1901-1902 by the editorial board of *Iskra*.

9. L.I. Petrazhitsky (1867-), an internationally recognized authority on civil law and legal philosophy, was a member of the Kadet Party and a deputy in the First Duma.

10. Geoffrey Hosking concluded that the Stolypin majority, created by the Law of 3 June, was an alliance that held together for only one issue, the agrarian reform. The keystone of the alliance was the defense of private property and its extension to the peasantry. The motive, of course, was to defuse the revolution. *Constitutional Experiment*, pp. 72-73.

11. The Law of 9 November cleared both chambers essentially in its original form. Rightists in the State Council introduced several amendments to weaken the bill, but the Council understood that the emperor wanted the law passed and did so without change. The hottest debate occurred on Prince A.D. Obolensky's amendment to preserve the traditional communal character of landholding by transferring communal lands to family rather than individual ownership.

12. Baron Alois Lexa Aerenthal (1854-1912) represented Vienna as ambassador to Russia in 1899-1906. He already had served as secretary of the Austro-Hungarian embassy to Russia in 1878-1883 and 1888-1894. He held the post of foreign minister from 1906 until his death in 1912.

13. While German ambassador to Russia from October 1907 to August 1914, Pourtales (1853-1928) worked energetically among monarchist circles to loosen Russia's ties with its two democratic partners. When the war broke out in 1914, he returned to Berlin as counselor to the German foreign office and retired in July 1918. Prior to his appointment to St. Petersburg he had been the ambassador to The Hague (1899-1902) and Prussian minister to Munich (1902-1907).

14. The British government was under pressure from the public and Parliament to achieve more radical reforms in Macedonia than those agreed upon by the great powers. Grey's plan was to make the three Macedonian provinces practically autonomous. Izvolsky, who was eager to play a more active role in the Balkans, wanted to cooperate with the British. The meeting at Reval on 9-10 June 1908 verified the improved

state of Anglo-Russian relations but seemed even more ominous to Berlin. That was mainly because the British delegation included Sir Charles Hardinge, the permanent under-secretary of the foreign office, and the commanders of the British army and navy, General Sir John French and Admiral Sir John Fisher. The discussions covered Macedonia, Persia, Crete, and the Balkan railways and were summarized in Hardinge's report, *British Documents*, V, No. 195.

15. Abdul Hamid II came to power in 1876 in the aftermath of a reformist coup. In March 1877 he dissolved Turkey's first parliament, elected under the liberal constitution of 1876. He then ignored the constitution and devoted himself to the restoration of his absolute power.

16. The sultan retained his throne by convincing the revolutionaries that he was a benevolent patriarch who had been led astray by evil advisors. He was deposed, however, in April 1909 and exiled to Saloniki where he died in 1918.

17. No minutes or other record was kept of the day-long Buchlau conference. What passed between the two foreign ministers has been a subject of controversy ever since. In sum, Aerenthal regarded the meeting as the final step that cleared the way for the annexation of Bosnia and Herzegovina, which he interpreted as a local matter. Izvolsky considered their meeting a stage in the negotiation of a "European question" that required the participation of all the powers before any definitive action became possible. Although both ministers were in an adventuresome mood, Izvolsky's position was well-founded in that the general European character of the disposition of the Ottoman Empire was a firmly established international principle. The conflicting interpretations are analyzed in detail in Bernadotte E. Schmitt, *The Annexation of Bosnia, 1908-1909* (Cambridge University Press, 1937), pp. 20-26; and in Luigi Albertini, *The Origins of the War of 1914*, 3 vols. (Oxford University Press, 1952-57), I, 206-10.

18. Apparently neither Izvolsky nor the tsar was aware of these promises at first. Nicholas wrote to his mother on 21 October 1908: "You will understand what an unpleasant surprise this is, and what an embarrassing position we are in." "Iz perepiski Nikolaia II i Marii Feodorovni, 1907-1910 gg." [From the Letters of Nicholas II and Maria Feodorovna, 1907-1910], *Krasnyi arkhiv*, 50-51 (1932), 185-86.

19. Izvolsky was making a leisurely tour of the European capitals to sound out the governments on a general conference. He arrived in Paris on 4 October and there received a letter from Aerenthal announcing that the annexation would be proclaimed on the 7th. The Austrian announcement actually came on the 6th. Izvolsky received another letter in Paris. That one, from St. Petersburg, informed him of the indignation of the Russian public and of Stolypin's complete disapproval of his policy.

20. Turkey insisted on compensation for its loss of territory. In February 1909 Austria-Hungary paid a large sum and made other financial considerations. Thereupon Turkey recognized the annexation. Meanwhile however, the Turkish government completely ignored Aerenthal in its negotiation with Bulgaria. As a result Izvolsky was able to offer a compromise and earn from Bulgaria the gratitude that Aerenthal had

sought for himself. Russia renounced forty years of the 1878 indemnity and allowed the Turks to capitalize the remaining 34 annuities at four percent. That was Izvolsky's only victory in the annexation crisis.

21. The Serbs wanted to have their fate decided by the great powers. Aerenthal insisted that Belgrade had to deal with Vienna directly. He refused to permit mediation by the powers and was even less willing to allow Russia to serve as Serbia's protector. In March 1909 he informed the Serbs that unless they recognized the Austro-Turkish agreement, he would issue an ultimatum and march on Serbia. At the same time he advised Izvolsky to exert pressure on Belgrade. If Russia would not give in, Aerenthal threatened to make public the secret protocol of 1878 and Izvolsky's note of July 1908. Publication of those documents would have been disastrous for Russian prestige, since they indicated that Russia was willing to sell out the Balkan Slavs in return for access to the Straits.

22. The author of the famous demarche of 21 March 1909 was Alfred von Kiderlen-Waechter who served as acting secretary for foreign affairs from November 1908 to March 1909, during Schoen's absence because of illness. The text of the note is published in *Grosse Politik*, XXVI (2), No. 9460.

23. To his mother Nicholas wrote that there was no alternative but to "swallow our pride." He believed, he said, that the sacrifice would be justified "if it will save Serbia from being crushed by Austria." *Krasnyi arkhiv*, 50-51 (1932), 188.

24. Alexis Alexandrovich Lopukhin (1864-) became a public prosecutor in the ministry of justice in 1886. In 1892 he was assigned by the ministry to supervise the activities of the Moscow Okhrana. That job introduced him to Zubatov and the efforts of the police to infiltrate the revolutionary movement. Later, as public prosecutor in Kharkov, Lopukhin's analysis of agrarian riots and pogroms in the Ukraine favorably impressed Plehve, who in 1902 made Lopukhin the director of the empire's police department. It was Lopukhin who with Plehve's approval permitted Azef to join the SR Battle Organization. Lopukhin was forced to resign after the assassination of Grand Duke Sergei Alexandrovich in 1905.

25. After Gershuni's arrest, Azef became undisputed chief of the Battle Organization; for other details see Volume 2, Chapter VIII, notes 12 and 21.

Boris Viktorovich Savinkov (1879-1925) was a prominent terrorist and member of the SR central committee. He was in charge of the groups that assassinated Plehve and Grand Duke Sergei in 1903 and 1905. In the fall of 1907 he attempted to revive the Battle Organization in order to assassinate the tsar and "rehabilitate the honor of the terror." He assembled twelve trustworthy old revolutionaries, but three subsequently proved to be traitors, and the last campaign of the Battle Organization collapsed.

Savinkov energetically supported the Russian war effort in 1914-1917 and then served as assistant war minister in the Provisional Government. He became involved in the abortive Kornilov putsch and was dismissed. After October he actively fought the Bolsheviks and in July

1918 organized the Yaroslavl revolt. He furnished the weapon that Dora Kaplan used to wound Lenin in 1918. Savinkov eventually fled to Western Europe, but in 1924 he returned secretly to the USSR and was arrested. The Soviet government sentenced him to death but then commuted his sentence to ten years at hard labor. In 1925 he reportedly took his own life. In an epilogue to Savinkov's *Memoirs of a Terrorist* translator Joseph Shaplen provides an account of this final chapter in his life.

Under the pseudonym of V. Ropshin, Savinkov wrote poetry and several novels of which the most important are *Pale Horse* (1909) and *What Never Happened* (1913). The former portrays the confusion that Azef's betrayal created among the revolutionaries.

26. Vladimir Lvovich Burtsev (1862-1942) pioneered the study of the history of the Russian revolutionary movement. After the 1905 revolution, he became particularly interested in how the Okhrana penetrated revolutionary organizations. He began to cultivate sources among the police. Among the valuable general information that he acquired was the clear indication that a police agent had penetrated to the very heart of the Socialist Revolutionary Party. That set him off on his long search to discover the traitor, and it eventually led him to the astonishing conclusion that the agent could be none other than Azef. Burtsev had no definite proof, however, until Lopukhin finally admitted to him that "I know nobody of the name of 'Raskin,' but I have seen the engineer, Ievno Aseff, several times." (Nikolaevsky, *Aseff the Spy*, p. 21.)

As a student in the 1880s, Burtsev was active in the Populist movement and was arrested and exiled in 1885. He escaped and in 1889 settled briefly in Geneva where he and others published the journal *Svobodnaia Rossiia* [Free Russia]. In 1891 he moved to London and began a systematic study of the revolutionary movement; in 1896-1897 he published his history, *Za sto let* [In the Course of a Hundred Years]. Arrested by the British police, Burtsev spent about eighteen months in prison. In 1900 he left England and began to publish the journal *Byloe* [The Past] first in Switzerland and then in France; he was deported from both countries, and *Byloe* temporarily ceased publication in 1904. Burtsev then returned to Russia in 1905-1907. Abroad once again, he resumed publication of *Byloe* (1908-1912). During this period, Burtsev exposed Azef and several other double agents, including Roman Malinovsky, a prominent Social Democrat.

Burtsev returned to Russia after the World War began, and in 1917 started a new journal, *Obshchee delo* [Common Affairs]. After the Bolshevik coup, he moved his journal to Paris and for several years participated actively in anti-Soviet organizations.

27. He lived abroad under an assumed name for about ten years and died of a kidney disease in Berlin in the spring of 1918. (Oldenburg's note)

28. The Senate later reduced his sentence to residence in exile. (Oldenburg's note)

According to Nikolaevsky, Stolypin was determined to make an example of Lopukhin in order to impress on other officials what would happen if they betrayed their trust. The tsar sanctioned the trial, which was certain to cause a sensation, because Nicholas never forgave Lopukhin for disclosing in January 1906 that the police were printing and distributing broadsides urging loyal Russians to participate in pogroms against Jews and socialists. Lopukhin's case was processed in record time. "On Stolypin's special instructions, Lopukhin was prevented both at the preliminary inquiry and in court from making his most important statement, which would have accused his opponents in the Police Department, and in particular Stolypin himself, of being chiefly responsible for Aseff's double game." *(Aseff the Spy*, pp. 280-81.) Nikolaevsky's evidence included the police department files for 1909-1910 and the papers of the examining magistrate who conducted the inquiry into the Lopukhin affair. According to Nikolaevsky, neither Lopukhin's testimony before the extraordinary commission of inquiry of the Provisional Government nor his memoirs *(Vospominaniia*, Moscow, 1923) are completely reliable.

29. Brief sketches of these SR assassins are provided above, Volume 2: Gershuni, Chapter VIII, notes 12 and 13; Kaliaev, Chapter X, note 17; and Schweizer, Chapter X, note 43. For Savinkov see this chapter, note 25.

30. Azef, also known occasionally as Lipchenko, appeared as the character "Lippenchenko" in Andrei Bely's novel *Petersburg*. (Oldenburg's note)

31. The author has stretched the facts to defend the Okhrana's use of Azef, for it was by no means the one-way street that is suggested. Although Azef was not the best judge of his own actions, he attempted to justify himself to Burtsev in a private meeting in Frankfurt in 1912: " 'I organized the assassination of Plehve, that of the Grand Duke Sergei . . .' —and with every new name his right hand dropped lower and lower like a scale when new weights are added to it—'And whom did I give up to the police? Only Sletoff, Lomoff, Vedenyapin . . .'—and as he mentioned these names he did not lower his left hand, but, on the contrary, raised it as if in illustration of the insignificance of his services to the police in comparison with those to the Revolution." And then he reproached Burtsev for exposing him: "If it had not been for you, I would have killed [the tsar] . . . ." Quoted by Nikolaevsky, *Aseff*, pp. 293-94.

32. Described as "one of the most brilliant studies ever penned of the world-thought of the Russian intelligentsia," a substantial part of *Vekhi* can be found in translation in Marshall Schatz and Judith Zimmerman, trans. and eds., "*Vekhi* (Signposts): A Collection of Articles on the Russian Intelligentsia," *Canadian Slavic Studies*, 2 (1968), 151-74, 291-310, 447-63; 3 (1969), 1-21; 4 (1970), 36-59, 183-98; and 5 (1971), 327-61. See also Leonard Schapiro, "The *Vekhi* Group and the Mystique of Revolution," *Slavonic and East European Review*, 34 (1955), 56-76.

33. Like Struve and Bulgakov, who also contributed to *Vekhi*, Nicholas Berdiaev (1874-1948) had once been a Marxist. Around the turn of the century, however, he abandoned Marx and developed his own nonconformist Orthodox Christianity. In 1899 he was exiled to northern Russia for criticizing the church for its subservience to the state. He continued his dissent as one of the founders and editors of *Novyi put*.

His attacks on the holy synod again led to his arrest and trial in 1914. After the revolution, Berdiaev was appointed professor of philosophy at Moscow University. Arrested twice for his attacks on Marxism, he finally was expelled from Russia in 1922. In 1924 he settled near Paris where he founded his own religious academy. He published several philosophical attacks on Marxism and Russian communism. See Nikolai P. Poltoratzky, "Berdiaev, Nikolai Aleksandrovich," *The Modern Encyclopedia of Russian and Soviet History* (hereinafter MERSH). (Gulf Breeze: Academic International Press, 1976-), Vol. 4, pp. 19-24.

34. Bulgakov's "Heroism and Asceticism" accused the intelligentsia of rejecting Christianity for a peculiar form of atheism, the religion of "man-Godhood," which envisioned the heroic Russian intelligent as the savior of mankind. Whereas Christ provided Christians an ideal or standard for self-examination, the intelligentsia hero had only his own ego projected in an heroic pose. The gulf between the intelligentsia and the people, Bulgakov explained, grew out of those conflicting attitudes toward religion.

Sergei Nikolaevich Bulgakov (1871-1944), the son of a priest, studied law and political economy. Originally a legal Marxist, he turned to the defense of Russian Orthodoxy around the turn of the century and in 1905 joined Berdiaev in founding *Novyi put.* Bulgakov became an ordained priest in 1918. In 1922 he was expelled by the Soviet government. He settled first in Prague and then in Paris, where he taught at the Russian Orthodox Theological Seminary and published several philosophic studies.

35. Michael Osipovich Gerzhenzon (1869-1925) was a prominent literary critic and historian and the editor of *Vekhi.*

36. Kistiakovsky, the least well-known of the *Vekhi* contributors, was a prominent figure in liberal intellectual and political circles.

37. Simon Ludvigovich Frank (1877-1950), recognized by his contemporaries as one of Russia's outstanding thinkers, was a professor of philosophy at Saratov and later at Moscow University.

38. Alexander Izgoev, a member of the Kadet Party, a prominent Kadet publicist, and frequent contributor to *Rech*, also was regarded as an outstanding thinker—until his participation in *Vekhi.*

39. Critics on the far left were even more caustic in their condemnation of *Vekhi.* Ekaterina Kuskovo wrote that "some contributors went so far as to ignore science and embrace the theology of the middle ages. They are probably the most harmless, for where would they find any followers in the twentieth century? If Peter of Amiens himself were to appear today, he could not rally five people for a crusade." (Oldenburg's note)

Because of its notoriety, *Vekhi* went through five editions in four months. The liberal response, mentioned by Oldenburg, was *Intelligentsia v Rossii* [The Intelligentsia in Russia] (St. Petersburg, 1909). Its contributors, besides Miliukov, included I.I. Petrunkevich, N.A. Gredeskul, M.M. Kovalevsky, M.I. Tugan-Baranovsky and others.

40. Alexander Suvorov (1730-1800), Imperial Russia's greatest general, inflicted crushing defeats on the Turks in 1789-1790 and in 1799 crossed the Alps in a brilliant campaign against the French.

Archbishop Anthony's letter, incidentally, was an unwelcome embarrassment to Struve and the other *Vekhi* contributors.

41. Oldenburg apparently meant that the authors did not follow their critiques to the *conservative* political conclusions that seemed implicit in them. The following statement then makes somewhat more sense.

42. In his memoirs Witte wrote: "I tore off Stolypin's mask and revealed how he wanted to limit the emperor's power in order to please the Duma majority." (Oldenburg's note)

43. *Krasnyi arkhiv*, 5 (1924), 120.

44. The Old Believers were Orthodox schismatics who refused to accept ritualistic reforms introduced into the Russian Orthodox Church in the middle of the seventeenth century. In 1901 an official survey set their number at slightly over two million, but unofficial sources estimated that the Old Believer population was closer to twenty million. Curtiss, *Church and State*, pp. 136-37.

45. Alexander Dmitrievich Protopopov (1866-1918), a very wealthy landowner in Simbirsk, was elected to the Third and Fourth Dumas as an Octobrist; he identified with the party's left wing. Protopopov was vice-chairman of the Duma in 1914-1916 and, through the influence of Rasputin, became the last minister of interior of the imperial government (September 1916-February 1917). He was executed by the Bolsheviks in 1918.

46. The Guchkovs are believed to have been Old Believers.

47. In the fall of 1909 in voting in St. Petersburg's second curia, N.N. Kutler won election to the Duma by polling only 12,500 votes. The quotation is from *Vestnik Evropy*, 1909, No. 11. (Oldenburg's note)

48. Reported in *Novoe vremia*, 3 October 1909. (Oldenburg's note)

CHAPTER FIFTEEN

1. The meeting occurred during the emperor's visit to France in 1901. The Imperial Rescript of 19 February 1911 marked the fiftieth anniversary of the Emancipation and provided a concise and thoughtful summary of the agrarian policy followed by the emperor throughout his reign: "I have adopted as our goal the fulfillment of the task set before us in 1861 to make the Russian peasant not only a free but also an economically viable landowner. Therefore, in addition to abolishing the system of mutual guarantees and the redemption payments, and besides expanding the activities of the Peasant Land Bank, I considered it timely, through the removal of the more basic restrictions on peasant rights, to facilitate their departure from the communes and their transition to *khutor* and *otrub* economies. With that in mind measures were introduced to provide the agricultural community with low-cost loans and to propagate agricultural improvements and knowledge." (Oldenburg's note)

"A consolidated farm upon which the peasant actually lived was called a *khutor*, while a similar holding cultivated by a family who still lived elsewhere (usually in the old house beside the village street) was called an *otrub.*" Robinson, *Rural Russia*, p. 236.

2. Russia and Italy shared a concern over Austro-Hungarian expansion in the Balkans. In addition, Italian foreign minister Tommaso Tittoni wanted to strengthen his country's position against the Habsburg Empire. In the fall of 1909 Nicholas paid a state visit to King Victor Emmanuel III. They met at Racconigi on 24 October 1909, and their foreign ministers drew up a top secret agreement which formed the basis of Russo-Italian cooperation in the Near East.

The Racconigi agreement committed each power to work to uphold the status quo in the Balkans; to support the principle of nationality and to exclude all foreign domination of the Balkan states; to employ common diplomatic action to oppose any move contrary to the preceding principles. Furthermore, they agreed not to enter into any new agreement affecting the Near East, beyond those already in existence, "without the participation of the other." And finally in the clincher, both powers agreed "to view with goodwill, the one the interests of Italy in Tripolitania and Cyrenaica, and the other the interests of Russia in the Straits Question." In 1911 Italy went to war with Turkey and as a result annexed Tripoli.

The text of the agreement can be found in *Un livre noir*, ed. René Marchand, 3 vols. (Paris, 1929-31), I, 357-58; and a detailed discussion in Albertini, *Origins of the War*, I, 306-11.

3. Izvolsky's daughter speaks of this episode in her introduction to her father's unfinished memoirs. (Oldenburg's note)

4. Sergei Dmitrievich Sazonov (1860-1927) entered the chancellery of the ministry of foreign affairs in 1883 but he brought only limited diplomatic experience to his new post. His foreign assignments included a few years as counselor of the embassy in London and Washington and head of the Russian legation at the Vatican (1906-1909). He became Izvolsky's assistant in 1909.

Sazonov offered several attractive qualities—affability, modesty, honesty, and lack of ambition—but he was also sickly, high-strung, mercurial, and too frequently impulsive. He was deeply religious, Orthodox and Russian to the core, and unswervingly loyal to the tsar. His first task as foreign minister, indeed the reason he was chosen, was to stabilize and redress the balance of Russia's foreign policy. In particular he was to repair the havoc of the Bosnian crisis by improving Russian relations with Berlin and Vienna.

Sazonov served as foreign minister until his resignation in July 1916. During the Russian Civil War, he represented various White organizations in Paris (1918-1920) and remained there as an emigre until his death.

Personal characterizations of Sazonov by his intimates include: Taube, *La Politique russe*, pp. 237, 248-49; and A.V. Nekliudov, *Diplomatic Reminiscences Before and During the World War, 1911-1917* (London, 1920), pp. 32-33. See also Sergei Sazonov, *Fateful Years, 1909-1916* (London, New York, 1928).

5. Germany recognized Russia's special interests in northern Persia and promised not to seek concessions there. The Russians promised to

seek a concession for a railway from Teheran to Khanikin, where it would be linked by a spur to the Bagdad Railway. If Russia failed to obtain the concession, Germany was free to seek it.

6. Sazonov's report apparently was inaccurate or incomplete, however. He told the tsar that the Bagdad Railway had not been discussed, and he failed to mention a Russian pledge (if it was given) not to support England in a hostile policy toward Germany. No minutes were kept of the ministers' meeting at Potsdam. Bethmann's report of the meeting differs from Sazonov's, and both differ considerably from the agreement drafted by Bethmann and sent to St. Petersburg on 15 November 1910. *Grosse Politik*, XXVII(2), nos. 10155 and 10159; S.D. Sazonov, "L'entrevue de Potsdam," *Un livre noir*, II, 331-34.

Before the Potsdam meeting, a special ministers' conference discussed the line to be followed. The ministers concluded that improved relations with Germany were essential but any commitments should be general in nature. To ensure Russia's economic preponderance in Persia, railways linking northern Persia to Russia were preferable to a Teheran-Khanikin link with the Bagdad Railway. For the minutes of this meeting of 15/28 October 1910 see "K istorii Potsdamskogo soglasheniia 1911 g." [On the History of the Potsdam Agreement of 1911], *Krasnyi arkhiv*, 58 (1933), 46-57.

7. It was the German who wanted the agreement in writing.

8. State Duma session of 2 March 1911. (Oldenburg's note)

9. The Entente powers had agreed in 1907 that the final agreement on the Bagdad Railway would be a four-power pact. The allies were obliged to inform one another of all negotiations with Germany on the question and to consult before concluding any agreement. Sazonov did keep London and Paris informed of the negotiation and communicated the final text of the agreement. The French, nevertheless, were miffed at what they regarded as a breach of the understanding in that Russia unilaterally had concluded an agreement with Germany. The British were no less upset because London felt that the Potsdam agreement weakened England's position in negotiations on the railway.

10. Sir George Buchanan (1854-1924) entered the diplomatic service in 1876 and held a series of junior positions in Rome, Tokyo, Vienna, Darmstadt, and Berlin. Then in 1904 he was designated minister to Sofia, a post that he held until 1908. He served as ambassador to St. Petersburg from 1910 until his expulsion by Soviet authorities in January 1918. He spent two years as ambassador to Rome and then retired to write his memoirs: *My Mission to Russia*, 2 vols. (London, New York, 1923).

11. *Novoe vremia*, 27 October 1910. (Oldenburg's note)

12. General Yuri Danilov gave a detailed explanation of these measures in his work, *Uchastie Rossii v mirovoi voine* [Russia's Role in the World War]. (Oldenburg's note)

General George Nikiforovich (Yuri) Danilov (1866-1937) served as quartermaster-general of the general staff from 1909 to 1914 and later as chief of staff to General Ruzsky. A French edition of his work is *La Russie dans la guerre mondiale 1914-1917* (Paris, 1927).

13. The four ships, all built in St. Petersburg, were the *Gangut, Petropavlovsk, Poltava*, and *Sevastopol*. Each had a displacement of 23,000 tons and main batteries of twelve 12-inch guns.

14. The "substance" of the convention was set forth in a secret treaty designed "to confirm and further develop the provisions of the Secret Treaty of June 17-30, 1907." The secret treaty of 1910 committed each power to non-interference in the other's sphere of influence. It stipulated that "in case these special interests should be threatened, the two governments will agree on the measures that may become necessary for the common action or mutual support in order to protect these interests." The treaty was kept secret from the United States and Germany but apparently confided, at least in general, to the British government. The text of the treaty, first published in the New York *American* on 17 April 1921, is given in Ken Shen Weigh, *Russo-Chinese Diplomacy*, pp. 137-38.

15. In a letter describing his Siberian journey Stolypin told the emperor that Siberia "is growing incredibly . . . in the last few months huge settlements, practically cities already, have sprung up." But he also foresaw problems as a result of transplanting the commune artificially into a country accustomed to private property. Private landownership had been overlooked and if precautions were not taken, Siberia would become "unconsciously and without direction, an enormous crudely democratic country capable of strangling European Russia." (Oldenburg's note)

16. In May 1911 a Mongolian delegation journeyed to Russia to appeal to the tsar to intervene against Chinese intrusions and the policy of assimilation, which Peking had been pursuing in Mongolia since 1906. The Russian minister at Peking protested in behalf of the Mongolians and notified the Chinese that Russia reserved the right to take whatever action seemed necessary to ensure the safety of the Mongolian frontier. The Chinese readily rescinded their aggressive policies and asked the Mongolians to recall their delegation from Petersburg and to urge Russia not to send troops into Mongolia. The Russians, however, were already on the way, and the opportunity was too good to miss. Within a short time the Chinese were distracted by the outbreak of revolution, and Russia was free to do as it pleased in Mongolia. Weigh, pp. 156-57.

17. According to Weigh, "there is every reason to believe . . . that the independence of Mongolia was initiated by the Russians and engineered by a few influential persons . . . ." The new government immediately hired 45 Russian officers and obtained large quantities of used weapons and ammunition to train and equip an army. The Russian government provided financial advisers and then a loan of two million rubles, guaranteed by Mongolia's mines. (The Mongolians used the money to build a temple.) With state finances under Russian direction, Russian capitalists then established a state bank whose assets were mortgaged by the entire mineral wealth of the country. Weigh, pp. 159-60.

18. The Chinese Republic at first refused to accept or acknowledge the secession of Outer Mongolia and, although the cards were stacked against them, the Chinese managed to outlast the imperial government on the Mongolian question. In July 1912 Petersburg and Tokyo concluded

yet another secret treaty "in order to more exactly determine and to complete the provisions of the secret treaties" of 1907 and 1910. The 1912 treaty delimited their spheres of influence in Inner Mongolia. The British and French governments were consulted during the negotiation, and therefore the final agreement was a product of entente diplomacy.

Thus armed, Russia on 3 November 1912 formally recognized the independence of Outer Mongolia in the Treaty and Protocol of Ugra. The intent and effect of this Russo-Mongolian agreement was to exclude China completely and to give Russia total influence and almost total control over nominally independent Outer Mongolia. Peking, however, refused to recognize the agreement. A Russo-Chinese war threatened. Negotiations began early in 1913 and an agreement, finally reached in November 1913, was confirmed by a joint declaration. The Mongolians were made part of the agreement by the Tripartite Agreement in Regard to Outer Mongolia, signed on 25 May/7 June 1915. As a result, Outer Mongolia remained under Chinese suzerainty; Mongolia was prohibited from concluding political or territorial agreements with foreign powers but was free to enter into commercial and industrial contracts with foreign governments or firms. Russia and China mutually pledged not to interfere in the internal administration of the country. Thus Peking retained the integrity of its empire, and Petersburg obtained the commercial advantages it sought. Two years later, after the collapse of the imperial government and with pressure from Peking, the Mongolians offered and China accepted their "voluntary" revocation of Outer Mongolia's autonomy. The latest chapter was written at the end of World War II, when the Soviet Union recovered its predecessor's "lost province."

This summary follows Weigh, pp. 164-84; the texts of the treaties, protocols, and declarations can be found in John V.A. MacMurray, ed., *Treaties and Agreements with and Concerning China,* 1894-1919 (Oxford University Press, 1919), II, pp. 992-94, 1066, and 1239.

19. *Golos Moskvy,* early February 1912. (Oldenburg's note)

20. The bank remained under the jurisdiction of the ministry of finance.

21. The new food distribution system provided a more rational approach to famine relief by supplanting the old system that supplied free food to every peasant in a region afflicted by crop failure. Under the new regulation prosperous peasants received food and seeds as a loan. Others were employed on public works such as road and canal construction. Only the "weak" received free assistance. As Stolypin declared in his speech of 9 September 1910, the new system restricted "the spreading corruption of state socialism." The regulations received their first successful application in the food distribution campaign of 1911-1912. (Oldenburg's note)

22. The Union of the Archangel Michael, formed in Petersburg in March 1908, represented the first formal schism within the parent group, the Union of the Russian People (note 23). Purishkevich's organization was named in honor of the founder of the Romanov dynasty, Tsar Michael (1613-1645). Its program differed little from that of the URP under Markov's leadership: preservation of the autocracy, supremacy of

Russian Orthodoxy, and defense of the property of the nobility. Like Purishkevich the Union proclaimed salvation through Great Russian chauvinism and militant anti-semitism. Its separation from the URP was occasioned by the latter's refusal to demand that the Third Duma disenfranchise all Jews and severely restrict the representation of Poles and Caucasians. The Union tended to support Stolypin's agrarian reform as a defense of the principle of private property.

A fourteen-member executive chamber directed the national organization. The most prominent local chapters were located in Moscow, Odessa, and Kiev; there was also an active student chapter in Odessa and a chapter of railway workers in Moscow. Supported by dues, donations, and government subsidies, the Union of the Archangel Michael conducted a full range of propaganda, including a daily newspaper and two weeklies. When the monarchy collapsed in 1917, the Union also collapsed, and the Provisional Government quickly suppressed its publications.

On Purishkevich see above, Chapter XII, note 53; for bibliographic references on the Russian right see Chapter XI, note 40 and also *Sovetskaia istoricheskaia entsiklopediia*, s.v. "Soiuz Mikhaila Arkhangela."

23. Plagued from the outset by personal, doctrinal, and tactical differences, the Union of the Russian People was reorganized in 1910 when N.E. Markov finally broke with and replaced Dubrovin. Markov with a majority of the organization held that the Duma, granted by the tsar, was to be exploited to discredit parliamentary institutions generally while yet serving as a forum to extol autocracy, Orthodoxy, and the Russian people and state. Dubrovin flatly rejected the Duma, which he saw as an alien abomination imposed on the tsar by the revolution. Dubrovin responded to his ouster by forming a small splinter group, the All-Russian Dubrovin Union of the Russian People in St. Petersburg.

24. The "liquidators" afford an example of a major distortion of history at the hands of Communist Party hagiographers. Certain Mensheviks, whom Lenin denounced as "liquidators," had concluded that the party's central committee had become thoroughly discredited and ineffective. Therefore they reasoned that the anti-Leninist party leadership should concentrate for the moment on building a mass revolutionary workers' movement and that on this foundation a new more responsible Social Democratic Party—legal, illegal, or both, as circumstances dictated—eventually might be formed. The fact was that the party had disintegrated under Lenin's leadership. Lenin, however, went to great effort to lay the blame on the Mensheviks, the "liquidators," who in turn made it clear that the rejuvenated party would have no room for Lenin's conspirators and "expropriators." Thus, after 1908 Lenin busily purged "his" party of all dissenters, and by 1910 the central committee of the Russian Social Democratic Workers Party consisted mainly of Latvians and Poles who saw eye-to-eye with Lenin.

The reader who wishes to explore the world of intra-party factionalsim can begin most profitably with Leonard Schapiro, *The Communist Party of the Soviet Union* (New York, 1960); on the "liquidators" see especially pp. 112-13. The "official truth" can be found in the History of the Communist Party of the Soviet Union, 2nd revised edition

Moscow, 1960). This version supersedes the truth as it existed from 1938 to 1956 in *A History of the All-Union Communist Party (Bolshevik): A Short Course* (Moscow, 1938; English-language edition, 1948). The revised edition (p. 142) "objectively" criticizes Stalin for failing to comprehend the significance of the vicissitudes of party life: "He regarded Lenin's struggle against the opportunists of every shade in the R.S.D.L.P. as 'a storm in a tea-cup' abroad." Less devout disciples of the great Lenin might conclude from this that Stalin already had the edge on his teacher. The efforts of the Mensheviks to gain control of the workers' movement in Russia are analyzed by the Western authority on Menshevism, Leopold Haimson, in "The Problem of Social Stability in Urban Russia, 1905-1917."

25. Anatole Vasilievich Lunarcharsky (1875-1933) was a member of a group of Bolshevik intellectuals who attempted to infuse Marxism with contemporary ideas and evolved a pseudo-religious theory of socialism as the religion of the future. Lenin and others ridiculed this anti-materialist conception of history and denounced its proponents as "godbuilders." In 1917 Lunarcharsky, a Social Democrat since 1897, returned to the Leninist camp and became the first People's Commissar of Education. He was by profession a literary critic and dramatist.

26. Based on a letter that he discovered in the Soviet archives, Hosking suggested that Stolypin supported Guchkov's ambition, possibly to revive his connections with the Octobrists and improve their relations with the tsar. The letter from Stolypin to Guchkov, dated 3 March 1910, read: "For the good of the cause, the new President of the Duma must be Alexander Ivanovich Guchkov. If you will call on me tomorrow, I will explain my reasons in detail." Hosking, *Constitutional Experiment*, p. 129, n. 63.

27. Gregory Efimovich, a starets or holy man from Tobolsk, was first known as *Novykh* (the New), but because of his debauched life his fellow peasants dubbed him Rasputin—the Dissolute. Born in the village of Pokrovskoe in 1872, Rasputin became either a member or an associate of an exotic heretical sect known as the *khlysty* or "flagellants". The *khlysty* sought salvation through debauchery on the theory that redemption was all the sweeter if it came to one thoroughly steeped in sin and degradation. Rasputin's life was a pattern of alternating orgies of sex and drunkeness and orgies of contrition and religious fervor. Around 1902, apparently, the local priest of Pokrovskoe complained to his bishop about Rasputin's activities, and the bishop ordered an investigation. At that point Rasputin abandoned his family to join Russia's immense fraternity of *stranniki* (holy wanderers). During the course of his travels, Rasputin came eventually to St. Petersburg. In a manner not entirely clear he gained access to the imperial family. His principal sponsors were Abbott (later Bishop) Theofan, Inspector of the St. Petersburg Religious Academy and confessor to the empress, Grand Duke Peter Nikolaevich, the tsar's cousin, and his wife Militsa Nikolaevna, the Montenegrin princess who already had sponsored the abortive spiritualist, Philippe Vachot. (Between Philippe and Rasputin came the astrologer Papus and the deranged mute Mitia, a peasant from Kaluga.) Also involved was Anna Vyrubova, the empress's confidante and client. Convinced that

he was sent from God, the empress arranged for "our friend" to obtain an official position as "the emperor's lamp-keeper," which carried the duty of maintaining the candles that burned before the icons of the palace.

Much has been written specifically on Rasputin, all of it fascinating but none entirely reliable; Rene Fulop-Miller, *Rasputin, the Holy Devil*, trans. F. Flint and D. Tait (Viking, 1928); Sergei Trufanoff [Iliodor], *The Mad Monk of Russia* (Century, 1918); Prince Felix Youssoupov, *Rasputin: His Malignant Influence and His Assassination* (Dial, 1927), an account by his murderer; Maria Rasputin, *My Father* (London, 1934); and others. One of the better sketches, with critical bibliographic references, is Curtiss, *Church and State*, pp. 366-407.

28. Hermogen's visit occurred one year later than the date given here by Oldenburg; the bishop's arrival was reported and discussed by *Russkie vedomosti* on 8 October 1911.

Hermogen, bishop of Saratov, was a reactionary fanatic and erstwhile champion of Rasputin. Although most Russian bishops muted their anti-semitism after 1905, the province of Saratov remained a tumultuous center of bigotry and reaction largely because of the inflammatory activities of its zealous bishop. In 1905 the zemstvo press had refused to print his diocesan newspaper because it was "sowing disorder and hatred among the population." In the following years Hermogen maintained close ties with the local Union of the Russian People and gave encouragement and support to the Black Hundreds. In September 1909 Rasputin visited Hermogen in Saratov, and in November they went together to Tsaritsyn to spend some time with Iliodor (below, note 40), a notorious Black Hundred incendiary under Hermogen's protection. Curtiss, *Church and State*, pp. 292-391, *passim*.

29. The entry in the emperor's diary for 1 November 1905 reads: "We have come to know a man of God, Gregory, from the province of Tobolsk."

30. "Fat Orlov"—Prince Vladimir Nikolaevich Orlov (1868-1927) was a reactionary court lackey and favorite of the tsar. He served from 1906 to 1915 as chief of the emperor's chancellery. His friendship with the tsar ended in a disagreement over Rasputin, and Orlov concluded his imperial career in the entourage of Grand Duke Nicholas Nikolaevich as assistant for civil affairs to the viceroy of the Caucasus.

31. How Rasputin controlled Alexis' bleeding has always been a mystery. Robert Massie, a lay expert on hemophilia, concluded that "if, technically, it was not hypnosis that he practiced. it was nevertheless a powerful suggestion . . . ." *Nicholas and Alexandra*, pp. 201-3.

32. Unfortunately, Rasputin's conduct left little room for slander and hardly tested the skill of the emperor's enemies. Rasputin's political meddling, beginning in 1911 with Sabler's appointment to head the holy synod (below), was reasonably clear at the time and well-documented since. The starets' continued influence and interference is substantiated in the letters of the empress herself. People from all walks of life sought to exploit Rasputin's influence at court. Women of all stations were attracted by his spiritual intensity, his crudity, or his sensuousity. They waited in line to get into his bedroom, or the "holy of

holies" as his most devoted admirers called it, and his business manager
Simanovich recalled that he had more offers than he could handle. Not
every woman, however, was interested in a romp with Rasputin, and
the starets was neither discriminating nor circumspect in his proposals
or conquests. Lecherous and boastful, he made mistakes and enemies.

33. P.G. Kurlov's memoirs maintain that Matsievich was an alleged
SR and that he intended to kill Stolypin during the flight but for some
reason decided against it. (Oldenburg's note)

Paul Grigorevich Komarov-Kurlov (1860-1923) served as director
of the police department from 1907 to 1909 after two decades of experience as a prosecutor and provincial governor. In 1909 he became
assistant minister of interior and commander of the gendarmes corps.
Responsible for security arrangements in Kiev where Stolypin was killed,
Kurlov was found negligent and forced to resign. He returned to governmental service after the outbreak of the world war, emigrated after
the revolution, and died abroad. His memoirs appeared as *Der Zusam-
menbruch des kaiserlichen Russlands* [The Collapse of Imperial Russia]
(Berlin, 1929).

34. The author (above, Vol. 1, p. 11) describes the "demophiles" as
those who minimized the importance of the nobility and sought to
anchor the state on the Russian masses. The "aristocrats" supported
the interests of the nobility as the traditional ruling hierarchy.

35. The problem of translating the Russian adjective "Russian" is apparent in Obolensky's phrase, ". . . *chto v Rossiskoi Monarkhii est
Russkii Tsar.*" *Rossiskaia monarkhiia* literally means "the monarchy of
(belonging to) the Russians," whereas *russkii tsar* means that the tsar *is*
a Russian—a member of the Great Russian nation. *Rossiskii* in other
words denotes both the Great Russian (russkii) and the non-Russian
people of the empire, including Ukrainians (Little Russians) and Belo-
russians (White Russians). Two paragraphs below in Struve's quotation,
when the form *rossiskii* is used, the word is italicized in the translation.
(Mihalap's note)

36. *Slovo*, 10 March 1901. (Oldenburg's note)

Vasily Berngardovich Struve (1854-1912) should not be confused
with his more prominent brother, Peter Struve. V.B. Struve directed
the Konstantinovsky Survey Institute from 1900 until his death.

37. In 1887 Louis Lazarus Zamenhof, a Polish Jew and a philologist
by profession, invented an artificial international language. It was based
on word stems common to many European languages, a standard system
of inflection and conjugation, and standard endings for each part of
speech. The new language made its debut in a pamphlet titled *La
Lingvo Internacia de la Doktoro Esperanto* or, as translated from Esperanto, "The International Language of Dr. Hopeful." Dr. Hopeful was
hopeful that a common language would strengthen the bonds of what
he and others perceived as a worldwide civilization. Esperanto was well
received during the international Paris Exposition of 1900, but views
like those of Bely prevailed.

38. The council for affairs of the local economy, created by Plehve
in 1903 and placed under the jurisdiction of the ministry of interior,
was revived by Stolypin as a sounding board of local opinion. It was a

consultative body consisting of local zemstvo representatives summoned by invitation by the prime minister. It served Stolypin as a "pre-Duma" from which he obtained the views of local officials on matters of immediate interest to them.

39. See Hosking, *Constitutional Experiment*, pp. 114-16, which indicates that only a few of the more liberal Octobrists attempted to amend and soften the bill. The Octobrist majority, anxious to demonstrate its patriotism, fell in with the right-wing chauvinists and voted with them. On the final vote an overwhelming majority of 164-23 carried the bill; at the time the Octobrist fraction claimed over a hundred members.

40. Oldenburg's modest account scarcely does justice to the flamboyant exploits of the fanatic young monk Iliodor (Sergei M. Trufanov). A gifted rabble-rouser, Iliodor had a large popular following and staunch supporters at the imperial court. His public career began in Volynia during the Revolution of 1905. As a monk in the Pocheveskaia Monastery, he headed a local branch of the Union of the Russian People and edited a couple of scurrilous and inflammatory papers. After his transfer to Tsaritsyn around 1907, he organized another URP branch and continued his outrageous campaign of slander against Jews, revolutionaries, and the "liberal" government. The governor finally obtained his exile to a monastery in Tambov, but Iliodor returned in disguise to Tsaritsyn where under the protection of Hermogen he defied the holy synod. In April 1911 the tsar himself ordered the synod "to leave the monk Iliodor in Tsaritsyn in response to the wishes of the people."

The emboldened Iliodor spent the summer of 1911 traveling along the Volga inciting mob action by urging his followers to free themselves from the Jewish yoke and calling on the masses to launch "a great and merciless struggle with all enemies of Faith, of Tsar, and of the Russian People." The turmoil finally became intolerable. Iliodor was arrested and incarcerated in the Florishchevo Monastery, and the civil chaos along the Volga diminished.

Curtiss, *Church and State*, pp. 255-375, passim; Pares, *Fall of the Russian Monarchy*, pp. 144-50.

41. Lukianov's dismissal is generally attributed to the fact that, alerted by the police, he initiated a thorough investigation of Rasputin's extracurricular activities. Stolypin approved of the investigation, and when it was completed and a report submitted to the tsar, he supported Lukianov's insistence that Rasputin had to go. Sabler, on the other hand, was regarded as Rasputin's stooge. If the starets did not secure his appointment, which appears doubtful, within a short time Sabler was under his thumb. Cf. M.V. Rodzianko, *Reign of Rasputin* (London, 1927; Gulf Breeze; Academic International Press, 1973), pp. 23-24; Kokovtsov, *Iz moego proshlago*, II: 32; and S.P. Beletsky, *Grigorii Rasputin* (Petrograd, 1923), p. 98.

Sergei Mikhailovich Lukianov (1855-) held the post of director-general of the holy synod from February 1909 to May 1911; he had served previously as assistant minister of public education (1902-1905).

Vladimir Karlovich Sabler (1845?-1923?) entered the civil service in 1873, serving until 1891 in the ministry of justice and then the emperor's chancellery. From 1881 to 1895 he worked in the holy synod as the head of various departments and became second in command to Pobedonostsev in 1892. He was transferred to the senate in 1896 and in 1905 was appointed to the State Council. He held the post of director-general of the holy synod from May 1911 to July 1915. When he left the government, he also changed his name to Desiatovsky.

42. Vladimir Feodorovich Trepov (1860-1918) was appointed to the State Council in 1908. He was an able conservative and a convinced monarchist, but he placed the interests of the empire ahead of those of the crown. He was assistant director and then director of the ministry of interior's department of general affairs in 1899-1902. He then served three years (1902-1905) as governor of the Tauride and moved to the first department (administration) of the senate in 1905.

43. Hosking's work, the latest on the subject, concludes that the right wing of the State Council definitely conspired to weaken or destroy Stolypin and that the rightists saw the defeat of this bill as a means to that end. He writes: "They therefore sent a letter to the Emperor expressing deep gratitude for the trust shown to them in the 'highest spheres,' but stating that they had many doubts about the bill before them; they would do their best to resolve these doubts and vote as conscience dictated. V.F. Trepov conveyed this letter to the Emperor and had an audience with him, from which he returned with the message that the Rights were freed from any external obligations and should vote each as his conscience dictated." *Constitutional Experiment*, p. 133.

That is the proof of "an intrigue." Stolypin's attempt to pressure the rightists was not an intrigue, but the rightists' assertion of "many doubts about the bill" was an attempt to dupe the tsar in order to get at Stolypin. Since they were "reactionaries" they must have been lying or in any case could have had no legitimate objections to the bill. Here Hosking provides an example of liberal historiography—statements by "reactionaries" are *ipso facto* untrustworthy and must be searched for ulterior motives (which are always there); statements by "liberals" or "constitutionalists" are to be taken at face value, since those notables are, by definition, "trustworthy, loyal, helpful . . . ."

44. A detailed account of this important interview in Stolypin's own words appears in the memoirs of Count V.N. Kokovtsov (*Iz moego proshlago*, I, 452-58). As far as is known, this is the only existing record. (Oldenburg's note)

In his research in the Soviet archives, Hosking found another handwritten transcription, which apparently accords with Kokovtsov's version. Ibid., p. 136, n. 83.

45. On learning of the defeat of the bill in the State Council, more than 200 members of the Duma signed a statement expressing their willingness to pass the bill again without delay. Ibid., n. 84.

46. Durnovo obeyed and did not return to the State Council until fall; Trepov resigned in protest and left governmental service for good. (Oldenburg's note) Trepov, a shrewd businessman, immediately became a director of the St. Petersburg International Bank of Commerce; he was shot by the Bolsheviks in 1918.

47. Bobrinsky's diary for 1910-1911 is found in *Krasnyi arkhiv*, 26: 127-50. An introduction by M. Murzanov also quotes excerpts from 1895 and 1904-1905.

48. Count Alexis Arakcheev (1769- 1834 was an influential official in the reign of Alexander I and virtually a dictator during the last decade of the emperor's reign. An able, ruthless administrator associated primarily with the formation of military colonies, his period of dominance came to be known as the *Arakcheevshchina*—the evil reign of Arakcheev.

49. Stolypin instructed Izvolsky to interpret the incident to the French press in that light. (Oldenburg's note)

50. Oldenburg's quotation of Maklakov's speech is amplified slightly from the fuller version given by Hosking, *Constitutional Experiment*, pp. 145-46. See Hosking for more detailed descriptions of the analysis of the issue by several deputies: Guchkov (pp. 139-40), V.A. Bobrinsky (p. 142), P.V. Kamensky, who was the main speaker for the Octobrists (p. 143), Baron A.F. Meyendorf (pp. 143-44), and Maklakov (pp. 144-46). An important account of the entire crisis is Edward Chmielewski, "Stolypin's Last Crisis," *California Slavic Studies*, 3 (1964), 95-126. The nationalities question and an important aspect of it is treated in Chmielewski's *The Polish Question in the Russian State Duma* (Knoxville, 1970). For a useful summary of the social and ethnic composition of the Duma see C.J. Smith, Jr. "The Russian Third State Duma: An Analytical Profile," *Russian Review*, 17 (1958), 201-10; and the somewhat different and broader analysis in Alfred Levin, *The Third Duma Election and Profile* (Archon, 1973), esp. pp. 95-111.

51. See above, note 6. In May 1911 W. Morgan Shuster, an American financial expert hired to reform Persian finances, created a Persian gendarmerie under British officers. Russia perceived these and other reforms as a threat to its interests in northern Persia. Having no interest in constructive reforms aimed at strengthening Persia, Petersburg in November 1911 sent two ultimatums demanding the removal of Shuster. When these were rejected, the Russians began an invasion of northern Persia and precipitated a crisis that threatened the Entente. Grey's policy was to preserve England's friendship with Russia at all costs. Shuster was dismissed. By February 1912 the crisis had subsided, and for the next two years Russian influence was dominant in Persia.

52. The Agadir or second Moroccan crisis was essentially an affair between Germany, France, and England. It found a solution because the two principals, Caillaux for France and Kiderlen for Germany, as well as French and German business and financial interests, sincerely desired to improve Franco-German relations. Although diplomacy succeeded, public opinion on both sides was left dissatisfied and belligerent. Russia's "pacific" role consisted of informing Berlin that it desired fruitful negotiations and of advising Paris that conciliation was necessary because Russia's military reorganization was incomplete and in any event Russian opinion would be unsympathetic to a colonial war. The relevant Russian documents can be found in *Mezhdunarodnie otnosheniia v epokhu imperializma* [International Relations in the Age of Imperialism], ser. 2, vol. XVIII (Moscow-Leningrad, 1931). This compilation of documents (fourteen volumes in all) from the Russian archives has been reorganized, translated, and annotated under the editorship of Otto Hoetzsch: *Die internationalen Beziehungen im Zeitalter*

des Imperialismus, 16 vols. (Berlin, 1931-43). The corresponding volume on the Agadir crisis is series 3, volume I.

53. The *poteshnie,* literally "playmates," refer to detachments of young boys training for military service. In 1683 Peter the Great formed his friends, mostly boys of common origins, into detachments of *poteshnie voiska*—play soldiers—whom he delighted in drilling. In 1691 he organized them into regular infantry regiments, the Preobrazhensky and Semenovsky, which became the elite units of the imperial guards.

54. That was the conclusion of Senator M.I. Trusevich. (Oldenburg's note) The results of a senate investigation conducted by Trusevich are summarized in Kokovtsov's memoirs (*Iz moego proshlogo*, II, 116-18). It is worth mentioning, however, that the authorities hanged Bogrov after a closed trial and before Trusevich had an opportunity to question him. For a detailed examination by a Soviet historian see A.Ya. Avrekh, *Stolypin i tretia duma* [Stolypin and the Third Duma] (Moscow, 1968), pp. 367-406.

55. Kuliabko gave Bogrov tickets to those affairs so that he could point out the assassins to the police. That, the official explanation, raised a critical question of why the police would put a potential assassin in close proximity to the tsar, since obviously they were not watching Bogrov closely enough to prevent him from shooting Stolypin. A possible explanation was furnished by Guchkov: V.V. Trepov, the governor of Kiev, told him that the police were concerned solely with the safety of the imperial family—despite the numerous threats against Stolypin. Guchkov, "Iz vospominaniia," quoted in Gurko, *Features and Figures of the Past*, pp. 723-24.

For the Okhrana the most charitable conclusion was that expressed by Empress Maria Feodorovna: "It is horrible and scandalous and one can say nothing good of the police whose choice fell upon such a swine as that revolutionary to act as informer and as guard to Stolypin. It exceeds all bounds and shows the stupidity of the people at the top." *Secret Letters,* p. 262.

56. The spread of this story abetted the willingness of the government's enemies to employ any weapon in their struggle, and it had one other consequence: In order to defend himself against charges of criminal negligence, Colonel Kuliabko did everything possible to enhance Bogrov's importance as an Okhrana informant. Thus Kuliabko unwittingly furthered Bogrov's aim. (Oldenburg's note)

In sum the murder of Stolypin remains unexplained, and three alternatives are available: 1) the official version, followed by Oldenburg, that Bogrov duped the Okhrana; 2) Kurlov, Kuliabko and others knew or suspected what Bogrov was up to but allowed him to continue because they knew it would please the court reactionaries; or 3) powerful court reactionaries actually conspired with the Okhrana to eliminate Stolypin.

57. In 1613, during the Time of Troubles, Ivan Susanin, a peasant from Derevenko, was seized by a group of Polish knights intent on murdering Russia's newly elected but yet uncrowned tsar, Michael Romanov. The Poles forced Susanin to lead them to the Romanov estate; instead he led them deep into a forest where they became lost and mired

in bogs. Susanin was tortured to death, but the tsar was saved and Romanov Russia had its first national hero. Susanin is celebrated in Russian literature and music, including an opera by Glinka and the play performed in Kiev on 1 September 1911, *A Life for the Tsar.*

58. Stolypin reportedly told Shulgin on more than one occasion: "You will see. I shall be killed. And I shall be killed by members of the secret police!"

CHAPTER SIXTEEN

1. Alexander Aleksandrovich Makarov (1857-1919) was an honest and even courageous but otherwise undistinguished official. His career began in the ministry of justice, but in 1906 he moved to interior as an assistant minister (1906-1909). He was appointed imperial state secretary in 1909 and held that post until he succeeded Stolypin in September 1911. After his dismissal in December 1912, he was appointed to the State Council. He was the Russian Empire's next-to-last minister of justice in July-December 1916.

Nicholas Alekseevich Maklakov (1871-1918) was the ultra-conservative brother of V.A. Maklakov, the prominent Kadet leader. He served in the state treasury from 1892 to 1908, rising to the post of director of the Tambov branch. In 1909 he was appointed governor of Chernigov. He became minister of interior in December 1912, was dismissed in July 1915, and appointed to the State Council. In 1918 he was arrested and shot by the Bolsheviks.

Alexis Nikolaevich Khvostov (1872-1918), a self-acknowledged scoundrel, began his career in the ministry of justice. He served as governor of Vologda from 1906 to 1910 and then as governor of Nizhni Novgorod. In 1912 he ran successfully for a seat in the Duma and became a leader and chairman of the rightist fraction. He acquired a reputation as one of the most reactionary and unscrupulous members of the right in the Fourth Duma. Through the influence of Rasputin, Khvostov eventually became minister of interior (September 1915-March 1916). He was arrested by the Provisional Government in 1917 and executed by the Soviet Government in 1918.

2. *Pravda,* the central organ of the Bolshevik central committee and presently of the Central Committee of the Communist Party of the Soviet Union, was founded in St. Petersburg on 22 April/5 May 1912. With a daily circulation of about 40,000 it became the first legal mass daily newspaper of the Bolsheviks. Established by Lenin, the paper was not only a vehicle for spreading Bolshevik propaganda but also an instrument for organizing and training party workers. During the first year of its existence, *Pravda* published the contributions of more than 11,000 workers.

The government suppressed the paper on 8/21 July 1914 on the eve of the world war. During its first 27 months of existence, the government confiscated 41 of its editions and closed its editorial offices eight times. During this period, therefore, the paper reopened and appeared under several different titles: *The Workers' Truth, Northern*

Truth, Labor Truth, For the Truth, etc. *Pravda* reappeared on 5/18 March 1917 but was suppressed by the Provisional Government in July. It has a continuous record of publication since 27 October/9 November 1917, and since March 1918 its editorial offices have been in Moscow.

3. Stolypin's daughter wrote of a warning that Kurlov was not to be trusted which was sent to her by the Russian consulate in Berlin. When informed of it, Stolypin replied: "Yes, Kurlov is only one of my fellow ministers not of my choosing. I do not have the heart to deceive him about this and I know of his behavior. Yet it seems to me that recently he has begun to recognize my authority and has become more devoted to me." Maria Petrovna von Bock, *Reminiscences of My Father, Peter A. Stolypin,* trans. and ed. Margaret Patoski (Scarecrow Press, 1970), p. 242.

4. Rasputin took a trip to Jerusalem possibly because of Lukianov's report and at Stolypin's insistence. He left for the Holy Land in March and returned in August. Then the empress's confidante, Anna Vyrubova, took him with her to Kiev. Shulgin related that Rasputin, observing Stolypin driving behind the imperial couple through a crowd, cried out, "Death is after him! Death is driving behind him!" He muttered the same idea through the night, and the next day Stolypin was shot. V.V. Shulgin, *Dni* [Days] (Belgrade, 1925), p. 106, quoted by Pares,'*Fall of the Russian Monarchy,* p. 143; Pierre Gilliard, *Thirteen Years at the Russian Court* (Doran, 1921), p. 49.

5. In 1911 at the insistence of the emperor and his minister, Sabler, the holy synod reluctantly confirmed the appointment of one Barnabas (Varnava) as bishop of Kargopol. Barnabas, a former gardner, was reputed to be illiterate, but Rasputin allegedly urged his appointment. Hermogen attacked the synod for its spineless capitulation to Sabler. He also opposed the creation of an order of deaconesses, desired by Grand Duchess Elizabeth Feodorovna, the tsar's aunt, on the grounds that a church council had forbidden the establishment of such organizations. Curtiss, *Church and State,* pp. 370-71; "V tserkovnikh krugakh pered revoliutsiei" [Life in Ecclesiastical Circles before the Revolution], *Krasnyi arkhiv,* 31 (1928), 204-13.

6. The generally accepted reason for the break among these religious notables was that Hermogen confronted Rasputin with testimony that he had raped a nun who had resisted his advances. Rasputin admitted his crime, whereupon Hermogen denounced him for his "unclean and shameful life," adjured him "in the name of the Living God to cease troubling the Russian People by your presence at court," and roughed him up. That version depends on the accounts of Iliodor and Rodzianko; the latter had access to official records, and in this instance cites an alleged eyewitness. Since Rasputin, Hermogen, and Iliodor had been on such close terms, Oldenburg's version, unfortunately undocumented, fails to explain why Hermogen and Iliodor needed "to establish their influence over Rasputin."

7. Soon afterward, Iliodor revealed his true nature when he declared that he was renouncing Orthodoxy. He told a correspondent of *Rech* (1 January 1913): "I was a sorcerer and fooled the people. I am a deist. Paganism is a fine religion." (Oldenburg's note)

The tsar's decree of January 1912 deprived Hermogen of his see and exiled him in disgrace—all without a trial and in violation of canon law. Hermogen's expulsion is generally attributed to the wrath of Rasputin. In 1915 Hermogen returned from exile and for a time resumed his campaign against the starets.

The synod, meanwhile, prepared to place Iliodor on trial, but he spurned and viciously denounced the council: "Godless, Antichrists, I will not be in spiritual communion with you. . . . You are animals fed with the people's blood." In November 1912 he was unfrocked, and a short time later he renounced Orthodoxy. He then "decided to start a revolution on October 6, 1913. I planned the assassination on that day of sixty lieutenant governors and forty bishops throughout Russia." When that fell through, he claimed to have formed an organization of women and girls wronged by Rasputin; its single aim was to castrate the starets.

Finally in August 1914, disguised as a woman, Iliodor slipped across the frontier into Finland, where he wrote a book about his relations with Rasputin (*Sviatoi chort*—The Holy Devil). His book featured letters from the empress and the grand duchesses that were given to him by or stolen from Rasputin. He tried to sell his narrative to the empress for 60,000 rubles. When his offer was rejected, Iliodor added "a bit extra" at the end and peddled the book to an American firm which published it as *The Mad Monk of Russia.*

See also Curtiss, *Church and State,* pp. 255-391, *passim*; Rodzianko, *Reign of Rasputin,* pp. 19-22; Pares, *Fall of the Russian Monarchy,* pp. 144-50.

8. "Why do the 'watchmen of Israel' keep silent, when in letters to me several of them openly call this servitor of lies a *khlyst* , an erotomaniac, a charlatan?" Novoselov was an expert on heretical sects, a lecturer at the Religious Academy of the Trinity and St. Sergius, and editor and publisher of the *Religiozno-filosofskaia biblioteka* [Religious and Philosophical Library].

9. Michael Vladimirovich Rodzianko (1859-1924) was a descendant of an old Russian noble family. He received his education in the elite Corps of Pages, served from 1877 to 1882 in Her Majesty's Regiment of the Cavalry of the Guard, and was designated a chamberlain of the imperial court. In his native province of Ekaterinoslav he served as marshal of the nobility and as chairman of the provincial zemstvo. He was elected from Ekaterinoslav to the State Council in 1906. Then, having joined the Octobrists, was elected to the Third Duma. In 1911 Rodzianko, who stood to the right of Guchkov, was elected chairman of the State Duma.

10. Investigations into Rasputin's alleged connections with the *khlysty* were conducted both by ecclesiastical authorities and by the prominent expert on sectarianism [Vladimir Dmitrievich] Bonch-Bruyevich [a Bolshevik publicist and editor closely associated with Lenin]. (Oldenburg's note)

Rodzianko claimed to have a photograph, which he showed to the tsar during their interview on 26 February. It depicted Rasputin surrounded by about a hundred young men and women, two of whom were holding a large placard inscribed with *khlyst* texts. At the conclusion of the interview Rodzianko asked whether the emperor would authorize him to say that Rasputin would not be permitted to return to court. The tsar thought for a moment and replied: "No, I cannot promise you that. Nevertheless, I fully believe all you have told me." The Duma chairman also claimed that the empress attempted to frustrate his investigation of the official dossier compiled by the holy synod. *Reign of Rasputin*, pp. 8, 45, 47, and 53.

11. On the eve of his departure for Livadia the tsar sent Kokovtsov a letter asking him "to inform the President of the Duma that I am unable to receive him, nor do I see any necessity for so doing, as I received him a week and a half ago. The Duma debates on the Synod's budget estimates have taken a turn of which I disapprove. I desire you and the President of the Duma to take steps to prevent a recurrence of this in the future." The report was written out and submitted to the emperor who read it later in Livadia. Ibid., pp. 59 (quoted), 60-62.

12. The approximate dates of the letters could be established because among them was a note from the tsarevich—a small cross and the initial "A", obviously made before he had learned to write. This affair is described in Kokovtsov's memoirs. (Oldenburg's note)

13. Colonel S.N. Miasoedov (1867-1915) was hanged as a German spy in 1915 (below, Chapter XVIII). It now appears that he was used as a scapegoat by the army high command to excuse Russia's defeats, and Guchkov's allegations of 1912 made the story all the more plausible. According to George Katkov, Guchkov accused Miasoedov of spying for Austria, but in his memoirs published in 1936 he referred to Miasoedov as a police spy (i.e. security officer) not as an Austrian agent. Despite Guchkov's charges, which attracted a great deal of publicity, Miasoedov was not prosecuted in 1912 but was requested to retire from active service as a counter-espionage officer. Katkov, *Russia 1917*, pp. 176-79.

14. From 1894 to 1907 Miasoedov served as a frontier guard. In 1907 he was called to testify in a trial of smugglers accused of having transported propaganda and arms into Russia. Under cross examination he admitted that the Okhrana commonly planted subversive literature and weapons on persons whom they wanted to compromise. As a result of Miasoedov's testimony, the state's case was lost. The Okhrana was furious at the betrayal of its secrets, even though Miasoedov had been compelled to make his revelations on the court's order. At the Okhrana's insistence, he was forced to resign. Later Sukhomlinov reinstated him and assigned him to special duties pertaining to security and the morale and political reliability of army officers. Ibid., p. 180.

15. Captain Alexander Vasilievich Kolchak (1873-1920), best known as a White leader in the civil war, was one of the imperial navy's abler and more promising officers. He was born in St. Petersburg, the son of a naval officer, and in 1894 graduated from the Naval School. Although his technical specialization was torpedoes and mines, he had broad scientific interests and spent 1900-1902 on a polar expedition. During the Russo-Japanese War he commanded a minelayer and a destroyer and was serving as a battery commander when Port Arthur fell. Between the wars, he worked energetically on the rehabilitation and modernization of the fleet.

When the World War began, Kolchak commanded the torpedo boat flotilla of the Baltic Squadron. In May 1916 he was promoted to rear-admiral in charge of mining operations in the Baltic and Black Seas. In July 1916 he was promoted again, to admiral, and given command of the Black Sea Squadron. He resigned his command in the summer of 1917, and the Provisional Government sent him to the United States as a specialist on mine warfare.

Kolchak returned to Vladivostok after the October Revolution. He became minister of war and navy in the anti-Soviet Siberian government and in November 1918 was recognized by several White and Allied factions as "Supreme Ruler of All Russia." In 1919 Kolchak led his forces into European Russia, but the Red Army repulsed the invasion, and the Allies abandoned him. The Czech Legion, operating along the Trans-Siberian Railway turned Kolchak over to the revolutionary "Political Center" in Irkutsk. In February 1920 he was shot and his body dumped into the Angara River.

Russian naval policy, 1905-1914, is a sorely neglected subject. In Western literature naval questions and the Duma are treated, if at all, as an adjunct to the "constitutional experiment." Therefore the best studies are by Soviet scholars: M.A. Petrov, *Podgotovka Rossii k mirovoi voine po more* [Russia's Preparations for the World War at Sea] (Moscow, 1926) and K.F. Shatsillo, *Russkii imperializm and razvitie flota* [Russian Imperialism and the Development of the Fleet] (Moscow, 1968). There is a brief sketch in Mitchell, *Russian and Soviet Sea Power* (pp. 271-82), but Shatsillo's work is missing from the bibliography.

16. The Lena massacre set off a wave of strikes that continued for over two years and culminated in the Petersburg general strike of July 1914. The strike movement gathered great momentum in late April 1912, after Makarov's tactless speech to the Duma. See Below, note 38.

17. Not trusting the government's inquiry, the Duma formed its own commission, headed by Alexander Kerensky. The two commissions worked side by side apparently with little friction. See Alexander F. Kerensky, *The Crucifixion of Liberty* (New York, 1934), pp. 134-36.

18. Guchkov was eliminated in Moscow's first curia. He received only 1300 votes compared to 2100 in 1907. The Kadets meanwhile garnered only 250 votes, implying that conservatives simply did not vote for Guchkov. (Oldenburg's note)

About a dozen other Octobrists failed to win election; they were mainly Left-Octobrists, and as a result that wing of the party was seriously crippled. The election of the Fourth Duma is not treated in any study in English comparable to Alfred Levin's work on the Second and Third Dumas. A basic Soviet account is E.D. Chermenskii, "Vybory v 4-uiu Gosudarstvennuiu Dumu" [The Election of the Fourth State Duma], *Voprosy istorii*, No. 4 (1947), 21-40.

19. The composition of the Fourth Duma (with comparable figures for the Third) was:

	Third Duma 1908	1912	Fourth Duma	Percent
Rightists	49	46	65	(15)
Nationalists	96		88	(20)

Centrists	—		32	(7)
Octobrists	148	120	98	(22)
Progressists	25	36	48	(11)
Kadets	53	52	59	(13)
National Groups	26	27	21	(5)
Trudoviks	14	14	10	(2)
Social Democrats	19	13	14	(3)
Non-party		27	7	(2)
Total	429	437	442	

The national groups consisted of six Muslims (down from 8 in 1908) and 15 Poles (down from 18 in 1908). The extreme right (Rightists and Nationalists) increased slightly over 1908 from 146 to 156; the center (Centrists and Octobrists) declined from 153 to 130; and the opposition increased from 141 to 154. (Oldenburg's note, adapted to tabular form and supplemented by Kalinygev's data in *Gosudarstvennaia Duma v Rossii*, p. 489.)

Kalinygev identified two majorities: The "primary majority" of Rightists, Nationalists, Centrists, and Octobrists controlled 283 votes; the "secondary majority" of Octobrists, Progressists, Kadets, Muslims, Poles, and Trudoviks controlled 236.

20. *Europe and Italy's Acquisition of Libya, 1911-1912* by William C. Askew (Chapel Hill, 1942) is the definitive study of the Italo-Turkish War and its impact on international relations.

21. Russia's complex relations with Turkey, including railway projects in Anatolia and the Caucasus which were linked initially to the Straits question, are treated in several places: William L. Langer, "Russia, the Straits Question, and the Origins of the Balkan League," *Political Science Quarterly*, 43 (1928), 321-63; which is supplemented and revised in the light of Russian documents published in the 1930s by Philip Mosely, "Russian Policy in 1911-12," *Journal of Modern History* 12 (1940): 69-86; and Edward C. Thaden, "Charykov and Russian Foreign Policy at Constantinople in 1911," *Journal of Central European History*, 16 (1956), 25-44. B. de Siebert, trans., and George Abel Schreiner, ed., *Entente Diplomacy and the World, 1909-1914* (London, 1921) is a dated but still fundamental monograph. A concise and expert survey can be found in Dwight E. Lee's chapter titled "From Agadir to the Balkan Wars" in *Europe's Crucial Years*, pp. 270-300. The Russian collection *Mezhdunarodnie otnosheniia*, previously cited, greatly expands but does not supersede E.A. Adamov, ed., *Konstantinopol i prolivy po sekretnym dokumentam byvshego Ministerstva inostrannykh del* [Constantinople and the Straits according to the Secret Documents of the Former Ministry of Foreign Affairs], 2 vols. (Moscow, 1925); a French edition is *Constantinople et les détroits* . . . . (Paris, 1930-32).

22. The impetus for a Balkan alliance came from the Bosnian crisis, which convinced Russia and Serbia that some sort of Balkan bloc was necessary to hold Austria in check. The disposition of Macedonia, an ethnic kaleidescope, prevented the Balkan states from making any headway toward an alliance until the propitious events of 1911 and 1912. At that point Russian diplomatic initiatives, the belligerent chauvinism of the Young Turks, and the Italo-Turkish War brought the Balkan nationals together.

The Serbian-Bulgarian alliance formed the cornerstone of the pact. Two months later (29 May 1912) Greece and Bulgaria concluded an alliance which stipulated full assistance if either were attacked by Turkey. In September and October Montenegro formed alliances with Bulgaria and Serbia, and those treaties completed the Balkan League. By then all of the allies were preparing for an assault on the Turks. The Bulgarian-Montenegrin alliance actually committed the signatories to war: Montenegro was to attack Turkey no later than 20 September, and Bulgaria was to enter the war no more than a month later.

Russian diplomacy, inspired principally but by no means exclusively by Izvolsky, aimed at the creation of a Balkan federation that included Turkey and that would serve to check any further Austrian expansion into the Balkans. Russia was not privy to all the secret negotiations that produced the four-power league, and the result—a predatory alliance that sought to destroy Turkey in Europe—was the antithesis of the original plan.

Since the cement of the league was a common hatred of the Turks, the mutuality of interest collapsed with the collapse of Turkish power in Europe. As historic national antagonisms reasserted themselves, even the lions could not restrain the jackals squabbling over the corpse of Turkey. The result was the Second Balkan War and the volatile powder keg that ignited the world in August 1914.

Nicholas Hartwig, the energetic Russian minister in Belgrade, was instrumental in the formation of the Balkan League, as was his counterpart in Sofia, Nekliudov. A brief but important biographical sketch of Hartwig is Marco [Bozin Simić], "Nikolaus Hartwig," *Berliner Monatshefte*, 6 (1928), 745-69; Nekliudov's memoir, *Diplomatic Reminiscences*, was previously mentioned. Miliukov's *Political Memoirs* contain a critical analysis of Russian policy (pp. 238-77). Long the standard work on the Balkan League and the Balkan Wars, and still useful, is Ernst C. Helmreich, *The Diplomacy of the Balkan Wars, 1912-1913* (Harvard University Press, 1938). A more recent work based on the Russian documents is Edward C. Thaden, *Russia and the Balkan Alliances of 1912* (Pennsylvania State University Press, 1965). For a broader picture of Balkan relations since the Congress of Berlin see L.S. Stavrianos, *Balkan Federation: A History of the Movement toward Balkan Unity in Modern Times* (Smith College, 1944); Stavrianos provides a brief history of the league and the Balkan wars in his general history, *The Balkans since 1453* (New York, 1958), pp. 532-43, which also includes an extensive but dated bibliography. H.R. Wilkinson, *Maps and Politics: A Review of the Ethnographic Cartography of Macedonia* (Liverpool, 1951) is an excellent introduction to the complexities of the Macedonian question, and Feroz Ahmad, *The Young Turks* (Oxford, 1969) covers Turkish policy in this critical period.

23. For a documentary record of the meeting at Port Baltic see *Grosse Politik*, XXXI, pp. 427-54.

24. The chiefs of the naval staffs initialled the convention on 3/16 July, and it was ratified by an exchange of notes a month later. The agreement provided for the close coordination of naval strategy and operations and stipulated that the two naval staffs would meet at regular

intervals. Other protocols to the convention dealt with the development of Bizerta in Northern Africa as a joint naval base to be linked by wireless to Sevastopol. France was to achieve naval supremacy in the Mediterranean and prevent the Austrian and Italian fleets from breaking into the Black Sea. England was to control the North Sea, and Russia the Baltic and Black Seas. The text of the convention, similar to the military convention of 1894 which was the foundation of the alliance, is given in the *DDF*, ser. 3, III, no. 206.

25. In the works of the revisionist historians Poincaré's visit to Russia in 1912 is interpreted as a critical point in the transformation of the alliance from a defensive pact into an instrument of aggression. Sidney B. Fay, for example, wrote that "the character of the alliance began to be changed. France began to support more actively Russia's aggressive policies in the Balkans, and assured her that France would give her armed support if they involved Russia in war with Austria and Germany, *The Origins of the World War* (New York, 1932), I, 330-31.

Sazonov disclosed for the first time the terms of the secret Serbian-Bulgarian alliance, and Poincaré exclaimed: "This is an instrument of war!" He protested at having been kept in the dark on a matter that might involve Russia, and therefore France, in a conflict with the Germanic powers. Sazonov tried to reassure him that Russia could control the Balkan states. Poincaré replied that French opinion would never support a war on a purely Balkan issue unless Germany intervened and provoked the *casus foederis*. Sazonov likewise repeated the position taken by Russia during the Moroccan crisis: Russia could not go to war over a colonial matter that did not directly affect the vital interests of France. In short, both ministers reaffirmed the traditional interpretation of their obligations under the alliance. The critical documents are Sazonov's report to the tsar, "Le voyage de Poincaré," *Livre noir*, II, 338-45; Poincaré's summaries for the foreign ministry, *DDF*, ser. 3, III, no. 264; and his memoirs, *Au service de la France* (Paris, 1926), II, 114-69.

26. In August Austria made two attempts to get concerted action in Constantinople and the Balkan capitals. In September Sazonov proposed joint pressure in Constantinople but not in the Balkans. Instead he urged restraint upon the Balkan states by himself. Finally Poincaré called for joint action on the part of Russia and Austria, who were to speak for all the powers.

A week before the war broke out Poincaré complained to Paul Cambon that Russia perceived the Serbo-Bulgarian treaty as "a means of assuring her hegemony in the Balkans. She perceives today that it is too late to wipe out the movement which she has called forth, and, as I said to MM. Sazonov and Izvolski, she is trying to put on the brakes, but it is she who started the motor." Quoted by Fay, *Origins of the World War*, I, 43.

27. Several dates in the author's account of the Balkan wars are incorrect; therefore correct dates have been provided without editorial marks.

In the Treaty of Lausanne of 18 October 1912 Turkey ceded Tripoli to Italy. Italy promised to withdraw from the Aegean Islands as soon as the Turkish evacuation of Tripoli was completed.

28. On 3 November the Russian government warned the Bulgarians not to occupy Constantinople and threatened to send the Black Sea Fleet to the Bosphorus if the warning was not heeded. Because Bulgaria was situated nearer to Constantinople, the Bulgarians bore the brunt of the fighting in the First Balkan War. Although their political objectives were Macedonia and the port of Saloniki, military strategy dictated the eastward movement of their army against Adrianople and Constantinople. Therefore, while the Bulgarians engaged the bulk of the Turkish army in front of the capital, the Greeks and Serbs moved behind them into the universally coveted region of Macedonia. The combined military operations produced a triumphal march through the peninsula, but they left in their wake a political stew that led to the Second Balkan War.

29. The cardinal goal of Austrian policy at that point was to create a viable independent Albanian state in order to safeguard the coast of the Adriatic and check the expansion of Serbia and Montenegro. Although Italy was sympathetic to Serbia's aspirations, Rome was more interested in cooperating with Vienna because of the impending renewal of the Triple Alliance.

30. The author has reversed the order of events. On 17/30 September Russia ordered a trial mobilization in Poland. Reserves were called up, and the third-year levy was kept under the colors past its normal date of discharge. Berlin and Vienna claimed to be satisfied by Sazonov's assurances that this exercise had been scheduled for some time. The move nevertheless made the Austrians nervous and on 6/19 November, as a test of Russian intentions, Austria reinforced its Galician army. Russia responded by extending for an additional six months the enlistments of the third-year levy. As a result of these maneuvers, the size of the Russian army expanded by about 350,000 men, the Austrian by about 225,000.

31. Rodzianko wrote: "I urged decisive action. Troops could be moved against Erzerum from the one side, and against Constantinople from the other. I repeated several times: 'Your Majesty, there is still time. We must take advantage of the popular enthusiasm. The Straits must become ours. A war will be joyfully welcomed, and will raise the Government's prestige.' The Emperor maintained a stony silence." *Reign of Rasputin,* p. 86.

32. The texts of the treaties are given in Ivan Geshov, *The Balkan League* (London, 1915), pp. 112-22, but need to be supplemented by later Russian materials incorporated in the studies of Mosely, "Russian Policy," pp. 74-76, and Thaden, *Russia and the Balkan Alliances,* pp. 86-93.

33. Russia's goal was to salvage the Balkan League; Austria meanwhile was working to tear it apart. Their allies generally sought to maintain the concert of Europe, to win Austria to a policy of moderation, and to prevent another humiliation of Russia.

34. The war lasted about a month. Montenegro joined Serbia immediately after the Bulgarian attack; Rumania declared war on 27 June/ 10 July; Turkey attacked on the 11th and declared war on the 12th. An armistice was concluded on 18/31 July.

35. A separate Bulgarian-Turkish peace treaty was concluded in Constantinople on 16/29 September. The Turks recovered the greater part of Thrace, including Adrianople and Kirk-Kilissa.

36. V.I. Nazansky gave a detailed description of the Romanov tercentenary celebration in *Krushenie Velikoi Rossii i Doma Romanovykh* [The Fall of Great Russia and the House of the Romanovs] (Paris, 1930), pp. 73-141. (Oldenburg's note)

37. Kokovtsov observed in his memoirs that the emperor did not encounter any "real enthusiasm" until he reached Kostroma. Then "the emperor and his family were surrounded by enormous crowds who expressed genuine rejoicing." (Oldenburg's note)

38. Data from the ministry of trade and commerce indicated eight political strikes in 1910; 24 in 1911; 1,300 in 1912; [1,034 in 1913; and 2,401 in 1914]. (Oldenburg's note, amplified by more complete official data provided by Haimson, "Social Stability," 627, n. 8.)

Just as the curve of strikes was rising from its nadir in 1910 (a total of 222), so too was the number of strikes called over political issues steadily rising, from about three percent of all strikes in 1910 to five percent in 1911, 64 percent in 1912, 43 percent in 1913, and 85 percent in 1914. Although these political strikes lasted an average of only 1-2 days, their frequency is taken to indicate the increasing politicization of the industrial worker force.

39. During the Duma's recess in the summer and fall of 1913, interior minister Maklakov tried to drum up support for a radical reorganization of state institutions—the abolition of the council of ministers and the dissolution of the Duma to be followed by a revision of the Fundamental Laws that reduced the Duma to an advisory body. Maklakov's plan was touted by Prince Meshchersky's *Grazhdanin*, which also sought to force Kokovtsov's resignation. See below, note 51.

40. This split marked the demise of the Octobrists as a significant political influence in the Duma. The 22 dissidents adopted the label of "Left-Octobrists" and moved into the opposition. The new fraction included N.A. Khomiakov, the former chairman of the Duma, and Baron A.F. Meyendorf; it elected S.I. Shidlovsky as its chairman with N.N. Opochinin as vice-chairman. A remnant of about a dozen former Octobrists chose to stand entirely aloof from any affiliation and thereafter identified themselves as "non-party" deputies.

41. The "blood accusation" was an anti-semitic doctrine that alleged the periodic consumption of the blood of a Christian in certain Judaic rites. The charge originated in the middle ages, had been condemned as slanderous by several popes, but still persisted into modern times. The Beilis trial was instigated and the case fabricated by Kievan reactionaries and officials with the complete endorsement, encouragement, and assistance of the minister of justice, I.G. Shcheglovitov.

42. Seen retrospectively, the Beilis trial is taken as the mark of the corruption of Russian justice under Shcheglovitov and a symbol of the utter degradation and obscurantism of the imperial court, including the tsar himself. See Hans Rogger, "The Beilis Case: Anti-Semitism and Politics in the Reign of Nicholas II," *Slavic Review*, 25 (1966), 615-29; Maurice Samuel, *Blood Accusation: The Strange History of the*

Beiliss Case (New York, 1966); A.S. Tager, *Decay of Tsarism: The Beiliss Trial* (Jewish Publication Society of America, 1935). Substantial documentary material on the government's conspiracy can be found in "Protsess Beilisa v otsenke departmenta politsii" [The Beilis Trial in the Estimation of the Police Department], *Krasnyi arkhiv*, 44 (1930), 85-125; "Tsarskoe pravitelstvo i protsess Beilisa" [The Tsarist Government and the Beilis Trial], ibid., 55 (1932), 162-204; and in *Padenie tsarskogo rezhima*, especially the testimony of Shcheglovitov and Beletsky. See Ralph T. Fisher, Jr., "Beilis Case," *MERSH*, 3, pp. 189-192. See also Ralph T. Fisher, Jr., "Anti-Semitism in Russia," *MERSH*, 2, pp. 30-39.

43. Baron Taube's memoirs include excerpts from unpublished letters sent by the emperor to Prince Meshchersky, who agreed on the necessity of improving Russo-German relations in order to avert a great catastrophe. (Oldenburg's note)

44. Davydov's conversation with the kaiser concerning the Russian press is recorded in detail in Kokovtsov's *Iz moego proshlago*, II, pp. 225-27.

45. Ibid., p. 242.

46. The appointment of Liman von Sanders to supervise the reorganization and training of the Turkish army was part of a general reform program introduced by the Young Turk regime. The British already had been invited to reform the navy and civil administration, and a French general had been placed in charge of the gendarme corps. On 17/30 June 1913 the Turkish government announced Lt. Gen. Liman's appointment for five years as inspector-general of the army, director of military schools, commander of the First Army at Constantinople, and member of the supreme war council. The Liman mission included 42 German officers.

The Russian government protested that the Turkish capital could not be placed under German protection. The Turkish government pointed out that the Straits were under British command and that Liman was subordinate in Constantinople to the minister of war. Neither England nor France sympathized with Russia's position, and Arthur Nicolson, the British under-secretary for foreign affairs, suggested that Sazonov had "completely lost his head." In December the German ambassador in Constantinople suggested the solution that Russia with some reluctance accepted in January 1914. The Liman von Sanders affair was another aggravation to the deteriorating relations between Petersburg and Berlin. The principal study is Robert J. Kerner, "The Mission of Liman von Sanders," *Slavonic Review*, 6 (1927-1928), 12-27, 344-63, 543-60; and 7 (1928-1929), 90-112.

47. Conrad von Hötzendorf (1852-1925) served as chief of the Austro-Hungarian general staff from November 1906 to November 1911 and again from December 1912 until the end of the war. From the autumn of 1913 on he held the opinion that the Dual Alliance ought to attack Russia before its military reorganization was complete. Oldenburg probably alludes to Conrad's memoirs, *Aus meiner Dienstzeit* [From My Service], 5 vols. (Vienna, 1921-1925). See also Norman Stone, "Moltke-Conrad: Relations between the Austro-Hungarian and German General

Staffs, 1909-1914," *Historical Journal*, 9 (1966), 201-28, which describes the coordination of war plans by the two chiefs of staff.

48. The conference of ministers met at the request of Sazonov to decide what to do if Germany refused to yield on the question of the Liman mission. The general conclusion was that Russia alone was not prepared to do anything in the way of military or naval measures. The minutes of the conference are given in Friedrich Stieve, *Isvolsky and the World War* (London, 1926), pp. 228-29.

49. Kokovtsov's memoirs emphasize that everyone, with the possible exception of Sukhomlinov, was aware of Russia's unpreparedness, and therefore no one, "and certainly not Sazonov, was thinking of starting a world war." *Iz moego proshlago*, II, pp. 253-56.

50. The diverse interests included Rasputin, Meshchersky, Witte, and Krivoshein. Witte, who originally created the state liquor monopoly, proposed that revenues from the sale of spirits be fixed at a certain sum with any excess committed to a campaign to combat drunkenness. Krivoshein believed that alcoholism threatened the agrarian reform. Therefore he wanted to restrict the sale of spirits and make up for lost revenues with an income tax.

51. Prince Meshchersky, an influential advisor in the early years of Nicholas's reign, had been eclipsed by Stolypin, but in the gloom that followed the prime minister's death he began to shine once again. He conspired with Maklakov to force Kokovtsov's resignation. During September and October 1913, when Kokovtsov was abroad on business, Meshchersky's *Grazhdanin* ran a series of articles that accused him of poaching on the emperor's autocratic power and seeking to introduce parliamentarianism in order to enhance his own independent position. Meshchersky called for the abolition of the council of ministers and the restoration of the old committee of ministers (each individually responsible to the tsar). He suggested that Goremykin would be suitable for the chairmanship of such a government. Hosking, *Constitutional Experiment*, pp. 199-201.

52. Kokovtsov, *Iz moego proshlago*, II, pp. 278-79.

53. Goremykin's complete statement, as given in Kokovtsov's memoirs, was: "I am being unpacked merely for the occasion; when it passes, I shall be put away again until the next time I am wanted." He had no portfolio other than that of chairman of the council of ministers, and thus the emperor broke the concentration of power enjoyed by Witte, Stolypin, and Kokovtsov. Goremykin's chief function was to sit on the Duma, and it was a job for which he was well-suited. Sometimes Nicholas is ridiculed by writers who erroneously identify Goremykin with the "man fresh for the task" in the tsar's letter to Kokovtsov. That man, described below by Oldenburg, was P.L. Bark who at 44 was Kokovtsov's junior by sixteen years.

54. Peter Lvovich Bark (1858-1937) was a protege of Krivoshein, the minister of agriculture. Bark had served in the ministry of finance from 1892 to 1906 and had risen to a position of responsibility with the state bank. In 1906, however, he left the government to become manager of the Volga-Kama Commercial Bank. In 1911 he returned to state service as assistant minister of trade and industry. He held the post of

finance minister from the end of January 1914 to the fall of the imperial government in February 1917, one of the few ministers to survive the vicissitudes of wartime politics. He emigrated to England in 1917, became manager of the Anglo-International Bank of London, and was knighted by George V in 1935.

CHAPTER SEVENTEEN

1. In 1890 the Russian postal service handled 384,127,000 letters and 57,046,000 telegrams; by 1910 the volume had increased to 2,056,085,000 letters and 195,457,000 telegrams. (Oldenburg's note)

2. Germany was Russia's chief trading partner and had enjoyed that position for several decades. In 1913 imports from Germany were valued at 642,800,000 rubles. Far behind in second place was Great Britain (170,400,000 rubles), followed by the United States (74,200,000) and France (56,000,000). The value of German goods purchased by Russia exceeded the combined value of all other imports.

Germany was also Russia's best customer. In 1913 Germans bought Russian goods valued at 452,600,000 rubles. The next three leading purchasers of Russian goods were Great Britain (266,900,000), Holland (177,500,000) (see below, note 43) and France (100,900,000). Overall Russia enjoyed a favorable trade balance; Germany was the only nation which sold more to Russia than it bought.

Data from *Vestnik finansov* [Messenger of Finance], No. 8, 1914, quoted by Miller, *Economic Development of Russia*, p. 77.

3. These figures included workers employed by state enterprises—war and naval factories and the railways. According to official statistics of the factory inspectorate, the average annual wage of industrial workers in 1912 was 225 rubles. This ranged from the high averages of 447 rubles for electrical power workers and 425 rubles in the machine tool industry to the lows of 180 rubles for processors of flax and hemp and 156 rubles for workers in the food-processing industry. In comparison in 1901 the average annual industrial wage was 201 rubles.

Unskilled day laborers in 1913-1914 earned 1 ruble 20 kopecks per day in Odessa, 1 ruble 10 kopecks in Petersburg, 60 kopecks in Kazan and parts of Saratov province, and 54 kopecks per day in the province of Tambov. (Those were the official rates used by insurance companies in calculating pensions awarded in accident cases.) (Oldenburg's note)

4. Zemstvo and municipal budgets increased during the same period at a rate far greater than that of the central government: the zemstvos from 60 million to 300 million rubles; the municipalities also from 60 million to 300 million rubles. (Oldenburg's note)

5. By 1 January 1912 Russia had 42,156 miles of railroad, and by 1 January 1915 the mileage increased to 43,669 (including tracks in Eastern China but not Finland). Telegraph lines expanded from 21,120 miles in 1895 to 206,580 miles in 1896 and to 435,600 miles in 1910. The number of steamships increased from 2,539 in 1895 to 4,317 in 1906. (Oldenburg's note)

6. Those were the *Gangut, Petropavlovsk, Poltava,* and *Sevastopol.* In addition four battle cruisers were under construction: *Borodino, Izmail, Kinburn,* and *Navarin.* With their completion (around 1917) the Russian navy with eleven of the newest battleships again would have achieved fourth place among the world's fleets (following England, Germany, and the United States). By that time Japan would have had ten dreadnoughts in service. (Oldenburg's note)

7. The *Imperatritsa Maria,* the *Imperator Aleksandr III,* and the *Imperatritsa Ekaterina II.* (Oldenburg's note)

8. Edmond Thery, *La transformation economique de la Russie* (Paris, 1914); the introduction, from which this quotation was taken, was dated January 1914. (Oldenburg's note)

9. W.D. Preyer, *Die russische Agrarreform* (Jena, 1914). (Oldenburg's note)

10. That was the equivalent of about 800 million gold francs or 28 million pounds sterling. In the same period France spent 347 million francs on education and the British 18 million pounds. (Oldenburg's note)

11. That represented about five percent of the population. (Oldenburg's note)

12. Including the four-year elementary course, the school-age population of Russia in 1912 was about 14 million (Oldenburg's note)

13. "Lectures on Russia" (hectographed by General E.K. Miller). (Oldenburg's note)

14. The latest available survey of Russian books and periodicals covered the year 1908 and indicated a circulation of 2,028 periodicals, including 440 daily newspapers. Excluding the publications of various associations, Russian publishers issued 70,841,000 copies of 23,852 titles of books and pamphlets. The value of all editions was set at 25 million rubles. Large publishing houses accounted for more than two-thirds of all book production. The largest firm, I.D. Sytin, published 12 million books worth nearly 3,000,000 rubles. (Oldenburg's note)

15. During its first three years, 1909-1911, the foundation sponsored 4,095 excursionists. The tours remained available with growing success until the summer of 1914. (Oldenburg's note)

16. V. Totomiants, *Kooperatsiia v Rossii* [The Cooperatives in Russia] (Prague, 1922). (Oldenburg's note)

17. *Zavety,* June 1914. (Oldenburg's note)

18. For a detailed account of the proceedings of the 1906 pre-sobor conference see F. Suetov's article in the *Uchenie zapiski Yurievskago universiteta* [Learned Papers of the Yuriev University], 1912, No. 1. (Oldenburg's note) J.S. Curtiss has summarized the numerous problems besetting the church and requiring reform in *Church and State,* pp. 287-318.

19. V.V. Rozanov (1856-1919) was a conservative writer, moralist, and social commentator—"the greatest writer of his generation" in the estimation of the literary historian D.S. Mirsky. Rozanov despised the morals and agnosticism of the contemporary left and consequently was welcome only among the small circle of independent conservative thinkers who still managed to survive in Russia. In 1899 he became a

permanent contributor to *Novoe vremia*. Although politics never held much importance for Rozanov, for a time after 1905 he was intrigued by the youthful vigor of the revolution. Thus without any sense of inconsistency he simultaneously contributed conservative pieces to *Novoe vremia* under his own name and radical articles to the liberal *Russkoe slovo* under the pseudonym V. Vavarin. Peter Struve among others found Rozanov's attitude incomprehensible and accused him of moral insanity. Struve's defense of Rozanov in connection with the Beilis affair therefore was all the more memorable as an act of conscience in defense of intellectual freedom.

20. B.K. Zaitsev (1881-1972), whose first stories were published in 1903, came to be regarded as one of Russia's great "impressionist" writers. He was associated with the revolutionary movement since his student days. In 1917 he became president of the All-Russian Writers Union, but he emigrated to France after the revolution.

21. Count Alexis Nikolaevich Tolstoy (1883-1945), a distant relative of Leo Tolstoy, gained some fame as a poet and novelist before the revolution. During World War I he worked as a war correspondent for *Russkiia vedomosti*. After the Bolshevik victory he went abroad for a few years but returned to the USSR in 1923. In the next two decades he produced a number of works that were read widely in the Soviet Union. Tolstoy's heroic nationalist themes earned him three Stalin prizes for literature: in 1941 for the historical novel *Peter the First*, Parts 1 and 2; in 1943 for the trilogy *The Way through Hell* (in English *The Road to Calvary*); and in 1946 (posthumously) for the play *Ivan the Terrible*.

22. Anna Akhmatova (1889-1966) attracted little attention with her first two collections of verse published in 1907 and 1912. In 1914, however, *Beads* received unprecedented acclaim and established her reputation as a major acmeist poet (below, note 23). Akhmatova lived in obscurity in Leningrad after the revolution. In 1940 her poetry once again began to appear in print with great success, but during the writers purge of 1946, her poetry was declared ideologically void and she no longer was able to publish. In 1958, however, during "the thaw," a new anthology of her poems appeared. See Sam Driver, "Akhmatova . . . Anna," *The Modern Encyclopedia of Russian and Soviet Literature* (hereinafter MERSL), (Gulf Breeze: Academic International Press, 1977-), 1, pp. 67-77.

Marina Ivanovna Tsvetaeva (1892-1941) was first published in 1910 *(Evening Album)*. Her highly individual style and originality deprived her poetry of the wider recognition that it may deserve. Tsevtaeva lived abroad from 1922 to 1939, when she returned to the USSR and where two years later she committed suicide.

23. The acmeists were a group of Russian poets united in a cult devoted to pure art. Their works stressed the themes of sensual perception, vitalism, and individualism, and they reflected a sentimental neo-romanticism. Their principal vehicle was the journal *Apollon* (1909-1917). Acmeism disappeared with the revolutions of 1917, and thereafter Akhmatova remained the only faithful representative of the movement. See Howard W. Tjalsma, "Acmeism," MERSL, 1, pp. 25-30.

N.S. Gumilyov (1886-1921) was educated in Russia and abroad, and he traveled widely and frequently in Western Europe. His first collection of poems was published in 1905. In 1911 he organized the Poets' Workshop, which brought together several important writers who were opposed to symbolism in its more extreme forms. Gumilyov married Anna Akhmatova in 1910, but the marriage lasted only a few years. In 1921 Gumilyov was executed for alleged participation in an anti-Soviet conspiracy.

24. I.F. Annensky (1856-1909), a classical scholar and school district superintendent, turned to poetry in 1904. However, it was only in 1909, the year of his death, that the symbolists discovered and acclaimed his originality. See Lubov Shapovaloff, "Annenskii, Innokenti Fedorovich," MERSL, 1, pp. 161-169.

25. Vladislav Khodasevich (1886-1939), a poet whose works were permeated with mysticism, achieved great but fleeting recognition and popularity among the depressed intellectuals of the immediate post-revolutionary period.

Osip Mandelshtam (1892-1940?), one of the original acmeists, became widely known only in 1922 with the publication of a poetic collection called *The Stone.* Sometime during the 1930s Mandelshtam was arrested and disappeared into the Soviet concentration camps where he is presumed to have died.

Boris Sadovsky (1881-1952) was classified as a symbolist though he wrote in the classical tradition of Pushkin.

26. V.V. Khlebnikov (1885-1922) was the poet most responsible for the development of Russian futurism. Khlebnikov's particular goal was to create an etymological poetic vocabulary that divorced words from their meanings. Although European futurism generally signified the search for "dynamic" art forms attuned to modern technology, industrialism, and urbanization, Russian futurists were not all so narrowly or easily defined. Some, like Khlebnikov, tried to recapture the ideals of an earlier natural life and searched for models in primitivism or the original culture of Orthodox Russia. All futurists, however, unreservedly rejected the artistic, cultural, and moral heritage of the more recent past. Thus in 1922 the literary manifesto of the cubo-futurists—"A Slap in the Face of Public Taste"—rejected Russia's entire cultural past from Pushkin to Tolstoy and called for revolutionary new art forms to express the modernity of technology and power. One of the founders and most prominent examples of the cubo-futurist movement was D.D. Burliuk (1882-1968).

For discussions and translated selections from the acmeist and futurist poets see: George Z. Patrick, *Popular Poetry in Soviet Russia* (Berkeley, 1929); Avraham Yarmolinsky, ed., *A Treasury of Russian Verse* (New York, 1949); Vyacheslav Zavalishin, *Early Soviet Writers* (New York, 1958); Vladimir Markov, *Russian Futurism* (Berkeley, 1968); and Leonid I. Strakhovsky, *Craftsmen of the Word* (Harvard University Press, 1949), which deals with the acmeists.

27. I.V. Severianin (1887-1942), who identified himself as an egofuturist, attempted to apply his genuine talent for song and rhythm to mundane subjects with a vocabulary drawn from the world of technology.

The literary world applauded his *Thunder-Seething Cup* in 1913 but quickly lost interest in his unique mode of expression. Severianin, however, captured a mass audience and for several years his works sold better than those of any other Russian poet. He emigrated after the revolution and died in 1942 during the Nazi occupation of Estonia.

28. V.V. Mayakovsky (1893-1930), a Georgian and one of the leading prerevolutionary futurists, became one of the best known and most widely read of the Soviet poets. Mayakovsky's original aim was to create a "poetry of the streets and public squares," and after the revolution he devoted his talents to popularizing the Soviet movement and its ideals. In 1923 he became one of the founders of the futurist literary association *Lef*—Left Front. But in 1930, disappointed in love and disillusioned by the course of the revolution, Mayakovsky killed himself.

29. The "wanderers," realist painters associated with the Society of Circulating Exhibitions, are introduced above, Volume I, p. 23.

30. See above, Volume I, pp. 142-43. For a survey of the prerevolutionary painters see Camilla Grey, *The Great Experiment: Russian Art, 1863-1922* (New York, 1962).

31. V.E. Meyerhold (1874-1942), a gifted, controversial, and influential avant-garde director, began his career in 1898 under Nemirovich-Danenko at the Moscow Art Theater. He worked with Kommissarezhevskaia in 1906 and 1907 and then left her to become director of the imperial theaters of drama and opera in St. Petersburg. After the Bolsheviks came to power, Meyerhold joined the Communist Party and as one of the foremost leaders of the "theatrical October" embarked on daring dramatic experiments. By the middle of the '30s the regime began to lose its taste for his inventiveness. He was accused of formalism and dismissed. In 1939 Meyerhold was arrested, and he died three years later in a labor camp.

32. The author's survey of the arts overlooks the field of music and the inestimable contributions of a host of composers and artists whose talents enriched the world in the twentieth century: Sergei Prokofiev, Sergei Rachmaninov, Nicholas Rimsky-Korsakov (who died in 1908), Alexander Scriabin (died 1915), Igor Stravinsky, Leopold Auer, Yascha Heifetz, Vladimir Horowitz, Nathan Milstein, Ephrem Zimbalist . . . .

33. Diaghilev's famous *Ballet Russe* had little in common with the traditional Imperial Russian ballet, except that Diaghilev drew heavily on the talent of the Imperial Mariinsky (now Kirov) and Bolshoi theaters of Petersburg and Moscow. Modern ballet as a distinctive art dates from the first performance of Diaghilev's company in Paris in May 1909. Freed from official rules and opinion and uninhibited by the classicism of the nineteenth-century European ballet to which the Imperial ballet had fallen heir, the *Ballet Russe* launched an artistic revolution that continues in the West.

The *Ballet Russe* performed mainly in Western Europe until 1929 when Diaghilev died and the company broke up. Throughout the two decades of its existence, the *Ballet Russe* was a magnet that attracted Europe's greatest artists. Its sets were designed by Benois, Bakst, Picasso, Matisse, and others. Its composers included Stravinsky, Georges Auric, Claude Debussy, Francis Poulenc, and Erik Satie. Michel Fokine, the *Ballet*'s unparalleled choreographer, was joined by Bronislava Nikinska, Leonide Massine, and George Balanchine.

Diaghilev's company made only two appearances in Russia, the last in 1911. Consequently the ballet in Russia remained largely unaffected by the creative departures of the *Ballet Russe*. Soviet ballet continues to stress technical perfection in the performance of strictly classical works.

The vibrant era of the *Ballet Russe* can be traced in *The Diaghilev Ballet, 1909-1929* by S.L. Grigoriev (London, 1953); in the memoir of Alexandre Benois, *Reminiscences of the Russian Ballet* (London, 1941); and in the autobiographies of two of its premier ballerinas: Tamara Karsavina, *Theatre Street: The Reminiscences of Tamara Karsavina* (London, 1930, 1950); and Mathilde Kschessinska, *Dancing in Petersburg*.

34. Baron Alexander Meyendorf, *The Background of the Russian Revolution* (New York, 1928). (Oldenburg's note)

35. Durnovo's famous memorandum of February 1914 appears complete in Frank A. Golder, ed., *Documents of Russian History*, 1914-1917, trans. Emanuel Aronsberg (New York, 1927), pp. 3-23.

36. *Aziatskaia Rossiia* [Asiatic Russia], Vol. II, p. 616. (Oldenburg's note)

37. This region included the Yakutsk and Kamchatka territories, the Kirensk and Olekminsk districts of Irkutsk province, and the Barguzinsk district of the Transbaikal. (Oldenburg's note)

38. Tomsk, the southern Yenisei region, Akmolinsk, and the Kustanaisk district of the Turgaisk region. (Oldenburg's note)

39. The land was sold to settlers at the nominal price of four rubles per desiatin with a 49-year mortgage. (Oldenburg's note)

40. In 1894 butter exported from the Altai had a value of 4,000 rubles; it increased to 23,600,000 rubles in 1904 and to 68 million rubles in 1912. (Oldenburg's note)

41. *Aziatskaia Rossiia*, Vol. II, p. 407. (Oldenburg's note)

42. Durnovo's memorandum was divided into several sections, the titles of which convey the essence of the document: 1) A future Anglo-German war will become an armed conflict between two groups of powers. 2) It is hard to discover any real advantages which have accrued to Russia as a result of its rapprochement with England. 3) Fundamental alignments in the coming war. 4) The main burden of the war will fall on Russia. 5) The vital interests of Germany and Russia do not conflict anywhere. 6) Russia's economic advantages and requirements do not conflict with Germany's. 7) Even a victory over Germany would place Russia in a very unfavorable position. 8) A struggle between Russia and Germany is profoundly undesirable as it can lead only to a weakening of the principle of monarchy. 9) Russia will be plunged into utterly hopeless anarchy, the outcome of which is difficult to foretell. 10) In the event of its defeat Germany is destined to suffer social upheavals no less serious than those of Russia. 11) Peace among the civilized world is imperiled chiefly by England's desire to retain its vanishing domination of the seas.

The Durnovo memorandum appeared in the Russo-German journal *Aufbau* (Munich) in 1921 and in the Soviet journal *Krasnaia nov* in 1922. [See above, note 35.] (Oldenburg's note)

43. Trade summaries for the final years were incorrect as a result of a statistical error: Russian exports which entered Germany by sea through the mouth of the Rhine were listed in Russia as "exports to Holland." About 90 percent of those goods simply passed through Holland in transit to Germany. (Oldenburg's note) [See above, note 2.]

44. That was the mood in Germany as early as the summer of 1910 as assessed by Yu.S. Kartsov, a member of the Russian Assembly [a right-wing nationalist organization], and reported in *Novoe vremia*, 29 June 1910. (Oldenburg's note)

45. At the urging of the Russian general staff, in 1912-13 French President Poincaré and his ambassador Paleologue personally began to press the tsar to devote greater attention to the development of strategic railways in western Russia. In 1913 the French government decided to provide annual loans of about 500,000,000 francs specifically for railway construction. A.M. Zaionchkovskii, *Podgotovka Rossii k imperialisticheskoi voine* [Russia's Preparation for the Imperialist War] (Moscow, 1926), p. 127.

46. The emperor ordered a halt to the proceedings against Chkeidze and noted on the report: "I hope that henceforth the Chairman of the State Duma will not tolerate the expression of opinions that violate the law and the oath [of the deputies]." (Oldenburg's note)

The gist of Chkeidze's remarks was that Russia could prosper and flourish only under a republican regime. The initiative for prosecuting Chkeidze came from interior minister Maklakov. Although the government previously had prosecuted deputies for illegal activities outside the Duma, this was the first time that official action was taken against a deputy for a speech within the assembly.

47. As a member of the Petersburg municipal duma, A.I. Guchkov recommended that the city disburse 100,000 rubles to assist the strikers' families. The mayor, however, strenuously opposed this ostentatious gesture. (Oldenburg's note)

48. See above, Chapter XVI, note 2.

49. The Malinovsky affair remains one of the skeletons in the Bolshevik closet. The leader of the six Bolsheviks in the Duma, Malinovsky was working with Lenin to split the Social Democratic faction. (Lenin already had "expelled" the Mensheviks from the party.) Therefore Lenin denounced as slander the Menshevik charge that Malinovsky was a police agent—and the corollary that Lenin's divisive tactics made the movement an easy target for infiltration by the Okhrana. Malinovsky fled to Lenin, who assembled a hand-picked party tribunal which exonerated Malinovsky of the Menshevik charges.

Malinovsky spent the war in Germany where with the approval of the German authorities he spread Bolshevik propaganda among Russian prisoners. In November 1918 he returned voluntarily to Petrograd and demanded either to see Lenin or to be put on trial. The Soviet authorities accomodated Malinovsky by taking him to Moscow where he was swiftly and secretly tried and executed. His repeated demand

224   *Notes to Pages 175—176*

that the court summon Lenin, whom he contended must have known of his police connections, were ignored.

Wolfe, *Three Who Made a Revolution* (pp. 535-57), rejects the possibility that Lenin knew of Malinovsky's dual role; Schapiro, *Communist Party of the Soviet Union* (pp. 134-36), holds open the possibility. See also A. Badayev, *The Bolsheviks in the Tsarist Duma* (New York, [1929]), pp. 154-63; Badayev was a Bolshevik deputy in the Fourth State Duma.

50. In July 1913 the conference of ambassadors, assembled in London to liquidate the Balkan wars, determined that Albania should become an independent principality. Then after several months they agreed on William of Wied to rule over their creation. Prince William was 35 years old, a captain in the German army, a nephew of the queen of Rumania, and a novice in political and diplomatic affairs. He arrived in Albania in March 1914 and spent the next six months trying to establish his position in a country whose internal dissension was aggravated by foreign intrigues emanating from numerous quarters. By September 1914 all of his international backers were at war with one another, and William left the country with only his title.

51. Ivan Stepanovich Mazepa (1644-1709) was hetman of the Ukraine from 1687 to 1709. In 1708 he allied with Charles XII of Sweden in order to win Ukrainian independence from Russia. His efforts collapsed in 1709 when Peter the Great defeated the Swedes at Poltava.

CONVERSION TABLE

Linear Measure
   1 *versta* (plur., *verst*) = 0.663 mile
   1 *arshin* = 28 inches

Land Area
   1 *desiatina* (plur. *desiatin*) = 2.7 acres
   1 *kvadratnaia versta* = 0.43957 square miles

Weight
   1 *pud* = 36.113 pounds
   1 *berkovets* (10 puds) = 361.13 pounds

Volume, Dry Measure
   1 *chetvert* = 6 bushels (approx.)

Volume, Liquid Measure
   1 *vedro* (plur., *vedra*) = 3.25 gallons
   1 *bochka* (40 *vedra*) = 131.5 gallons

Currency
   1 *rubl* (gold ruble, 1896-1914) = $0.50 (approx.)
      (The "Witte" or gold-standard ruble of 1896-97 was equal to two-thirds the value of the old silver ruble.)
   1 *kopeika* (kopeck) = 1/100th ruble

from Academic International Press

The Russian Series

1 S.F. Platonov *History of Russia*
2 *The Nicky-Sunny Letters. Correspondence of the Tsar and Tsaritsa, 1914-
    1917.* 2 Volumes
3 Ken Shen Weigh *Russo-Chinese Diplomacy, 1689-1924.* Out of print
4 Gaston Cahen *History of the Relations of Russia with China under Peter the
    Great, 1689-1730.* Out of print
5 M.N. Pokrovsky *Brief History of Russia.* 2 Volumes
6 M.N. Pokrovsky *History of Russia from the Earliest Times to the Rise of
    Commercial Capitalism*
7 Robert J. Kerner *Bohemia in the Eighteenth Century*
8 *Memoirs of Prince Adam Czartoryski and His Correspondence with Alexander I.*
    2 Volumes
9 S.F. Platonov *Moscow and the West*
10 S.F. Platonov *Boris Godunov*
11 Boris Nikolajewsky *Aseff the Spy*
12 Francis Dvornik *Les Legendes de Constantin et de Methode vues de Byzance*
13 Francis Dvornik *Le Slaves, Byzance et Rome au XIe Siecle*
14 A. Leroy-Beaulieu *Un Homme d'Etat Russe (Nicolas Miliutine) d'apres sa
    correspondance inedite. Etude sur la Russie et la Pologne pendant le
    regne d'Alexandre II*
15 Nicholas Berdyaev *Leontiev* (In English)
16 V.O. Kliuchevskii *Istoriia soslovii v Rossii*
17 *Tehran Yalta Potsdam. The Soviet Protocols*
18 *The Chronicle of Novgorod, 1016-1471*
19 Paul N. Miliukov *Outlines of Russian Culture.* 3 Volumes
21 V.V. Vinogradov *Russkii iazyk. Grammaticheskoe uchenie o slove*
23 A.E. Presniakov *Emperor Nicholas I of Russia. The Apogee of Autocracy*
24 V.I. Semevskii *Krestianskii vopros v Rossii v XVIII i pervoi polovine XIX veka.*
25 S.S. Oldenburg *Last Tsar! Nicholas II, His Reign and His Russia* 4 Volumes
26 Carl von Clausewitz *The Campaign of 1812 in Russia*
27 M.K. Liubavskii *Obrazovanie osnovnoi gosudarstvennoi territorii velikorusskoi
    narodnosti. Zaselenie i obedinenie tsentra*
28 S.F. Platonov *Ivan the Terrible*
29 Paul N. Miliukov *Iz istorii russkoi intelligentsii. Sbornik statei i etiudov*
31 M. Gorky, J. Stalin et al. *History of the Civil War in Russia* (Revolution) 2v.
43 Nicholas Zernov *Three Russian Prophets: Khomiakov, Dostoevsky, Soloviev*
45 Anton I. Denikin *The White Army*
55 M.V. Rodzianko *The Reign of Rasputin: An Empire's Collapse. Memoirs*
56 *The Memoirs of Alexander Iswolsky*

Central and East European Series

1 Louis Eisenmann *Le Compromis Austro-Hongrois de 1867*
3 Francis Dvornik *The Making of Central and Eastern Europe.* 2nd edition
4 Feodor F. Zigel *Lectures on Slavonic Law*
20 Paul Teleki *The Evolution of Hungary and Its Place in European History*

Forum Asiatica

1 M.I. Sladkovsky *China and Japan—Past and Present*

The Modern Encyclopedia of Russian and Soviet History
The Modern Encyclopedia of Russian and Soviet Literature
Soviet Armed Forces Review Annual
USSR Facts & Figures Annual
Military-Naval Encyclopedia of Russia and the Soviet Union
S. M. Soloviev *History of Russia* 50 vols.